MW00462187

THE DRAGON'S TEETH

THE DRAGON'S TEETH

The Chinese People's Liberation Army
—Its History, Traditions, and Air, Sea and
Land Capability in the 21st Century

BENJAMIN LAI

CASEMATE
Philadelphia & Oxford

Published in the United States of America and Great Britain in 2016 by
CASEMATE PUBLISHERS
1950 Lawrence Road, Havertown, PA 19083, USA
and
10 Hythe Bridge Street, Oxford OX1 2EW, UK

Hardcover Edition: ISBN 978-1-61200-388-7
Digital Edition: ISBN 978-1-61200-389-4 (epub)

A CIP record for this book is available from the British Library

Printed and bound in the United States of America

For a complete list of Casemate titles, please contact:

CASEMATE PUBLISHERS (US)
Telephone (610) 853-9131
Fax (610) 853-9146
Email: casemate@casematepublishers.com
www.casematepublishers.com

CASEMATE PUBLISHERS (UK)
Telephone (01865) 241249
Fax (01865) 794449
Email: casemate-uk@casematepublishers.co.uk
www.casematepublishers.co.uk

All images, unless otherwise specified, are sourced from the author's own collection.

To my daughter, Faith Ying Lai

CONTENTS

ACKNOWLEDGEMENTS

This book would not have been possible without the encouragement and support of George Jiao, who helped with the photos and the preparation of maps and diagrams, without which this book would be so much duller. Special thanks to David Burke for proofreading my drafts and for their valuable comments.

Throughout this volume, Chinese names are written in the original format: surname/family name followed by given name. In the Romanization of Chinese names, I have adopted the international standard—the Hanyu Pinyin system, which has been adopted by the UN and all international bodies. Chinese is a tonal language, and when Romanized can cause confusion unless it is made clear with the original Chinese script, thus "*ma*" can mean a horse or "mother"! Historical names that are better known in the older Wade-Giles system are maintained; thus for example, "Chiang Kai-Shek" in Wade-Giles is used here, rather than "Jiang Jieshi" in Hanyu Pinyin. In writing Chinese names, I follow the Asian naming system where family names precede that of given name. In Chiang Kai-Shek, therefore, Chiang is the surname, while Kai-Shek is the given name.

ABBREVIATIONS

2iC	Second in Command
AA	Anti-Aircraft
AAA	Anti-Aircraft Artillery
AAH	Active Acoustic Homing
AAM	Anti-Air Missile
ACV	Armored Command Vehicle
AD	Air Defense
AEW	Airborne Early Warning
AEV	Armored Engineer Vehicle
AFB	Air Force Base
AFV	Armored Fighting Vehicle
AGL	Automatic Grenade Launcher
AGM	Air to Ground Missile
AIFV	Armored Infantry Fighting Vehicle
AKE	Auxiliary Cargo Explosive
ALCM	Air Launched Cruise Missile
AOE	Auxiliary Oiler Explosive
AOR	Auxiliary Oil Replenisher
APC	Armored Personnel Carrier
APFSDS	Armored Piecing Fin Stabilized Discarding Sabot
ARH	Active Radar Homing
ARV	Armored Recovery Vehicle
ASBM	Anti-Ship Ballistic Missile

ASEAN	Association of Southeast Asian Nations
ASM	Anti-Submarine Missile
ASW	Anti-Submarines Warfare
AShM	Anti-Shipping Missile
ASuW	Anti-Surface Warfare
ATG	Antitank Gun
ATGM	Antitank Guided Missile
AVLB	Armored Vehicle Launched Bridge
AWACS	Airborne Warning& Control System
AWOL	Absent Without Leave
Bn	Battalion
CAAC	Civil Aviation Administration of China
CAPTOR	Capsulated Torpedo
CCD	Charge-Coupled Device
CET	Combat Engineer Tractor
CO	Commanding Officer (Battalion Commander)
COMPASS	A Chinese Navigation Satellite System
DoD	Department of Defense (US)
DSMAC	Digital Scene-Mapping Area Correlator
ECM	Electronic Counter Measures
ELINT	Electronic Intelligence
ERA	Explosive Reactive Armor
ERFB	Extended Range Full-bore
ERFB HB	Extended Range Full-bore, Hollow-Base
FLIR	Forward Looking IR
GPMG	General Purpose Machine Gun
HE	High Explosive
HEAT	High Explosive Antitank
HESH	High Explosive Squash Head
HMG	Heavy Machine Gun
ICBM	Intercontinental Ballistic Missile
IR	Infrared
ImIR	Imaging IR
INS	Inertial Navigation System

JNCO	Junior NCO
KIA	Killed in Action
LACM	Land-Attack Cruise Missile
LAW	Light Antitank Weapon
LRRP	Long-Range Recce Patrol
LMG	Light Machine Gun
LSW	Light Support Weapon
MANPAD	Man-Portable Air-Defense
MBRL	Multi-Barrel Rocket Launcher
MBT	Main Battle Tank
MCLC	Mine Clearance Line Charge
MCLOS	Manual to Command Line of Sight
MIRV	Multiple Independently Targetable Re-entry Vehicle
MMW	Millimeter Wave
MR	Motor Rifle
MRBM	Medium Range Ballistic Missile
MSR	Main Supply Route
NATO	North Atlantic Treaty Organization
NBC	Nuclear Biological Chemical
NCO	Non Commissioned Officer
OC	Officer Commanding (Company Commander)
ORBAT	Order of Battle
PAH	Passive Acoustic Homing
PAS	Passive/Active Sonar
PLA	People's Liberation Army
PLAAF	People's Liberation Army Air Force
PLAN	People's Liberation Army Navy
POL	Petroleum, Oil, Lubricants
PRH	Passive Radar Homing
QRF	Quick Reaction Force
RC	Radio Controlled
SACLOS	Semi-Automatic to Command Line of Sight
SAGL	Semi-Auto Grenade Launcher
SAM	Surface-to-Air Missile

SAR	Surface Air Rescue
SARH	Semi-Active Radar Homing
SATCOM	Satellite Communication
SEAL	Sea-Air-Land (US Navy special force)
SLBM	Submarine Launched Ballistic Missile
SMG	Sub-Machine Gun
SNCO	Senior NCO
SPG	Self-Propelled Gun
SPATG	Self-Propelled ATG
SPAAG	Self-Propelled AA Gun
SRBM	Short-Range Ballistic Missile
SS	Surface-to-Surface
SSBN	Ship Submersible Ballistic Nuclear
SSM	Surface-to-Surface Missile
SSN	Ship Submersible Nuclear
TEL	Transporter Erector Launcher
TERCOM	Terrain Contour Matching
TVM	Track-vis-Missile
LVT	Landing Vehicle Tracked
UAV	Unmanned Aerial Vehicle
UN	United Nations

PREFACE

When Mao Zedong proclaimed The People's Republic of China on October 1, 1949, China was a poor society, wrecked from years of warfare and civil strife. After a brief liaison with the Soviet Union broke down, China became hermetic for some thirty years until the early 1980s, when Deng Xiaoping instigated a liberation policy that totally transformed the country. Since then, in less than three decades, China has risen to become the second largest economy in the world, poised to overtake the United States, the world's current economic superpower, in the foreseeable future.

The enduring images of the Chinese People's Liberation Army (PLA) are of massed human waves, and of soldiers goose-stepping in military parades wearing ill-fitting uniforms and bearing hand-me-down weapons. For many in the West, the PLA's bark is louder than its bite. By the early 1980s, even the Chinese admitted that their army was in a terrible state. Deng accused the PLA of "bloating, laxity, conceit, extravagance and inertia." However, Deng deliberately placed modernization of the armed forces behind that of farming, industry and science. It was not until the Gulf War in the early 1990s that the Chinese woke up to what modern war was all about and realized that the modernization of the PLA was an urgent matter that they could delay no longer. Military modernization began with a series of shopping sprees; much of the weaponry came from Russia and Ukraine, especially after the embargo by the West following the Tiananmen Square incident in 1989. These imported weapons were soon taken apart and worked on, such that by the late 1990s much of the PLA's armory appeared to comprise modern locally made armament. Today the PLA is a quasi-modern fighting force armed with a formidable arsenal that includes nuclear submarines, intercontinental ballistic missiles and stealth fighters. How has the transformation of China really affected the PLA, what is the Chinese PLA like in the 21st century? These are some questions many in the West would like answered.

For years China's military has been an opaque organization, but as China itself is opening up, cracks are appearing in the once-mysterious PLA which allow glimpses into the force. In writing this book, I have had to rely entirely on open-source material available to the public. China is one of the few countries to have a national TV channel dedicated to military matters; and defense-related magazines and newspapers are readily available. In the preparation of this book, I tried to avoid dutifully parroting government propaganda, but this book is in essence a book on the Chinese Army, written from a Chinese point of view, which some readers may find "different" from mainstream Western commentaries. My aim is to give the reader a short and succinct guide to the modern PLA and address some key questions: "What is the modern Chinese Army really like? Where and how does the PLA recruit its soldiers and officers? What weapons does the PLA use, how were they built and developed?" To answer these questions, I have explored the history of the PLA, its traditions, history, battles and glory, uniforms and equipment. Finally, this book ends with a chapter that provides a brief strategic outlook on how the Chinese and PLA see the world and the various threats to their national security.

CHAPTER I

EARLY YEARS OF THE CHINESE PLA

The Chinese People's Liberation Army (PLA) is the armed wing of the Chinese Communist Party (CCP). It owes its origin to the "Workers' and Peasants' Red Army," more popularly known as the Red Army, which was established on August 1, 1927 during the Nanchang Uprising by men of the Kuomintang (KMT, or Chinese Nationalist Party) 24th Army. As such, August 1 is still regarded as PLA Day in China and the emblem of the PLA still bears the Chinese characters "8" (八) and "1" (一), representing the 1st day of the 8th month—the day when the PLA was established.

The history of the Chinese PLA is essentially the history of China in the 20th century, so to understand the PLA one must know the history of modern China. In the 50-year period prior to 1949, when the People's Republic of China was founded, the country was essentially in a continuous state of war. During the last three decades of the Qing Dynasty, the last Imperial regime faced foreign aggression, while the Taiping rebels and republican revolutionaries threatened the country from within. In the early years of the 20th century, the Chinese Nationalist Party also known as the Kuomintang (KMT), became a dominant political force after the 1911 revolution and founded a new regime, the Republic of China (ROC). In its formative years the ROC was weak and prone to fractional fighting. Most of the country was essentially ruled by local warlords. The leader of the KMT, a medical doctor by the name of Dr. Sun Yatsun tried to get aid from the West but was rebuked; salvation came from the Soviets bearing gifts of guns and money. The KMT soon adopted Soviet ideals, and during this period the Chinese Communists and Nationalists cooperated, to the extent that members of the CCP were even allowed to join the KMT. Mao Zedong, later the founder of the People's Republic of China, was a member of the KMT. With aid from the Soviets, the KMT founded the Whampoo Military Academy and with a trained army, the Nationalists began a series of campaigns to eliminate all opposition, mainly regional warlords, in a bid to unite the country.

After the death of Dr. Sun in 1925, Chiang Kai-Shek, a soldier of the KMT, became its leader. The capture of Shanghai on March 23, 1927 by the KMT meant that it now had access to finance. Flushed with money and arms, by April of the same year the KMT decided to eliminate its unwanted "baggage," the Chinese Communists and its Soviet advisors. Soon Communists were simply executed or assassinated. The Communists fought back by instigating a series of uprisings across China.

All these uprisings were failures for the Chinese Communists. A column of rebels from the Nanchang Uprising, led by Zhu De, later Field Marshal of the PLA, retreated to Jinggang Mountain in Southeast China. Later this force was joined by another defeated rag-tag army from the failed Autumn Harvest Uprising, led by Mao. After many debates, Mao was recognized as a leader of the Chinese Communists in the Jinggang mountain area and, using the rugged terrain as a shield, the Communists established a "liberated zone" known as the "Chinese Soviet Republic" outside the control of the Nationalist government. The Communists also established an army, using the Soviet model as a guide, which became known as the Fourth Corps of the Chinese Workers Farmers Revolutionary Army, later better known as the "4th Red Army." Soon the Red Army expanded to 300,000 strong and managed to outmaneuver the Nationalist Army in four separate attempts at encirclement. In the fifth encirclement campaign, the Nationalists got wise. Unlike in previous campaigns when they had penetrated deeply in a single strike, the KMT troops patiently built blockhouses, around 8 km apart, to surround the Communist areas and cut off their supplies and food sources. The Communists were truly routed. Blame was laid on a Li De, who was better known in the West as Otto Braun. Braun was a Soviet-trained German Communist sent to China by the Comintern as a military advisor. Otto favored conventional tactics and direct attacks in set-piece battles. However, as the Chinese Communists were still largely a guerrilla force, pound for pound they were no match for the far better equipped Nationalists. As a result, the Communists suffered great casualties, so many that the number of soldiers in the encirclement fell from a high of 86,000 to about 25,000 within the space of 12 months.

Soon after the defeat, a soul-searching meeting was held in the town of Zunyi in January 1935. Enemies of Mao tried to pin the blame on him, but Mao with the support of his allies successfully defended himself and deflected the blame onto Otto Braun and his clique of supporters. Mao rightly argued that the Communists were not in a position to fight set-piece battles and that he instead favored a hit-and-run form of guerrilla warfare, for which Mao was to become famous. The result of the meeting was that Mao's strategy and leadership held sway and Braun was sacked. After this conference, the Comintern, the foreign Communists, were pushed aside, and "Native Communists" took control of the Chinese Communist Party.

The Red Army eventually broke out of the Chinese Soviet Republic using gaps in the ring of blockhouses (manned by the troops of a warlord, an ally of Chiang's, rather than the KMT themselves). The warlord armies were reluctant to challenge the Communists directly for fear of wasting their own men. In addition, the main KMT forces were preoccupied with annihilating the army of Zhang Guotao,[1] a fellow Communist who at that time had a larger army than Mao's. In October 1934 Mao and other Communists embarked on their historic "Long March" that would end a year later in the high mountain desert plateau of Yanan in Shaanxi province, northwest China. Of the 100,000 or so who began the march, only around 7,000–8,000 made it to Shaanxi. Zhang's army, which took a different route, was largely destroyed. The great retreat made Mao the undisputed leader of the CCP. Yanan and the surrounding area soon became a CCP-controlled zone, despite continuous pressure from the Nationalist Army of the KMT.

Chiang, who saw the CCP as a greater threat, continued to place his main effort on attacking the Chinese Communists despite the Japanese invasion and occupation of Manchuria in 1931. Infuriated by his inaction against foreign invasion, in 1936 two KMT generals held Chiang hostage in what was later known as the Xian Incident, in an attempt to force Chiang to fight the Japanese. However, by July 1937 Imperial Japan embarked on an all-out invasion of China after what was known as Marco Polo Bridge Incident, and this brought about a temporary "united front" between the CCP and KMT. The truce was not universally observed, however, and there were frequent infringements between the two belligerents. During this time, the Red Army was "absorbed" into the Nationalists' camp as the National Revolutionary Army, 18th Army Group, based largely in northwest China operating out of Yanan; whereas the Communist guerrillas south of the Yangtze River became the National Revolutionary Army's New Fourth Army. The Communists was able to expand their control outside of Yanan rapidly. Soon the KMT was faced with a two-front war, on one hand fighting Imperial Japan and on the other hand having to divert resources to contain the ever-expanding CCP influence over rural China.

With hindsight, it is clear that the all-out invasion of China by Imperial Japan helped the CCP. Not only was Chiang busy fighting Imperial Japan, thus giving the Communists some respite, but the latter were able to expand their armies and gain support from the rural population. In 1945 the war suddenly ended after the dropping of two atomic bombs on Japan. While the rest of the world began to rebuild in 1945, China plunged into war again, this time between the Nationalists and the Communists. The Eighth Route Army and the New Fourth Army was reorganized as one force under a new name: The Chinese People's Liberation Army. Moving rapidly and with some help from the Soviet Army in Manchuria, the PLA was able to take advantage of large quantities of abandoned Japanese weapons and ordnance, and as a result its military capability expanded considerably, transforming a guerrilla force into a standing army with tanks and heavy artillery.

On July 20, 1946, Chiang launched a large-scale assault on Communist territory with 113 brigades (1.6 million troops). Knowing their disadvantages in manpower and equipment, the CCP executed a "passive defense" strategy: they avoided the strongpoints of the Nationalist army, and were prepared to abandon territory in order to preserve their forces. In most cases, the surrounding countryside and small towns came under Communist influence while the Nationalists held the cities, the PLA strategy was to use hit-and-run tactics to wear out the KMT forces as much as possible. After a year of fighting, the power balance was more favorable to the CCP. They wiped out 1.12 million Nationalist troops, while the PLA's strength grew to about two million men.

With heavy armament in support, the PLA took on the KMT in three set-piece battles, at Liaoshen, Huaihai, and the Pingjin Campaign, where they wiped out 144 regular and 29 irregular divisions, eliminating some 1.5 million troops from the Nationalist Army. It was these key campaigns that essentially broke the backbone of the Nationalist Army and sealed the victory for the CCP. Despite military and financial aid from the United States, the Nationalist Army and the KMT was by then seriously hampered by widespread corruption, coupled with factional infighting, and a series of poor military judgments led the Nationalist Army from defeat to defeat. In December 1949 Chiang Kai-Shek, having escaped to the island of Taiwan with some two million loyal supporters, proclaimed Taipei as the temporary capital of the Republic of China (ROC) and continued to assert his government as the sole legitimate authority over all of China. With the mainland under the Communists, the CCP with Mao Zedong at the helm was to establish The People's Republic of China (PRC) on October 1, 1949.

Even when the ROC was forced to retreat to Taiwan, no peace treaty was ever signed, and the PRC continued to threaten ROC with invasion. Today, tension between the Communist mainland and republican Taiwan has lessened tremendously, and open travel and trade between the two former belligerents has helped to lessen cross-straits tension.

1.1 Establishment of the PLA Navy

At the foundation of the PRC on October 1, 1949, the PLA was 5.5 million strong. This force was essentially an infantry-heavy ground force organized into five field armies, each composed of several corps. By comparison the Chinese People's Liberation Army Navy (PLAN) was in its infancy; not only junior in terms of history but also in size. Whilst the PLA's roots date back to 1927, the PLA's naval history reaches back only to the 1940s. On April 4, 1949, whilst preparing for a major river crossing operation, the Third Field Army was instructed to establish a specialist team to handle this operation and to incorporate a group of recently defected Republic of China Navy (ROCN) personnel and ships into the PLA's order of battle (ORBAT). On April 23, 1949, the Central Military Committee of the CCP officially ordered elements of the Third Field Army, then part of the Eastern Military District, with defectors from the ROCN and selected volunteers from universities, to form the People's Navy with General Zhang Aiping as its first Commander and Political Commissar. Since then, April 23 has been celebrated as the PLAN Day in China.

In the early stages of the Chinese Civil War (1927–50), the Chinese Communist force never maintained a permanent boat fleet in its ORBAT. Instead, when there was a need for waterborne operations, boats, sampans and junks were amassed from local civilian sources. In 1941, a coastal defense unit equipped with boats was created by the New Fourth Army, and later in the 1944 rebellion by elements of the pro-Japanese puppet regime of Wang Jingwei[2] became the only true "marine" units of the Chinese Communists before 1949. However, it was only in 1949, the latter period of the Civil War that the PLA began to amass a permanent flotilla of boats and later on even warships, mostly through defection from the ROCN.

Three notable defections occurred in 1949, including the largest ship of the ROCN, the ROCS *Chung King*, formerly HMS *Aurora*, an *Arethusa*-class light cruiser of the British Royal Navy, in February 1949. Another was the *ROCS Chang Chi*, an ex-IJN *Hashidate*-class gunboat, the IJN *Uji*, given to the ROCN as a war prize, which defected in September and was renamed the CNS *Nanchang* with pennant number 210. In October, the ROCS *Lien Rong*, a former USS LCI (*M*) *632* war surplus boat, also defected to the Communists and was renamed the CNS *Yonggan* (*Brave*). In 1949 alone 9.5% of ROCN personnel and

111 vessels, accounting for 22.7% of the total ROCN fleet, defected to PLAN. A further 86 vessels were abandoned when the Nationalists withdrew to Taiwan; a serious blow to the Chinese Nationalist Force, but a welcome addition to the fledging PLAN.

Just one month after the founding of the People's Republic of China on November 11, 1949, No. 1 Naval Academy was formed in Dalian City (today it is known as PLA Dalian Naval Academy) with Soviet instructors. Later in 1950 the National Naval Command in Beijing was established by consolidating various regional marine forces. Two years later a separate Naval Aviation Force was created, also with Soviet assistance. Secondhand Soviet ships were added to the fleet and the PLAN was reorganized into three forces, the Northern, Eastern and Southern Fleets; with headquarters in Qingdao, Ningbo, and Zhanjiang respectively. At their peak in the mid-1950s, it was estimated there were more than 2,500 Soviet advisors in China.

During the 1960s and 1970s the Navy was the darling of the PLA. Some 20% of the defense budget was allocated to naval forces, and as such, the Navy grew rapidly. The conventional submarine force increased from 35 to 100 boats; the number of missile-carrying ships grew from twenty to 200. Nuclear-powered attack submarines (SSN) and nuclear-powered ballistic missile submarines (SSBN) were added to the fleet. By the mid-1980s PLAN boasted two *Xia*-class SSBNs armed with 12 CSS-N-3 missiles and three *Han*-class SSNs armed with six SY-2 cruise missiles, and was ranked third largest fleet in the world.

In additional to the PLAN, China has built up a formidable paramilitary marine force. The China Coast Guard (CCG) is the maritime branch of the Public Security Border Troops, a paramilitary police force under the leadership of the Ministry of Public Security (MPS). It is staffed by People's Armed Police (PAP) whose personnel consists of some twenty regimental-level flotillas. Another paramilitary element of the marine force is the China Marine Surveillance (CMS), a maritime law enforcement agency under the Chinese Oceanic Administration, operating US Coast Guard-style oceangoing cutters. There is also the China Maritime Safety Administration (MSA), a maritime search and rescue force and part of the Ministry of Transport, thus officially not part of the armed forces. Finally, there is the China Fisheries Law Enforcement Command (FLEC) which is a vital part of the Fisheries Management Bureau under the Ministry of Agriculture. It is responsible for the enforcement of laws concerning fishing and maritime resources in Chinese territorial waters and exclusive economic zones (EEZ).

Today, PLAN is the second largest naval force in the world with a fleet of some 500-plus combat vessels and 235,000 personnel, maintaining the three fleet structures. PLAN has six PLA naval aviation divisions as well as two marine brigades of 56,500 men. There are 34,000 in the Naval Air Force and 38,000 in Coastal Defense. Today the PLAN is a nuclear capable force and for the first time has real capacity for power projection in the form of an aircraft carrier, CNS *Liaoning* (the ex-Soviet Navy aircraft carrier *Riga*, later renamed as *Varyag (Варяг)*. For the first time in 400 years, the Chinese navy is once again seen patrolling in the waters of Eastern Africa, and the Chinese PLAN also conducted operations in the Mediterranean Sea as part of the international effort surrounding the 2011 Libyan Civil War. The Chinese PLAN is no longer restricted to Asian waters but is fast becoming a true blue water navy.

1.2 Establishment of the PLA Air Force

As early as 1925, promising individuals of the Whampoa Military Academy were selected for pilot training in the Soviet Union, and it was while there that many of these students became members of the CCP. On September 28, 1930, the Chinese Communists had a windfall when a Nationalist O2U-4 Corsair Biplane got lost and landed in the "Soviet Zone" by mistake; it was promptly captured and renamed "Lenin." Later, a Tiger Moth biplane fell into Communist hands more or less in the same way and thus these two planes constituted the token airpower of the CCP for most of the 1930s. In 1937, after the Marco-Polo Bridge Incident, the need for an air force became urgent and 43 Communist soldiers of the Eighth Route Army were selected for the Xinjiang Airlines Training School in northwest China under the auspices of a pro-Soviet warlord, Sheng Sichai. Eventually twenty-five graduated as pilots and eighteen became flight mechanics, learning their trade on planes such as the Polikarpov Po-2, Polikarpov I-15, I-16 and Polikarpov P-5. In 1942, Sheng suddenly defected to the Nationalist camp, and as expected the Soviets immediately withdrew all aid and planes, so the fledging Chinese Communist air force was stillborn.

As the Soviet Army struck at the occupying Japanese forces in Manchuria towards the end of World War II, the Chinese Communists encountered and detained some 300 members of the 4th Flight Training Group of the Imperial Japanese Kwantung Army who had been on the run from the Soviets for nine days. Under the leadership of Lieutenant Colonel Hayashi Yayichiro, they struck a deal with the Communists, and in exchange for security and shelter these ex-Japanese aviators/ground crews agreed to help the Chinese build an air force. Supported by a few aviators who had defected from the Wang Jingwei puppet regime, they all became instructors in the newly established Northeast Democratic United Army Aviation Corps (NEDAAC). With 46 abandoned Japanese planes, many of which were rescued from the scrap heap, and with former enemies as instructors, the Communist Chinese had a real air force.

The end of World War II also marked the beginning of the Chinese Civil War, and like the PLAN, the PLAAF was also boosted by captured equipment and defections from the Nationalist Chinese. By Nov 1949, the Chinese Communists could boast 130 airplanes; all were defections from the Nationalists and the puppet government of Wang Jingwei. These defections included P-51 Mustangs, B-25 Mitchells, B-24 Liberators and Canadian Mosquitoes, as well as a mix of trainers and transporters. These Western birds soon replaced the dilapidated Japanese warplanes[3] to become the mainstay of the fledging PLA Air Force. On August 15, 1945 on Nanyuan airfield on the outskirt of Beijing, the Chinese Communists fielded their first air combat unit, which incidentally predated the official formation of the PLAAF. On October 1, 1949, nine P-51D fighters, three C-46 Commando transporters, two Mosquito bombers, two PT-19 Fairchild trainers and one L-5 Sentinel made a historic first fly-pass over the foundation parade of the People's Republic of China.

On November 11, 1949, the PLA Aviation Bureau was abolished and the People's Liberation Army Air Force (PLAAF) was established with Liu Yalou[4] as commander. Soon after, the PLAAF was immediately thrown into the Korean War. The PLAAF grew rapidly with assistance from Soviet trainers as well as Soviet technology. From 1951 to 1953, the PLAAF expanded rapidly by adding twenty-eight divisions and seventy aviation regiments to its ORBAT with MiGs replacing the World War II US and British cast-off warplanes. Soon China was also building its own planes, from the MiG 17F (NATO: Fresco-C) (J-5) to MiG 21F-13 (NATO: Fishbed-A) (J-7). These new planes were vital to the PLAAF, as throughout the 1950s and 1960s the PLAAF was almost continuously in combat with the ROCAF. These air combats were not limited to dogfights but also included its newly equipped Surface-to-Air Missile (SAM) anti-aircraft force. On October 7, 1959, the PLAAF created history by successfully downing a ROCAF plane using a SAM, making the PLAAF the first air force in the world to do so. In the following decade, the PLAAF missile force shot down a further five U-2 spy planes and three US reconnaissance drones.

As China opened up again in the late 1980s the PLAAF began to reorganize and streamline its organization. Instead of four separate branches—Fighter, Ground Attack, Bomber, and Independent Regiments—it was reborn into a series of divisions that comprised a mix of fighters, bombers and other specialty functions. Focus switched from quantity to quality. Cooperation with the West in areas of aviation technology began to develop throughout the 1980s, but this rapport came to a sudden halt over the Tiananmen Square incident in 1989. Denied of Western technology, the PLAAF once again turned to the East. Help came from Russia, Ukraine, South Africa and even Israel. The 1991 Gulf War made a lasting impression on the PLA, and as a result spurred a surge in developing indigenous military technology. Today, there are approximately 398,000 personnel in the air force operating some 1,500 combat aircraft, many of which are locally developed warplanes such as the JH-7 *Flying Leopard* and J-10 *Vigorous Dragon*. Not content with restricting itself to aviation development, the PLAAF is branching out into space. In 2007, the PLAAF demonstrated its space operational capacity by shooting down a defunct satellite.

Today the PLA is a nuclear-capable army that includes a potent missile force, with increasingly sophisticated weaponry, and which has become more "Western" in its outlook. The once bloated Soviet-style organization was trimmed and transformed in a series of culls and re-organizations, losing more than a million soldiers, although much of these surplus was absorbed by the People's Armed Police (PAP), a paramilitary force focused on internal security.

Notes

1   Co-founder of the CCP with Mao. He competed for the leadership of the CCP, but lost to Mao, defected to the Nationalists and later moved to Hong Kong. He retired and died in Canada, and is buried in Scarbourgh, Toronto.
2   Wang Jingwei was once the Premier of China, but in March 1940 he defected to the Japanese to form a pro-Japanese regime of the ROC.
3   Nikkoku Ki-86 biplane trainer (10), Tachikawa Ki-55 "Ida" Adv. Trainer (30), Mitsubishi Ki-30 Lt-Bomber (3), Mitsubishi Ki-46 "Dinah" Command Reconnaissance Plane (1), Tachikawa Ki-54 "Hicholy" Trainer (5), Nakajima Ki-43 "Oscar" fighter (4), Kawasaki Ki-45 "Nick" Fighter (3).
4   Liu Yalou is one of few Communist Chinese who received formal military training. He attended the famous MV. Frunze Military Academy, under the name Sasha. A fluent Russian speaker, he served in the Soviet Armed forces and participated in the Defense of Leningrad, attaining the rank of major. He also later served with the Soviet 88th Division serving on the Asian front at Khabarovsk.

CHAPTER 2

POST-1949 DEVELOPMENTS

2.1 Early Years

2.1.1 The Army

After four years of civil war, the Communists prevailed and the People's Republic of China was proclaimed by Mao on October 1, 1949. This did not mean the end of fighting; for most of the next year, and stretching into 1951, the PLA was engaged in mopping-up operations against Nationalist forces in southern and western China: Fujian, Guangdong, Guangxi, Xinjiang, Yunnan and Guizhou provinces.

The PLA's attempt to control the island of Jinmen, also known in the West as Quemoy, only 2 km away from the city of Xiamen on the coast of Fujian Province was thwarted in the battle of Guningtou, sometimes known as battle of Jinmen. The Jinmen debacle was a major PLA defeat during the Chinese Civil War. Other Nationalist successes included the battle of Dengbao Island on the east coast of China, November 3–6, 1949, where the Nationalists thwarted a landing by the Communists through superior airpower and sustained naval bombardment. However, that victory was short-lived and the Nationalists had to evacuate all the islands off east China by May 1950.

The Jinmen Debacle

The defeat at Jinmen (Quemoy) was a wakeup call for Mao that the Communists needed to develop a navy. With an attacking force of 30,000, the Communists were unable to defeat a relatively small garrison of 15,000 Nationalist soldiers on the island. Following establishment of the PRC on October 1, 1949, the government of the ROC under Chiang Kai-Shek began withdrawing its forces from mainland China to Taiwan. However, ROC garrisons remained stationed on the islands of Jinmen and Matsu, located off the coast in Fujian Province. To "liberate" Taiwan, Mao first needed to take Jinmen and Matsu. The PLA planned to attack Jinmen by launching an initial attack with 9,000 troops to establish a beachhead, before landing a second force of roughly 10,000 on Jinmen, expecting to take the entire island in three days from an ROC garrison not expected to be larger than two divisions. Expecting that a PLA attack was imminent, the Nationalists ordered the immediate construction of various fortifications. By October, the Nationalists had laid 7,455 land mines and constructed roughly 200 bunkers on the shores of Jinmen, as well as several beach obstacles as defense against amphibious landings. Unknown to the Communists, the Nationalist garrison on Jinmen was also reinforced with armor. In the opening hours of October 25, the PLA's armada (consisting of hundreds of wooden fishing boats and junks) set sail for Jinmen from Xiamen, about eight kilometers distant across a narrow strait.

They intended to land near the village of Longkou on the narrowest part of the island. However, due to the crudeness of their craft, choppy waters and winds (which caused seasickness in the troops); many of them were scattered and carried past Longkou and northwestwards toward the shore of Guningtou instead.

Around 0130 hours on October 25, a Nationalist patrol accidentally set off one of the land mines. The blast alerted other units all along the northern shore and the PLA's quiet approach was detected by the alerted Nationalist defenders. Backlit by flares, the

PLA became silhouetted sitting ducks. Later, at about 0200 hours, when the tide started to recede, PLA troops from the 244th, 251st, and 253rd Regiments landed on the north side of Jinmen Island at Guningtou, Huwei, and Longkou. The 244th Regiment was the first ashore, landing near Longkou where the Nationalists were the strongest. The defenders sprayed the invaders with machine-gun and artillery fire, causing heavy casualties. The 251st and 253rd Regiments fared better, landing near Guningtou and Huwei where they broke through Nationalist defenses and continued inland. Arriving at high tide, many of the PLA landing vessels became immobilized by beach obstacles; when the tide went out, the PLA junks became stuck and were unable to return to the mainland to transport the second wave of troops. Although the Communists were initially supported by artillery from the mainland, it had to cease firing once the infantry disembarked. Some of the troops, stranded offshore in their vulnerable landing craft had to swim or wade some 600 m in order to reach the beach. The beached PLA junks were destroyed by two ROCN vessels, as well as by the Nationalists who used flamethrowers, grenades, and burning gasoline and oil on the surface of the sea.

The advancing PLA forces were met by the ROC 18th Army and US-made M5A1 tanks of ROC 1st Battalion, 3rd Tank Regiment. The PLA's 244th Regiment held high ground at Shuangru Hill, but were beaten back by ROC armor by early morning. The PLA's 253rd Regiment holding Guanyin Hill and the Huwei Highlands were also forced to fall back by 1200 hours after an overwhelming Nationalist counterattack. The PLA's 251st Regiment managed to break out of the attempted encirclement, enter the village of Guningtou and dig in at Lincuo. Shortly afterwards, the 251st was attacked by the Nationalists' 14th and 118th Divisions, but stiff resistance by the Communists managed to beat back the Nationalists, with the 118th suffering heavy casualties. Despite heroic last stands by the invaders, by the end of the day, the PLA had lost its beachheads at Huwei and Lungkou, and was fighting a desperate battle.

At 0300 hours on October 26, around 1,000 troops in four companies from the PLA 246th Regiment landed on Jinmen to reinforce the troops already on the island. At dawn, the 246th managed to break through to the village of Guningtou, making a rendezvous with the surviving PLA troops. Soon after, the Nationalists' 118th Division launched a counterattack on PLA forces in Guningtou. The resulting battle was extremely bloody, house-to-house fighting in the streets. With air support from ROCAF, the Nationalists eventually prevailed, taking Lincuo by noon and Nanshan by mid-afternoon, whereafter the surviving PLA forces began falling back to the coast. By the morning of the 27th, the surviving 1,300 or so PLA soldiers, having exhausted their food and ammunition, had retreated to the beaches north of Guningtou for a last stand. The Nationalists came in for the kill and after a brief battle, the remaining PLA troops surrendered.

The defeat at Jinmen effectively blunted further attempts to achieve a final victory over the Nationalists, giving rise to the current status quo, as well as informing the PLA leadership that a strong naval force with amphibious capability, as well as strong coastal defense capability, was needed before any attempt at the "liberation" of Taiwan.

2.1.2 The Navy

Prior to 1949 the Chinese Communist Naval force was nothing more than infantry on junks and sampans. The only trained "naval" personnel were a few former members of Wang Jingwei's river patrol force that came to the Communists in 1944 along with their gunboat. In 1946, with Soviet aid, a Naval Officer Academy was started in Dalian, and an enlisted men's school, Jiamusi, in Heilongjiang Province. Many of the graduates later infiltrated into the Chinese Nationalist Navy, with devastating effect fomenting rebellions and defections. Towards the end of the Chinese civil war, the PLA captured a Chinese Nationalist landing craft, making this the first true naval vessel of the PLA, but the joy was short-lived as it was soon destroyed by the Chinese Nationalist Air Force.

2.1.3 The Air Force

January 1, 1946 saw the establishment of New Democratic United Army Aviation Academy, and on August 15 of the same year, the first official PLA aviation combat unit was established. Just over a month after the founding of the PRC, on November 11, the PLAAF was officially founded.

2.2 The 1950s

2.2.1 The Army

Mao first raised the question of cutting the bloated PLA to four million men at the beginning of the 1950s; however, this plan was put on hold with the outbreak of the Korean War. Instead of cutting numbers, the PLA grew into a massive 6.27 million force. In late 1951, the question of cutting PLA numbers was again on the agenda. A proposal was to cut the numbers to three million, but by October 1952 the force was only down to 4.2 million and for many years this was the size of the PLA. In 1952 the PLA was biased towards the Army, which numbered some 3.76 million men. The Air Force had 304,000 while the Navy was only 126,000 strong. Demobbed soldiers were found employment in the Public Security (Militia) Force and Construction and Agriculture Force, while a sizable number return to their families in villages and found work in local areas. By the middle of the 1950s, the PLA was downsized from 3.83 million in 1956 and a further reduction took the force to its lowest yet, 2.5 million men, by the end of 1958. In cutting numbers, the PLA was also restructured. Previously there were five different force of arms (Army, Navy, Air force, Air Defense, Public Security) and up to eight headquarters (Chief of Staff, Inspectorate of Training, Armed Force Inspectorate, Political, Logistics, Finance, Armaments, Officers Administration) and these were reduced to three forces of arms (Army, Navy, Air Force) and three headquarters departments (Staff, Political, Logistics).

In October 1950, the Chinese People's Volunteer Army (PVA)[1] crossed the Yalu River into Korea under the leadership of General Peng Dehuai. The PVA soldiers, battle hardened following many years of fighting initially gained early success against the UN troops. The Chinese were superbly fit,[2] had excellent field craft skills, and were able to withstand hardship while relying on minimum resources. Lightly armed but able to move at great speed over almost impossible terrain, the PVA were able to close with and "hug" the enemy in close combat where the UN's superior firepower was mitigated by their fear of blue-on-blue fire. Using superior infiltration tactics, the PVA were able to surround the UN forces, creating panic and the wholesale collapse of entire units. However, as the war went on, the lack of effective air cover and inability to match the superior firepower of the US-led UN forces, coupled with a lack of effective cold weather protection[3] and poor communications (a PVA battalion had only two telephones; communications in the field were based on bugles, whistles and runners), meant that the PVA suffered tremendously. Poor logistics was also a key reason for the failure of the PVA. Used to foraging and gaining help from locals and the countryside during the Chinese Civil War, the PVA were surprised to find that in wintery Korea there was nothing much to forage, and withdrawing UN troops destroyed much of the remaining food stock. It was not until the stalemate period in the latter days of the war, when both sides settled on fixed lines, that the PVA was able to guarantee regular food supplies. Despite the material setback, the PVA was able to hold the much superior UN force at bay, culminating with a truce in 1953. Mao's son, Mao Anying, serving as a staff officer in General Peng's command HQ team, died in one of the many US air attacks.

For years the actual PVA combat commitment and loss in the Korean War has been a mystery to the West. According to reliable Chinese sources, China committed 1.9 million troops to Korea, and another half a million as combat replacements, giving a total of 2.4 million troops over the three years of the war. Militias, mostly in non-combat roles in rear areas, added another 600,000, giving a grand total of three million. China reported 115,786 combat deaths, 221,264 combat injuries, and 29,085 captured/surrendered, providing a total of 366,145.

Non-combat loss to the PVA was as high as 556,146, with almost 38% loss to hospitalization, Accidental deaths account for 10,808, while 73,686 men were deemed unsuitable and were returned to civilian duties, 786 committed suicide, 64 were executed, 3,089 were incarcerated for criminal activities, 450 dismissed/sacked, 17,715 went AWOL, and 4,202 died of illness. However, of the many that were hospitalized 173,405 eventually returned to active military duty, reducing the actual non-combat loss to 382,741.

For most of the 1950s the main task of the PLA was to complete the liberation of China by mopping up remnants of the KMT-led Nationalist Army holed up in the many islands on the southern and southeastern coasts of China. In April 1950 the PLA completed the conquest of the Island of Hainan, retaking the Wanshan Archipelago off Guangdong Province near Hong Kong and Macau in the summer months of 1950 and liberating Zhoushan Island off Zhejiang Province in May 1950. In 1952 the PLA conducted the Battle of Nanpeng Archipelago in the coastal areas of Guangdong Province and the Dongshan Island Campaign in 1953. In 1955, it led a combined-arms force in an air, sea, and land battle to take the Island of Yijiangshan, which saw the elimination of the last major KMT forces in the coastal areas of China, bar the islands of Jinmen (Quemoy) and Matzu off the Fujian coast, which are still controlled by Taiwan. Besides fighting the Nationalist Chinese, the PLA also exerted a large force, up to 1.5 million men, in pacification operations against bandits, pirates and outlaws within the Chinese mainland and coastal waters. These operations only came to an end by late 1953.

In the late 1950s both sides entered into a new phase of struggle. In 1958, on the coast of Fujian Province, a twenty-year artillery duel began with the Nationalist Army garrison on Jinmen Island, known by the Chinese as the "Jinmen Artillery Duels." The most intensive period occurred between August and October 1958, but from late 1958 to 1979 both sides transformed the military contest into a political wrestling match that lead to an almost comical farce with both sides only shooting on odd number days of each month, deliberately aiming at unmanned zones to minimize casualties. By the 1970s most of the shells were propaganda shells containing only leaflets. During much of the 1950s air battles over the Taiwan Straits were also common, with Chinese MiGs of the PLAAF conducting dogfights against the ROCAF's American-supplied F-86 Sabers.

From 1950 to 1961, the PLA saw action in a series of intermittent border clashes initiated by some of the surviving KMT troops who had escaped to Burma and Laos. These die-hard anti-communists vowed to continue the struggle under the banner of the Nationalist Revolutionary Army. Supplied by Taiwan using CIA logistics capacity, they fought a guerrilla campaign around the border areas of southwest China, in the Sino-Burmese frontier zone. By the 1970s, with support from Taiwan dwindling, some turned to opium cultivation to survive, creating the infamous Golden Triangle Drug Zone in the border area of Laos, Thailand, and Burma. However, by the 1980s many of these old soldiers and their descendants had tired of the criminal/guerrilla lifestyle and began to settle in Taiwan through an amnesty program, although some chose to stay in Thailand, where they remain today.

For more than twenty-five years, 1950–78, China provided unending military, economic and political support to the Communist Vietnam. In 1950 Ho Chi Minh, then the leader of the Vietnamese Communists, asked China for help and Mao agreed to assist Ho by forming the Chinese Military Advisory Group (CMAG). Over the period between the last weeks of July and the first week of August 1950, a total of 281 senior PLA officers under the guise of "South China official work teams" infiltrated into Vietnam. The CMAG was headed by a senior PLA officer, General Wei Guoqing, and Mao also appointed a special envoy, General Chen Geng, as his personal representative. One of the reasons Chen was selected was that he knew Ho personally from his days as a cadet at Whampoa Military Academy, and Mao thought that personal rapport was critical in establishing a good working relationship with the Vietnamese. The CMAG primary mission was to advise, guide and train the Vietnamese forces, from the use of heavy weapons and small unit tactics to military planning and strategy as well as complex combined-arms tactics. In 1950, from April to September, the Chinese gave the Vietnamese enough supplies to equip 16,000 soldiers. Their training was held mainly in China in Yunnan and Guangxi provinces. The CMAG worked closely with the Vietnamese, but at no times did the CMAG enter into direct command or combat operations. The CMAG's role remained strictly advisory and under direct orders from Mao, it would never share the limelight in any success and in all circumstances let the Vietnamese take all the glory from any military victories. In addition to training, China also provided substantial material support, which would peak at 4,000 tons a month just before the decisive battle of Dien Bien Phu. To prepare for the showdown at Dien Bien Phu, the People's Army of Viet Nam (PAVN) went from two to seven divisions, and to sustain this much larger force, the PLA military support team expanded to over 15,000 men, including substantial numbers of logistics, technical and political advisors posted at all levels of the PAVN's command.

General Chen provided key input in the development of the master plan that led to the French evacuation of Lao Kay, Lang Son, and Hoa Binh, abandoning virtually all of Vietnam north of the Red River Delta, as well as destroying seven French battalions. Meantime, Chen's tenure in Vietnam was cut short and in June 1951 he was recalled to Beijing and appointed as deputy commander of the PVA in August 1951. With the departure of Chen, Wei and the CMAG bore the sole responsibility of advising the PAVN.

The signing of the Korean Armistice in July 1953 allowed even greater resources to be devoted to supporting the Vietnamese struggle. For example, during the battle of Dien Bien Phu, the PLA was to provide some extra 8,000 tons of war materials a month to the Vietnamese. A new rush of battle-hardened PLA officers, fresh from the Korean War, proved to be invaluable to the Vietnamese during the run up to the Battle of Dien Bien Phu, and newly captured American equipment was also made available to the Vietnamese. For example, it was the Chinese who insisted that all Vietnamese artillery must be hidden in shell-proof dugouts, valuable experience learned the hard way in Korea. These hideouts prove to be a key battle-winning factor for the Vietnamese at Dien Bien Phu. To counter French air superiority, China furnished the PAVN with four battalions of 37 mm AA guns, and engineering experts with experience from Korea were sent to assists the PAVN to construct hundreds of kilometers of trenches. China also sent snipers, artillery crews to operate some of the guns, and the fire-coordination cells, and by April 1954, to facilitate the final strike against the French, China provided enough 75 mm recoilless rifles and "Katyusha" rockets to create two fire-support battalions. On the conclusion of the battle of Dien Bien Phu, CMAG ended its mission in Vietnam, though Chinese military aid continued.

After the Gulf of Tonkin incident with the United States, the Vietnamese Communists once again asked China for help, and this time, unlike the war with France, the PLA participated directly in combat support roles. This support mainly came in the form of anti-aircraft units, transportation by trucks and railway, and engineering and construction troops. From June 1965 to March 1968, over 15,000 PLA troops entered North Vietnam. According to Chinese sources, these troops participated in 2,153 direct engagements with the American/South Vietnamese forces, shot down 1,707 planes and helicopters, damaged 1,608 other aircraft, and achieved the capture of forty-two pilots. Overall, up to 320,000 PLA troops served in Vietnam in various capacities, which can be split into the following categories:

Anti-aircraft artillery (AAA) troops proved to be the single largest group—the PLA provided two dedicated AAA divisions and one independent AAA regiment for air defense of Vietnamese key points. In addition, there were AAA troops dedicated to protecting PLA construction, railway, engineering, and logistics troops, so that if these are included, China sent to Vietnam some sixteen divisions worth of air defense assets, equivalent to sixty-three AAA regiments numbering 150,000 troops.

Construction and engineering troops constituted some 100,000 soldiers, making them the second largest category of PLA troops in Vietnam. During the Vietnam War, PLA construction troops were responsible for the building and repair of 1,778 railway facilities, 577 km of railway tracks, 1,206 km of major roads, 305 bridges, 4,441 underground air raid shelters and two military airfields at Yen Bai and Noi Bai (for many years the main international airport in North Vietnam, and the principal civilian and military airport for Hanoi) with associated hardened shelters. The PLA also constructed nine semi-permanent and permanent ports/harbor facilities, 123 hardened bunkers and underground military facilities, laid 103 km of undersea communication cables and five petroleum pipelines to a total distance of 159 km.

The third category was transportation and logistics troops. China dispatched the 2nd and the 13th Divisions of its Railway Corps, a specialist PLA troop category responsible for railway transport and maintenance of railway facilities into Vietnam in 1965. These troops were formed into two specialist corps, No. 1 and No. 6. Later on, after troop rotation, the 12th Division, 58th Regiment and 10th Independent Regiment of the Railway Corps also entered Vietnam.

The last, and smallest, major category was the naval mine clearance specialists from the PLA Navy (PLAN). In May 1972, the Nixon administration ordered the renewal of bombing and the mining of Haiphong Harbor as well as inland waterways in North Vietnam. Responding to urgent requests from North Vietnam, China dispatched a total of 318 sailors and ten minesweepers to the country. From 1972 until 1974, the PLAN successfully cleared forty-two sea mines from 201 square km of coastal areas around key ports such as Haiphong, Hongay, and Cam Pha for the cost of one dead and one minesweeper damaged.

Over the eight years of the American war in Vietnam, the PLA suffered 5,270 casualties of whom 1,070 were killed. In addition to its activities in Vietnam itself, China also provided free training and education for more than 6,000 Vietnamese cadres. On top of that, China facilitated the delivery of military aid from other Communist bloc countries, most of which was carried out free of charge. The majority was routed from the USSR through the Trans-Siberian railway and delivered into Vietnam by the PLA Transport Corps. For example, in the latter part of 1972, three PLA transport regiments were mobilized, and some 2,100 trucks transported 62,500 tons of military aid to Vietnam.

According to Vietnamese sources, the North Vietnamese government received 160 million tons of military aid from China, the most generous aid provider. Second on the list was the Soviet Union with 51 million tons and third on the list was 24.5 tons from other Communist countries, mostly in Eastern Europe. Between 1950 and 1978, 93.3% of aid given by China to Vietnam was free of charge, and of that which had to be paid for, China provided interest-free loans to help Vietnam. The military aid can be broken down to the following categories: 2.2 million rifles and machine guns; 74,000 pieces of artillery of all calibers; 1.2 billion rounds of small arms ammunition; 18.7 million rounds of artillery shells; 176 naval vessels (mostly torpedo and gunboats); 552 tanks (mainly T-59s, 62s, and 63s) and 320 APCs; 170 different types of warplanes (mostly Chinese-made MiG-17s (J-5), MiG-19s (J-6) and MiG-21s (J-7)); 16,000 trucks and other military vehicles; three battalions of SA-2 equipment, and an extra 180 SA-2 missiles; two units of early warning radars; two units of pontoon bridging; 18,240 tons of explosives; one million radio and telephone sets; 130 tons of diesel fuel; 11.2 million sets of military uniform.

In the 1970s the Chinese/Vietnamese relationship began to sour. First, the death of pro-Chinese Ho Chi Minh in 1969 meant that China had lost a friend in Vietnam. However, the killer blow that broke the Sino-Vietnam relationship was the sudden arrival of the US President Richard Nixon in China in 1972. Vietnam was caught unprepared and felt betrayed by China making friends with America, North Vietnam's enemy. However, cooperation between Vietnam and China continued unabated. The material losses that resulted from the failed 1972 Spring Offensive were soon made up by China, and after the American withdrawal the Vietnamese were ready for another strike in 1974 or 1975. Flushed with new Chinese weaponry, in 1973 China withdrew all its PLA soldiers in Vietnam, feeling that Vietnam were able to go it alone. After the Vietnamese Communists gained victory in 1975, direct military aid from Beijing ceased, but Chinese support continued in the form of assisting with military infrastructure instead. China gave aid to help Vietnam establish a torpedo boat building yard, light- and heavy-machine gun factory, AA gun factory, ammunition factory, etc. and that aid continued right up to 1978, just before the Sino-Vietnam War of 1979.

Less prominent than the wars in Vietnam was another conflict in eastern China. In the 1950s, there were two attempts at an uprising in Tibet—one in 1954, which was easily suppressed, and a more serious one carried out by exiled Tibetans under the banner of the National

Volunteer Defense Army (NVDA), with CIA support, which occurred in October 1959. Better known as the Lhasa Uprising, the revolt was put down with ferocity by the PLA, which resulted with the 14th Dalai Lama escaping to India, where he remains today. In October 1961, an ambush carried out by the NVDA scored a major hit by killing a deputy regimental commander and capturing his papers.[4] The CIA continued to support the insurgency with airdrops until 1965 and intelligence until 1969. However, sporadic guerrilla attacks conducted by more militant members of the Tibetan exiles continued right up to 1974.

2.2.2 The Navy

The PLAN took no part in the Korean War and focused on building its strength and mopping-up operations in coastal waters against bandits and Nationalist raiders. At the start of the decade, there were only two fleets, the Northern and Eastern. The Eastern Fleet consisted of 134 vessels (fifty-one gunboats, fifty-two landing crafts) divided into two escort flotillas, the 6th and 7th, augmented by one landing and one minesweeping flotilla. Later in 1950 a Southern Fleet was formed, providing a three-fleet navy.

Upon the conclusion of the Chinese Civil War, the defeated Nationalists withdrew to Taiwan but also held on to thirty-two offshore islands around China's eastern and southern coasts. By holding on to these islands, the Nationalists were effecting a partial closure of mainland ports. They could also inconvenience normal fishing activities and commercial traffic. From 1950–53, there were ninety incidents of international shipping being held up in open seas by the Nationalists, two-thirds of them British vessels, which led to London filing numerous diplomatic protests. In addition to interdiction in the open seas, the Nationalists also laid mines around the mouth of the Yangtze River and the surrounding seas. Throughout the 1950s, the Chinese PLAN was engaged in a series of demining operations using a mixture of military and commandeered civilian craft. The Nationalists made numerous raids from their offshore islands and the Nationalist Navy harassed the PLAN and fishing craft and maintained a partial blockade on key coastal cities.

From October 11–15, 1952, 5,000 Nationalist commandos made a successful raid on Nanri Island off the coast of Fujian and held on to it for days before withdrawing with prizes and POWs.

The early 1950s was dominated by coastal skirmishes. Pirates and Nationalists were the two main scourges. In 1951 alone the PLAN conducted over fifty anti-pirate engagements resulting in over 600 kills and the capture/sinking of fifty-two pirate vessels. Meantime the Nationalists remained the main foe, and in April 1950 the Wanshan Archipelago campaign was regarded as the PLAN's first naval battle. The archipelago consists of forty-eight islands strategically located at the mouth of the Pearl River, a chokepoint on the communication lines to the British colony of Hong Kong and Portuguese enclave of Macau. The 4,000 Nationalist army personnel and forty vessels of the ROCN 3rd Fleet were in defense against a 10,000 PLA force backed up by a regiment-plus of long-range artillery and a Riverine Defense Force[5] from the Canton Military Region. Using the cover of darkness, the CNS *Liberation* gunboat entered into the harbor of Laurel Mountain (Guishan) Island and seriously damaged the Nationalist flagship, the frigate ROCS *Taihe*, severely wounding Qi Hongzhang, the Nationalist commander-in-chief. With Qi wounded and most of his staff killed, the Nationalist defense was thus effectively paralyzed. Without command, the loss of Guishan Island soon followed and other surrounding islands also soon fell to the PLA. This setback forced the Nationalists to withdraw their fleet and wait for reinforcements.

The next day saw the arrival of three frigates, two landing ships, four minesweepers and several gunboats from Taiwan; with superior vessels and strength in numbers, the Nationalist attempted to lure the PLAN into open waters but the PLAN did not take the bait and withdrew further into the protection of shallows. In desperation, a detachment of Nationalist vessels ventured carelessly too close to the islands and three ships suffered damage from hidden PLA shore batteries. By keeping the Nationalist Navy away from the islands and out of range of naval support, the PLA was able to isolate the Nationalist troops on the remaining islands in the archipelago. They were soon picked off by the PLA using leapfrog tactics, forcing the Nationalist to withdraw even further to the remaining outlaying islands. By clever use of tactics, the PLAN successfully laid a trap and once again lured the unsuspecting Nationalist ships too close to shore and thus into an ambush by accurate artillery fire, resulting in one gunboat sunk, and one destroyer, two large patrol craft, two minesweepers and two gunboats damaged. Finally, on August 7, 1950, the PLA succeeded in taking all of the Wanshan Archipelago. During this campaign the Chinese Nationalists suffered 700-plus casualties, with the loss of four gunboats sunk and eleven other vessels captured, while the PLA had one landing craft damaged and three hundred casualties.

Other notable naval engagements of the 1950s include the battle of Tanhu Hill Island at the mouth of the Yangtze River near Shanghai. A shallow draft ex-IJN river gunboat conducted shore bombardment that resulted in capturing forty-six POWs and four Nationalist craft. The year 1950 also saw the capture of Shengsi Island, the battle of Phishan Island, and the retaking of Zhoushan Island. In 1952 the PLA conducted the battle of Nanpeng Archipelago in the coastal areas of Guangdong province and the Dongshan Island campaign in 1953.

The air battle of Sanmen Bay in March 1954 is regarded as the first air-to-air combat mission of the newly formed PLANAF. Two of the four ROCAF's P-47s intercepted by a flight from the PLA Naval Aviation's 6th Regiment, 2nd Division were shot down, making the first recorded kills by the PLANAF.

A major naval success of the PLAN in November 1954 was the sinking of ROCS *Tai-Ping, F22* (the ex-USS *Decker, DE-47*, an *Evarts*-class destroyer escort), which at 1,520 tons was one of the largest vessels of the ROCN. This incident is sometimes known as the Yushanlie Island Sea Battle.

Despite the defeat in the Chinese Civil War and evacuation from mainland China, the Nationalist Chinese still held on to some outer islands west and southwest of Shanghai and continued to use these as a base to harass Communist Chinese shipping. The situation developed to a level where Mao specifically ordered the PLAN to sink one or two of the larger Nationalist naval vessels as a show of strength, as well as to lay the foundation for the capture of these islands from the Nationalists. The PLAN decided to lay an ambush and deployed its newly established

Soviet-trained and -equipped torpedo flotilla by sneaking eighteen torpedo boats from the 31st Fast-Attack Craft Squadron, an elite unit under the command of Mu Hua.

The eighteen vessels sailed from Qingdao in the north to the operation area by sailing in the shadow of larger transport or merchant vessels, so that they did not show up on radar. The boats used for the attack were P4 aluminum-hulled torpedo boats. The Chinese P4 was based on the Soviet K-123 hydroplane design and was armed with twin 14.5 mm machine guns, and two 18in (43cm) torpedoes. As preparation for this attack, the fast-attack craft flotilla trained for three months in nearby waters in order to distract the Nationalists from patrolling towards the area in which the torpedo boats were hiding, PLANAF made constant attack and harassment patrols around the Nationalist-controlled islands so that the ROCN were constantly alert for air attacks and neglected effective watch against sea attack. Finally, six boats were selected to spearhead the attack.

After a number of false alarms, an opportunity occurred on the night of November 14–15, 1954. Shore radar detected the movement of ROCS *Tai-Ping*, and instructed the four torpedo boats from the first section (boat nos. *155*, *156*, *157*, and *158*) that were on standby to attack. On the night of November 15 at 0005 hours, radar detected ROCS *Tai-Ping* moving at 12 knots on a bearing of 62 degrees. The four boats were ordered to lay an ambush on the homeward leg of *Tai-Ping*'s voyage back to its base at Taichen Island, an offshore island on the coast of Zhejiang Province still in the hands of the Nationalists. By 0050 hours, the four PLAN torpedo boats were lying in wait at the ambush point. At 0128 hours, the PLAN lookout spotted a flash of light off his starboard bow, a case of poor light discipline of the ROCN sailors. The four boats formed up line abreast to attack. Boat *155* was first to release its torpedoes, though at almost 2,000 meters and in rough seas, the release was premature and missed its target. The other boats each released one torpedo each, and also missed. In unison all four boats turned and came around for a second run at 0135 hours. This time Boat *158* scored a direct hit on the bow of ROCS *Tai-Ping*. The 150 kg warhead exploded and the *Tai-Ping* immediately lost all power and came to a stop. After drifting for two hours, Nationalist Navy boats arrived in an attempt to place *Tai-Ping* under tow, but before it could reach Taichen Island, at 0724 hours the *Tai-Ping* sank. This battle marked a key turning point in the PLAN's history, and from this point onward the PLAN began to dominate its eastern shores, eventually culminating with the capture of Yijiangshan Island on January 18, 1955, forcing the Nationalists away from eastern China. Torpedo Boat *158* was awarded the accolade of "People's Hero" and is today displayed in the PLA Military Museum in Beijing.

In 1958, to supply the island of Jinmen during artillery duels, the Nationalists had to run a dangerous gauntlet, resulting in frequent naval skirmishes. Losses occurred on both sides. Success went not just to the PLAN but also in some actions to the ROCN. In what is known by the Nationalists as "9.2 Sea Battle," the gunboat ROCS *Tuojiang* (ex-USS *PC-1247* sub-chaser), while escorting a landing craft (LSM *249*) came under attack from twelve PLAN boats and managed to sink ten of them, but was damaged so severely that despite reaching home port in Taiwan, the vessel had to be scrapped.

2.2.3 The Air Force

The early 1950s saw frequent Nationalist bombing raids on Shanghai. The Soviets came to the aid of the Chinese by dispatching General Batitskiy along with the 52nd AAA Division and the 106th Fighter Division, which comprised the 29th Guard (forty MiG-15s), 351th Fighter Regiment (forty La-11s), 829th Mixed Regiment (ten Tu-2s, twenty-five Il-10s), and an independent transport group (four Li-2s). In a period of eight months, the Soviets shot down seven ROCAF and one USAF planes with no combat loss. At the end of the emergency deployment, the Soviets "sold" all the planes and equipment to the Chinese at a fire sale price.

With increasing training and confidence, the PLAAF began to take on the ROCAF/USAF intrusions themselves. From 1952 to 1967 the PLAAF claimed twenty-seven kills with twenty-three damaged. A notable engagement occurred on September 20, 1952, when the PLAAF successfully intercepted an ROCAF B-29 bomber. In

1953, the PLAAF claimed a US Lockheed Neptune P2V-7 maritime reconnaissance aircraft. In 1956 the PLAAF scored its first night kill with a ROCAF B-17G bomber, followed by an American Martin P4M-1Q Mercator electronic reconnaissance aircraft and an RF-84F Thunderjet in 1957.

PLAAF involvement in the Korean War lasted two years and eight months. According to Chinese archives the PLAAF claimed 330 planes destroyed and ninety-five damaged in exchange for 231 Chinese planes shot down and 151 damaged. Like the land force, the PLAAF was deployed into Korea under the overall banner of CPV (Chinese People's Volunteers) with the air force element named CPVAF. The initial concept was for the CPVAF to protect the main supply routes (MSRs) and also to support ground operations. To achieve this aim, six fighter regiments (five MiG-15, one La-11), two Il-10 attack and four Tu-2 bomber regiments, a total of 360 planes, was deployed for combat. This was later expanded to 1,300 planes by the end of 1951. As the MiG-15 and IL-10 were both short-range aircraft, airfields needed to be constructed inside North Korea, and with the CPVAF came a large engineering corps in support.

The CPVAF had to face the Americans and their allies, a mighty foe with over 1,200 planes, often piloted by World War II veterans, many with 1,000 flying hours or more. By comparison, at the beginning of 1950, the PLAAF had fewer than 200 planes in total, and the Chinese pilots had only at most 100 hours of flying time. Of those lucky enough to have jet experience, most had just started to fly solo! Initially the PLAAF was held back from combat to focus on training, and much of it was done on the job. On December 21, 1950, the PLAAF sent one fighter group from the 4th Division—ten pilots along with their MiG-15s—to Langtou airfield at Andong under the supervision of the Soviets. The first engagement between the PLAAF and the Americans took place a month later, on January 21, 1951, and the embryonic PLAAF succeeded in wounding an F-84 Thunderjet. The first kill took place a week later when they downed an F-84 over the sea. However, the PLAAF lost two MiGs and one pilot due to inexperience. The Chinese leadership realized that the PLAAF was not yet ready for large-scale combat operations.

It was only on March 15, 1951 that the CPVAF was established in Andong with Liu Zhen as its commander. Initially the ORBAT consisted of three fighter divisions (2nd, 3rd, and 4th) and two bomber divisions (8th and 10th). Despite intensive training, the CPVAF was still no match for the US/UN force; as such the Soviets were often asked to provide top cover for CPVAF operations, but the language barrier stifled combat effectiveness. Without air cover the CPV logistics columns were hit hard by the US/UN air force. The forward airfields inside North Korea so vital to the CPVAF's strategy of close-air support for ground operations were rendered unserviceable due to constant attack by US/UN forces. In essence, the CPVAF failed to achieve both its primary missions.

By the summer of 1951, the ground war had become a stalemate along the 38th Parallel. Realizing the likelihood of a protracted conflict, the Chinese leadership decided to adopt new strategies to use the Korean War as a live training school for the entire PLA. Eighteen CPV armies were divided into two groups for rotation through the front line every two to three months. For the air force an entire division was be rotated through the theater one at a time; new airfields would also be constructed closer to the front line. In total twelve aviation divisions consisting of twenty-one fighter and three bomber regiments were rotated through the war in Korea. To keep the pressure on the US/UN force during negotiations, at any one time the PLAAF maintained as many as three or even four divisions, totaling some 200 MiGs, at airfields on the Chinese side of the Yalu River.

By June 1952, the US/UN policy to strangle the Chinese lines of communication by airpower was proving futile given the vigorous defense and rapid repair of damage. As such, US/UN forces changed strategy and proceeded to target selected key strategic points, such as bridges and dams, in the hope of forcing the Chinese to the negotiating table. In defending its strategic assets, the CVPAF became more aggressive, and the experience they had gained along with new tactics provided the CPVAF with its best records against the US/UN air force. In December 1952, Lu Mi of the 12th Division became an ace by shooting down five F-86s, and Han Decai of the 15th Division claimed Captain Harold E. Fischer, USAF, a double jet ace of the 39th Squadron, 51st Wing.

Meantime, Zhao Baotong of the 7th Regiment, 3rd Division, became China's top ace with seven confirmed kills and two damaged. By 1953, another eight Chinese pilots had reached ace status with five or more confirmed kills.

After the Korean War ended in armistice, the ever-present conflict with the Chinese Nationalists continued. The Yijiangshan Island campaign was the first ever combined-arms operation by the PLA. The PLAAF deployed four regiments of Tu-2s from the 20th Bomber Division and three regiments of Il-10 ground attack aircraft from the 11th Attack Division escorted by La-11s from the 3rd, 12th and 29th Fighter Divisions, and the whole operation was supported by the 2nd Reconnaissance Regiment. The PLANAF also participated in this campaign, committing three Naval Air Divisions (1st Bomber, and 4th and 6th Fighter), altogether some 200 planes to the landing operation.

The Chinese Nationalist ROCAF-controlled airspace over southeast and southern China frequently harassed Communist China, and the shelling of Jinmen (Quemoy) Island sparked a series of intensive air battles between July and October 1958. To interdict the frequent ROCAF harassment, the Communist Chinese secretly relocated two fighter regiments (10th Regiment, naval aviation, 46th Regiment PLAAF, 74 MiG-17s) to southwest China. Under cover of poor weather, the two regiments laid an ambush. On July 29, four MiG-17Fs of the 18th Division, 54th Regiment surprised four F-84G Thunderjets over Nanao Island, 330 km northeast of Hong Kong. In a three-minute battle the PLAAF claimed three F-84Gs and one damaged, with no loss of its own. The ROCAF stepped up its act by placing armed escorts on reconnaissance sorties. These high-profile sorties resulted in three air clashes in August, with the PLAAF (9th Division/27th Regiment) and Naval aviation (4th Division/10th Regiment) claiming four F-86s and damaging four (two RF-84s) including shooting down an F-86 flown by the deputy commander of the ROCAF in exchange for one MiG-17. The air superiority suddenly tilted toward the Communists. By mid-August, seventeen PLAAF regiments (fourteen fighter, two bomber, and one reconnaissance), some 520 planes, were deployed in south and southwest China. On August 23, the PLA began shelling Jinmen, firing 30,000 rounds on the first day alone. This marked the beginning of the second phase of the air battle.

America responded with three aircraft carriers in the area as well as transferring USAF fighters and one marine squadron, a total of 144 F-100s and F-104s, to Taiwan, as well as reinforcements from Japan. Backed up by America, the ROCAF increased from 100 to 200 flights a day along the coast of China, but the PLAAF responded by doubling its force from one to two aviation divisions deployed to the front (replacing the 1st Division with the 14th and 16th Divs.). This period saw three major air battles as the PLAAF tried to use superior numbers to contain the Nationalists. Despite new tactics, ground coordination remained a problem. On August 25 an AAA unit shot down a J-5 (indigenous MiG-17) piloted by Liu Weimin of the 27th Regiment, 9th Division over Zhangzhou in Fujian Province. This was known in the PRC as the "Zhangzhou 8.25 Air Battle." On September 24, the single largest air battle occurred with 126 Sidewinder-equipped F-86Fs escorting fourteen RF-84s flying over Jinmen, anticipating a Communist assault on Jinmen Island. This was the world's first successful use of air-to-air missiles in combat in history. The PLAAF responded with 250 sorties and in three separate engagements the PLAAF claimed one damaged for both sides while PLAN naval aviation claimed two F-86s shot down. The appearance of the Sidewinder missile was certainly a shock to the PLAAF. The Nationalists claimed nine MiG-17 kills, but without gun camera footage, it is impossible to prove. From this battle, the PLAAF obtained an unexpected windfall when a Sidewinder AIM-9B with a faulty fuse became lodged in a MiG. The dud missile was recovered, along with fragments from missiles that had landed on the ground; and after much bargaining the Soviets obtained missile parts for reverse engineering that resulted in a Soviet copy known as the K-13 (NATO: AA-2 Atoll). Later when the technology was transferred to China, the Chinese produced it as the PL-2.

In late September the Nationalists mounted a massive airlift to resupply Jinmen; each day up to 120 transports flew some 600 tons of supplies to the island protected by USAF and ROCAF fighters. On October 3, twenty-four C-46s protected by forty-eight F-86s flew to Jinmen, and the PLAAF scrambled forty-eight MiG-17Fs to distract the fighters while vectoring a separate flight of four MiG-17Fs onto the C-46s, which succeeded in downing two. In the air battles from July to October 1958, the PLAAF claimed fourteen kills, while the Nationalists claimed over forty MiGs downed. Despite the fact that PLAAF lost more planes than the Nationalists, the PLAAF regained control of the airspace over southeast and southern China; although losing a tactical battle they won the strategic war. Throughout this period, the Americans were unwilling to engage the Chinese Communists directly; the so-called military support for Taiwan was limited to technical and logistical support. Without direct US involvement, the ROCAF soon found that it could not carry on the fight alone, and began curtailing and eventually stopped entirely its flights over the mainland.

On October 7, 1959, the PLAAF made aviation history by shooting down a Nationalist Martin RB-57D Canberra, piloted by Captain Wang Ying-Chin, over Beijing, with three SA-2 (NATO: Guideline) SAM missiles at an altitude of 20 km (65,600 feet). This was the first-ever successful SAM engagement in the world. It was claimed that Wang became careless and made a premature descent while turning back toward Taiwan. The RB-57 program ended around 1964, when fatigue problems with the wing spars forced the retirement of the surviving aircraft, which were then returned to the United States.

2.3 The 1960s

2.3.1. The Army

In the fall of 1962, India and China fought a month-long border skirmish that ended in a Chinese military victory. After the 1959 Tibetan uprising, India had granted asylum to the 14th Dalai Lama, which had irritated the Chinese. At the same time India initiated a forward policy and placed a number of outposts north of the McMahon Line, which the Chinese regarded as their territory. One disputed area in the west was Aksai Chin in the northeast of Ladakh District in Jammu and Kashmir, but regarded by China as part of the Xinjiang Uygur Autonomous Region of China. The other claim was known by the

Indians as Arunachal Pradesh. In the fight over these areas, the PLA overpowered the Indian troops completely, and the war ended when the PRC declared a ceasefire and withdrawal from the disputed area. In 1967 the PLA had a brief one-day skirmish with the Indians in the border area of China and Sikkim, known as the Chola Incident.

In October 1964, China detonated its first atom bomb, followed by a hydrogen bomb in 1967. Missile development took a further four years when the PLA deployed its first land-based medium-range nuclear missile, DF-3A (DF Dong Feng/East Wind) in 1971.

For a period of almost ten years (1966–76), China entered into a long period of internal chaos with the onset of Mao's Cultural Revolution. Political factional infighting hindered economic, social and military development. Numerous new weapon developments were delayed, and some were even cancelled, which severely hampered the development of the PLA. Instead of military training, soldiers spent hours on political indoctrination focusing on political correctness. To further the chaos, military ranks were eliminated.

In the winter of 1969, a border incident with the Soviet Union almost turned nuclear with disastrous consequences for the whole world. It was all about a tiny island along the Ussuri River, where the borderline should be drawn. To the Chinese it was Zhenbao Island, but it was known to the Russians as Damanskii Island. The dispute was not a new one, dating back to the days of Imperial China and Czarist Russia. During the 1950s and much of the 1960s, in the era of Communist solidarity, Chinese and Soviet frontier patrols often met and exchanged greetings, and the unsubstantiated border was never a problem between the two Communist giants. With increasing tension between the two socialist camps after the Sino-Soviet split in the mid-1960s, these cordial exchanges drifted into shouting matches and later brawls.

On March 2, 1969, these skirmishes turned violent and shots were exchanged for the first time. According to the Soviets, the Chinese provoked an incident by crossing the line of separation en masse. The Chinese accounts related that on the night prior to the shooting, the Chinese sent two infantry companies with four recce platoons, one recoilless gun, and one HMG platoon to the island. At 0840 hours on the 2nd, two thirty-man patrols pushed forward to the ice in a pincer move, the left pincer hidden in the woods and the right pincer in the open. On seeing the right flanking patrol, the Soviets dispatched two APCs, a truck and jeep to confront the Chinese. Some pushing and shoving was involved and it seems (according to the Chinese account) that the Soviet side panicked when they saw the other "hidden" group of Chinese appearing from the rear and begin to "surround" them. At 0917 hours the Soviets opened fire. The first Chinese patrol was taken by surprise and six were killed immediately. The second patrol, hearing gun shots, returned fire and killed seven, including Lieutenant Strelnikov, the leader of the Soviet border guard. The Chinese supporting group opened up with recoilless artillery and small arms fire, destroying one of the APCs. The remaining Soviet border guards then retreated in their last remaining APC and by 1030 hours the battle was over. The Soviets claimed thirty-one dead and fourteen wounded from the seventy-one involved, and the Chinese admitted to seventeen dead, thirty-five wounded and one missing.

The next encounter occurred on the 15th, and this time both sides came prepared. Although both sides had a similar number of men, the Soviets had tanks, APCs, and helicopters while the Chinese were mainly infantry, without armor or air support. Since the last encounter, both sides had stepped up their patrols and adopted a more aggressive stance, until on the night of the 14th, in order to deter the Soviets, the Chinese laid mines on the southern tip of the island. On the morning of the 15th, the Soviets sent sixty men supported by six APCs to the northern tip of the island and laid in wait in the bushes. Two patrols from the 1st Battalion, 217th Regiment, 73rd Division PLA crossed to the island and by 0802 hours made contact with the Soviets in the bushes—shooting started immediately. After an hour, the PLA successfully drove the Soviets to retreat to their bank. Thus ended the first encounter.

The second encounter began almost as soon as the first ended. At 0946 hours, three Soviet planes made aggressive maneuvers over the Chinese positions with the aim of diverting the Chinese attention while the Soviets deployed tanks. Six (some say four) tanks and five APCs in two columns moved towards the Chinese. Four tanks made it across the ice and attempted to flank the Chinese, but one tank was blown up by mines and the other three retreated under a hail of artillery, RPGs and recoilless rifle fire. Two APCs were destroyed. Again, the Soviets retreated and thus round two of the battle ended.

After recuperating, unknown to the Chinese the Soviet brought up their divisional artillery (378th Artillery Regiment) plus a rocket battalion from the 13th Independent Rocket Artillery (less one battery) and launched a massive artillery barrage with over 10,000 rounds from 122 mm howitzers and 100 mm towed antitank guns, as well as BM-21 "Katyuska" rockets 10 km to the rear of the front line. The Soviets reported that up to 800 Chinese were killed.

At 1500 hours the second attack began, this time with 100 or so troops backed up by ten tanks and fourteen APCs which rushed the Chinese positions. The Chinese artillery responded and at approximately 1700 hours, the Soviet commander Major Leonov was killed. A T-62 tank, one of the latest Soviet tank of that era, fell into Chinese hands after it was disabled by an RPG attack. PLA soldier Hua Yujie with Yu Haichang, his number two in the RPG team, were able to destroy four Soviet tanks or APCs and achieved more than ten kills by using a combination of assault rifle/grenades as well as their 40 mm RPG-2. Hua and Yu were awarded the accolade "Combat Hero" by the Central Military Commission, and their action was commemorated in a stamp. The Soviets made successive attempt to recover the T-62, but each time were thwarted by the PLA artillery, and eventually the tank fell through the ice and sank into the river. It was eventually recovered using Navy divers, and after intensive study became the blueprint for the PLA's future MBT development. The result was an up-gunned T-59, known as the T-69 MBT. This captured T-62 is now displayed at the Beijing Military Museum. Over the three days, the PLA successfully halted Soviet advances onto Zhenbao Island, and according to the Chinese eventually evicted all the Soviet troops from the island.

Other notable border incidents of this period include Tielieketi Incident. Tielieketi is located in western China, Xinjiang Province (around Lake Zhalanashkol) and the incident took place in August

1969. According to the Chinese, three patrols with a total strength of 100, including three accompanying journalists, were patrolling in the Tielieketi area, a disputed zone, when they were attacked by a superior Soviet force. One of these patrols, of twenty-two soldiers and the journalists, was ambushed and surrounded by approximately 300 Soviet troops and attacked with supporting arms including BTR-60PB APCs, T-62 tanks and two armed helicopters. The PLA patrol was annihilated. This incident and the Zhenbao Island skirmish almost led to all-out war between China and the Soviet Union with each side massing millions of troops at the border. However, tensions eventually cooled, and both border disputes are now solved: China and Russia, and China and Kazakhstan have signed agreements to ratify the former borders between the nations. Zhenbao Island is recognized as Chinese territory by Russia and the disputed territory along Tielieketi has been formalized as part of China.

In the midst of tensions with the Soviet Union, the size of the PLA grew and by 1966 it was back to more than four million soldiers. By 1975 this number had grown to a massive 6.1 million. In 1975, Deng Xiaoping instigated a program to reduce the PLA by 1.6 million over three years. However, before the job was completed Deng was purged and the PLA only managed to reduce to 5.3 million.

2.3.2 The Navy

During the 1960s the PLAN's major focus was on yet more coastal skirmishes against the Nationalist Chinese, who by this time were fully entrenched on the Island of Taiwan. These naval battles moved to mainly around the waters of the Taiwan Straits. In 1965 the battles of August 6 and November 13 were a case in point. In both cases, smaller PLAN vessels were able to sink much larger Nationalist warships. Working in groups, PLAN torpedoes and gunboats sunk two ROCS sub-chasers, the *Zhengjiang (ex-*USN MSF-*387)* and the *Jianmen (ex-*USN PC-*1232)* in the August 6 battle (known in China as 8.6 Sea Battle), and a ROCS escort, the *Linhuai,* in the "November Chongwuyidong Sea battle."

2.3.3 The Air Force

After the Gulf of Tonkin incident, the Chinese were increasingly concerned about a possible Sino-American war over Vietnam. To guard against possible US intrusion, the PLAAF moved forward air defense assets to the Sino-Vietnam border. The 17th (less its 49th Regiment) and 26th Divisions were deployed forward while the 9th Division was put on alert. On the other hand, US President Johnson was equally suspicious about the real intentions of the Chinese. The US's biggest fear was that the Chinese would intervene in the Vietnamese conflict as they had in Korea. From August 1964 to December 1969, the Chinese detected ninety-seven drone intrusions into southern China. To avoid escalation, Beijing authorized shooting down these UAVs but not manned aircraft, and from late August 1964, PLAAF J-6s (Chinese MiG-19s) were placed on alert. On November 15, a J-6 from the 1st Division, piloted by Xu Kaitong, claimed a kill, a BQM-147 Dragon UAV. The Chinese claimed twenty UAV kills during the Vietnam War (PLAAF: seventeen, naval aviation: three).

The Chinese soon realized that such restraint would not halt the American escalation of hostilities. On April 8, 1965, two USN F-4B Phantoms flew over Yulin naval base on Hainan Island. The next day eight F-4Bs in two groups intruded over Hainan. Four J-5s of the Chinese Navy's 8th Division were scramble to intercept the second group of Phantoms. The rules of engagement stated that the Chinese pilots were not to fire unless fired upon. On the next day, April 10, the Chinese claimed that the Americans fired an AIM-7 missile but missed. This escalation marked a key turning point, and from then on standing orders were to try to shoot down all intrusions, manned or otherwise. PLAAF records show that from August 1964 to November 1968 there were 383 incidents of manned US intrusion into Chinese airspace. The first kill of a manned US plane, an F-104C, occurred over Leizhou Peninsula, just north of Hainan Island on September 20, 1965, and was made by a J-6 from the Navy's 4th Division. From September 9–17, 1966, PLAAF J-6s from the 18th Division claimed two F-105 Thunderchiefs, and these were followed by an F-4B Phantom, two A-4 Skyhawks and another F-4C Phantom in April, May, and June 1967. The first was a PLAAF kill, the two A-4s were taken down by AAA fire, and the last one was a PLAN kill. In August 1967, a J-6 from the 18th Division achieved a double kill of two A-6A Intruders somewhere close to the Sino-Vietnam border. Despite the list of combat tallies, overall the Chinese air force and naval aviation only engaged American forces if they intruded too deeply into Chinese airspace. Beijing had no intention of being dragged into another war with the United States, and when in 1968 President Johnson halted bombing in North Vietnam, Beijing saw it as an opportunity to withdraw from the war and began pulling its troops from Vietnam in early 1969.

Whereas the PLAAF aviation involvement with Vietnam was limited to homeland defense, up to three divisions of PLAAF air defense troops were dispatched to Vietnam from August 1965 to March 1969, where they were deployed to front-line locations and saw constant action against the American forces. In the three years and seven months when Chinese AAA troops were deployed in Vietnam, the Chinese claimed 597 kills in exchange for 280 KIA and 1,166 wounded. Fifteen AA guns and four sets of radar were also destroyed. As the Indochina war spread into Laos, the Chinese were a reluctant player in this secret war. From December 1970 to November 1973, Beijing dispatched up to two PLAAF air defense divisions, the 15th and 19th, into Laos. As they had with Korea, the top brass of the PLAAF saw the war in Laos as a training opportunity for the PLA, and throughout the three years of war, fifteen PLAAF AAA regiments, nineteen AA battalions and two independent HMG companies were rotated through Laos. Partly due to the lower intensity and scope of the battles, and fewer troops on both sides, the Chinese claimed only seventeen planes shot down in Laos, and three damaged.

In the late 1950s the Nationalists intensified their air reconnaissance over mainland China. Initially, converted B-17 bombers were the main reconnaissance platform of the ROCAF, until the PLAAF brought in the MiG-17PF night fighter. After a series of losses, the ROCAF turned to Lockheed Neptune P2Vs in 1960. At first, the PLAAF was unable to deal with the P2V, but as the PLAAF tactics improved and more sophisticated inceptors like the MiG-19 came online, overflights into mainland China became increasingly dangerous. To beat the increasingly sophisticated PLAAF, the Nationalists turned to using more sophisticated planes such as the RF-101 Voodoo and RF-104G Starfighter. For strategic reconnaissance, the Nationalist Chinese cooperated with the CIA under the code name "Project Razor," using U-2 spy planes to fly over the mainland. A specialist formation, the "Black Cat" 35th Squadron, was formed to conduct this secretive operation, and so secret was this unit that all supporting US personnel had false names and wore no uniforms.

The main purpose of the U-2 flights was to find out more about the Chinese A-bomb project, much of it located deep within mainland China, totally out of range of conventional reconnaissance planes like RF-101 and RB-57. The first overflight of mainland China by U-2C (No.385) was made in January 1962. This flight lasted some 8 hours and 40 minutes and succeeded in detecting China's first Tu-16 bombers. To avoid using a regular flight pattern, some of the missions had the U-2s flying from or to other US air bases such as K-8 (Kunsan) in South Korea, or Tikhli in Thailand. All US AFBs in the region were accessible by the "Black Cats" as emergency alternate recovery points in addition to the squadron's home base at Taoyuan Airbase in Taiwan.

Due to the high altitude, the only way to defeat the U-2 was by SAM. On September 9, 1962 the PLAAF scored a hit on a Nationalist U-2 No. 378, piloted by Major Chen Huai over Nanchang in central China (see "U2 kills and The Black Cat Squadron"). Learning a valuable lesson, subsequent U-2s were all upgraded with new electronic devices to evade the PLAAF's SA-2 high-altitude SAM. With these countermeasures in place, the Nationalists became careless and began to develop a flight pattern, entering mainland China via the southeast and using Nanchang City as a waypoint/navigation checkpoint before proceeding to the target. After analyzing the data, the Chinese Communists decided to lay an ambush with four SAM battalions. On November 1, 1963, a U-2 was detected over Shangrao City on its return leg from Jiuquan in the northwest, China's Cape Canaveral. The 2nd Battalion let loose three SA-2s and one found the mark, downing the U-2. Major Yeh Changti (Robin Yeh) was captured and was held for twenty years before being released in 1983. In July 1964, the 2nd Battalion scored another kill, earning the honorific title of "Air-Force Hero." ROCAF pilot Major Lee Nanping failed to eject because his ejector seat was not properly armed.

After China exploded its first A-bomb on October 16, 1964, U-2 flights intensified, especially toward the northwest area where China had its secretive nuclear facilities. Initially, the Nationalists were again able to circumvent PLAAF's SAM tactics by using new electronic interference, but by 1965, after intensive study of previous failures, the PLAAF changed tactics and the 1st SAM Battalion scored a hit over Baotou in Inner Mongolia on January 10, 1965, capturing pilot Major Chang Liyi. Like Yeh, Chang was not released until 1983. The last U-2 kill was brought down by the 14th SAM battalion using the locally made SA-2 (HQ-2) on September 18, 1967 close to Nanjing in eastern China; pilot Huang Jungbei failed to eject and was killed. U-2 flights continued throughout the 1960s, though by the 1970s, with the deployment of more sophisticated spy satellites, the U-2 was no longer considered necessary. The last U-2 flight took place on July 29, 1974. From 1962 to 1974, the "Black Cat" Squadron flew about 220 missions, with 102 over mainland China. Of nineteen U-2s operated by the 35th Squadron, five were shot down, with three pilots killed and two captured. A further six U-2s were lost in training with six pilots killed.

- September 9, 1962, U-2 No. 378, pilot Major Chen Huai KIA.
- November 1, 1963, Major Yeh Changdi piloting No. 355 U-2C was shot down while on a mission to Communist China, northwest Gansu province to check on China's missile manufacturing facilities. Yeh captured and released via Hong Kong in October 1983. Lieutenant Colonel Yue Zhenghua and his 2nd Battalion took the credit for this kill.
- July 7, 1964, Lieutenant Colonel Lee Nanpin, flying from NAS Cubic Point in the Philippines, was on a mission to reconnoiter PLA supply lines into North Vietnam. His U-2G No. 362 was shot down by PLAAF SAM in Fujian Province on his return

to Taiwan. Lieutenant Colonel Lee was killed despite ejecting. Once again Lieutenant Colonel Yue Zhenghua and his 2nd Battalion took the credit.

- January 10, 1965, Major Chang Liyi flew No. 358 U-2C from Taiwan on an IR photography mission to spy on PLA's nuclear bomb production facilities. He was shot down but survived and was released in 1983 with Major Yeh, both settled in the United States after release. The kill was credited to Wang Lin, commanding officer of the 1st Battalion.

- September 8, 1967, Captain Huang Jungpei piloting No. 373 U-2A was shot down over Jiaxing City in Zhejiang Province by a Chinese Red Flag HQ-2 SAM (copy of SA-2). Deputy battalion commander and temporary commissar[6] Xia Cunfeng and the 14th Battalion were credited with this kill. The first recorded success using a Chinese-made SAM.

- May 16, 1969 Major Chan Hsieh was on a night mission in northern China; when entering the Yellow Sea the plane lost control some 185 kilometers south of Cheju Island in Korea. He did not survive.

U-2 kills and The Black Cat Squadron

Throughout the early 1960s the Communist Chinese had no luck with the formidable U-2; catching one was like fishing for a needle in a haystack. The authorities of the PLAAF decided to move some of the SAM units around Beijing, the nation's capital, to lay an ambush along the regular route of the U-2s. The trap was laid around Nanchang City after analyzing radar tracks from previous U-2 flights. At that time Chiang Kai-Shek, the leader of the Nationalist Chinese, was still planning to retake mainland China, and he was desperate to seek information on recent troop concentrations, especially in the southeast. To force the Nationalists to act, the PLAAF deliberately made a series of high-profile announcements of major military redeployments in Fujian province, in southeast China.

On September 8, 1962, a U-2 flight (Mission code: GRC 127) piloted by Yang Shihchu "Gimo" turned back when over Guilin City due to electrical problems. (The aircraft would also have flown past Nanchang where the 2nd SAM Battalion was deployed). A backup U-2 was immediately deployed, piloted by Major Chen Huai. It lifted off from Taoyuan AFB near Taipei at 0600 hours on September 9 and entered Communist China's air space at 0732 hours local time. However, the U-2 No.378 was heading on a track north-northwest at 70 km east of Nanchang where the 2nd SAM battalion was located; out of range of the SAM, and Major Yue Zhenghua, the commanding officer of the 2nd Battalion, reluctantly switched off the radar. However, Chen made a U-turn after reaching Jiujiang City and backtracked to Nanchang, directly along the path that led right over 2nd Battalion's location. The PLAAF 228th Regiment, which was operating 406 early-warning radar systems in the area, acquired the U-2 some 78 km from the SAM. When Chen and his U-2 spy plane closed to about 39 km from the missile base, three SA-2 (NATO: Guideline) SAMs were launched. One missile found its mark and destroyed the U-2. Major Chen did successfully bail out but died later of injuries in a PLA hospital. He was thirty-two years old. For making the first U-2 kill, all eighty-nine members of the 2nd Battalion were decorated, and the entire 228th Radar Regiment received a unit citation. For making the world's first SAM kill of a U-2, PLA Major Yue was promoted to lieutenant colonel.

2.4 Reformation Era: 1970s–1980s

2.4.1 The Army

By the time Deng Xiaoping returned from exile in 1978, the PLA was massively overstaffed. The total ORBAT stood at just over six million strong. In 1979 there was a brief war with Vietnam and this delayed the much-needed cut in numbers. It was not until 1982 that Deng was ready to put into action his plan of 1975.

For most of the 1970s the PLA saw very little action except for the punitive one-month war against Vietnam in the spring of 1979. The PLA invaded Vietnam under the pretext of avenging Vietnamese incursions that had resulted in civilian deaths and damage to property,[7] with the incident on February 8–12, 1979 being particularly damaging. That was how the Chinese made the PR spin. However, the strategic aim of the invasion was twofold: one was to contain Vietnam, previously a staunch ally of China but which had recently sided with the Soviets, as witnessed by the Vietnam–USSR friendship treaty[8] in 1978. With the backing of the USSR, Vietnam felt it would be protected against potential Chinese retaliation. China's second motivation was a response to the Soviet-supported 1977 Vietnamese invasion of Cambodia, which at the time had a pro-China regime.

After the decision for war was confirmed by the Central Military Commission (CMC) on December 8, 1978, the engines of the PLA went into overdrive. Preparation was completed as early as January 8, 1979, and the PLA was to amass a force of 560,000 with some 700 tanks (T-59 MBTs, T-62 light tanks, T-63 amphibious tanks) and APCs for the invasion. This force consisted of twenty-nine infantry divisions, six tank regiments, one MBRL battalion, two artillery divisions, two AA divisions (supported by the Railway Corps), engineers, and a construction corps, as well as local militias, etc. The main thrust supported by tanks entered North Vietnam from two directions, from Yunnan Province in the west and from Guangxi Province in the east. The attacking force from Yunnan, some 100,000 strong, was commanded by Yang Dezhi, and another 100,000 from Guangxi were led by Xu Shiyou. H-Hour was in the morning of February 17, 1979. Facing the Chinese were six Vietnamese infantry divisions (3, 316A, 337, 338, 345, 346), plus sixteen local and four artillery regiments, giving a total of 100,000 troops. The principal objective of Xu was the capture of Cao Bang from two directions in a pincer movement with 41st Corps from the southeast, spearheaded by the 122nd and 123rd Divisions, and 42nd Corps attacking from the northwest with the 125th and 126th Divisions in the lead. In the first three hours the eastern attacking force under Xu broke through to Thông Nông but slowed when they met heavy resistance at Trà Lĩnh. A second objective of Xu was Lang Son with the 55th Corps and 43rd Corps[9] in the lead. The Chinese were able to annihilate stubborn resistance in an old French Fort in Dong Dang, and then proceed to Mong Cai, Lộc Bình, and later Khau Ma.

From the western sector Yang's objective was Lào Cai. Main forces in this sector were the 11th, 13th and 14th Corps[10] facing the Vietnamese 316 and 316A Divisions. After the loss of Lang Son, the PAVN (People's Army of Vietnam) counterattacked with the 308th Division but was beaten back. On March 5, the PLA declared a cease-fire and started to withdraw, with the last vehicle crossing the Sino-Vietnam border on March 15 at 2230 hours.

Despite achieving strategic objectives and overwhelming Vietnamese resistance, losses to the PLA were heavy. According to Chinese sources, this brief war cost the PLA 9,987 KIA and around 40,000 injured. The Chinese believed Vietnamese casualties were as high as 80,000, but from a translated Vietnamese publication, the Chinese loss was put as high as 62,500, with the loss of 280 tanks and APCs as well as 118 artillery pieces. Whatever the truth, the PLA was mauled and this became a valuable lesson for the Army as well as a pretext for Deng to overhaul the forces. Organization-wise the havoc caused by the Cultural Revolution with a rankless military proved to be a disaster, creating unnecessary confusion and administrative chaos. In tactics the PLA was still using Korean War/Chinese Civil War-style mass frontal assaults that created huge and unnecessary casualties.

Equipment-wise: lack of effective wireless communication[11] and poor coordination caused many "blue on blue" incidents; poor logistics and rear-echelon support, especially for medical facilities, caused many unnecessary deaths, and often units were faced with running out of supplies and even ammunition in the midst of battle. There was also no rapid bridging equipment. The air force lacked the ability to operate at night and was unable to provide adequate support to ground attack units. Infantry support was left mainly to artillery and tanks but T-59 MBTs were too heavy for mountainous terrain while T-62 light tanks were too lightly armored to defend against RPG teams. Lack of APCs forced the infantry to ride on top of tanks, and to prevent falling off the soldiers tied themselves to the handrails on the turret with their leather belts, but were thus unable to react quickly when ambushed. Poor combined arms coordination created much confusion that greatly reduced combat efficiency. Most of all, the PLA lacked real combat experience, having not waged a war for twenty years or more. The tactics used were often old and unsuitable for mountainous and wooded terrain; compared with the PAVN which had been in almost constant combat since 1944, the PLA were clearly out of touch with modern warfare. In a closed meeting of the CMC, Deng Xiaoping, the leader of China at that time, made the following remarks about the Sino-Vietnam War of 1979:

> The PLA still used human wave massed infantry heavy tactics as their main fighting means that resulted in huge casualties. Combined arms operations were tried but without success. The senior commanders are old and still mired in old-style defensive tactics. Even though there were numerous incidents of supreme heroism, in general we were totally unprepared for modern warfare. Despite meeting some limited objectives, the Chinese PLA had never developed any offensive doctrine, and the lack of heavy weapons and equipment combined with theory of warfare were totally outclassed by the Vietnamese.

Despite the tactical and operational setbacks, the Chinese were strategically able to meet two key aims: the debunking of Soviet aid to Vietnam, which turned out to be a "paper tiger" in that it became apparent the Soviets would never go to war with China over Vietnam. Without the backing of the Soviets, Vietnam subsequently stopped baiting China. Second, on the insistence of General Obaturov, the Soviet military advisor,[12] the Vietnamese forces withdrew a whole corps from the Cambodian front to reinforce the defense of Hanoi, partially achieving China's aim of supporting Cambodia in their war against Vietnam.

2.4.2 The Navy

During most of the Vietnam War, the Chinese navy was deployed, at the request of the North Vietnamese government, to provide naval mine clearance specialists to clear Haiphong Harbor as well as other harbors and inland waterways. From May 1972 to 1974, 318 sailors and over ten minesweepers were used to clear forty-two naval mines in which one Chinese sailor lost his life and a minesweeper was damaged.

However, towards the end of the Vietnam War, China had a relatively serious naval action against the South Vietnamese Navy over a dispute of sovereignty over the Xisha Islands (known in the West as the Paracel Islands). The brief engagement resulted in the sinking of one South Vietnamese Navy corvette and three damaged frigates with no cost to the PLAN. The 1979 Sino-Vietnam War was essentially a ground force affair. The only naval action recorded was the capture of three Vietnamese patrol boats around the Spratley Islands. There were no casualties reported from this minor action.

The battle of the Paracel Islands

In 1974, South Vietnam and China fought a brief but deadly naval action over the Paracel Islands,[13] expelling the South Vietnamese forces and resulting in their total evacuation from the entire archipelago. This was a significant event because it was the first naval battle in which the Chinese PLAN fought against external forces. The Paracel Islands are part of an archipelago in the South China Sea southeast of Hainan Island and roughly equidistant (330 km) from that island and Vietnam.

At that time, the western section of the Paracel Islands, known collectively as the Crescent Group, was controlled by South Vietnam while China controlled the Amphitrite Group in the east. Three islands on the northwest corner of the Crescent Group—Robert (Chinese: Ganquan Island, Vietnamese: Đảo Hữu Nhật), Pattle (Chinese: Shanhu Island, Vietnamese: Đảo Hoàng Sa), and Money Island (Chinese: Jinyin Island, Vietnamese: Đảo Quang Ảnh)—were under control of Vietnam, while Chinese forces controlled the southeast side of the Crescent Group, consisting of Drummond, Duncan, and Palm Island. China's interest in this area centered on Drummond and Duncan Island—on the latter was a Chinese-built fish-processing factory.

On the morning of January 15, a Chinese militia force on an island of the archipelago urgently reported the arrival of the South Vietnamese Navy (SVN) frigate RVNS *Lý Thường Kiệt (HQ-16)*[14] harassing Chinese fishing vessels and sporadically shelling Robert Island (Chinese: Ganquan Island, Vietnamese: Đảo Hữu Nhật). The South Vietnamese had dispatched a warship to the Paracels due to reports of armed Chinese fishing vessels and militia activities on Drummond and Duncan Islands.

In 1974, the PLA Navy was in a very poor state after almost eight years of political turmoil as a result of the Cultural Revolution. The flagship of the Southern Fleet was the CNS *Nanning*, an ex-IJN ship that was so old that it spent more time in dry docks than at sea. The three other newer vessels of the fleet were Type-65 escorts, but they too were unfit for duty due to various mechanical/technical problems. The commander of the Southern Fleet, Zhang Yuanpei, ordered Commander Wei Mingsen of Yulin naval base (located at the southern tip of Hainan Island) to dispatch a force to counter the Vietnamese. With the main force out of actions, Wei was left with no choice but to dispatch two of the better-conditioned Type-*6604* submarine chasers (No. *271* and *274*) to Paracel (Type-*6604* was a Chinese-built Soviet *Kronshtadt* submarine chaser). It was comparatively small at only 49.5 m in length, displacing 319 tons. It had originally been capable of 18 knots, but by 1974 could only do 12 knots. It was armed with a manual deck-operated Soviet Model-1941 85/L52 gun (15,000 m, 15–18 rounds per minute, eight crew), two single-barrel 37 mm guns and various 12.7 mm HMGs and depth charges.

The departure of the vessel was delayed by a sudden additional request by the militia on the island for more supplies. Vessels *274* and *271* left Yunlin Naval Base on January 16, 1974 at 1900 hours local time. Both eventually arrived on Woody Island, a part of the Amphitrite Group, at 1000 hours. On the 17th, at 1500 hours, the two sub-chasers left with additional stores and two additional platoons of militia to reinforce the troops already on the Crescent Group. At 1755 hours, as the Chinese approached their destination, they detected the South Vietnamese Escort Destroyer RVNS *Trần Khánh Dư* (HQ-4)[15] in the area. After challenging each other, HQ-4 retreated and eventually dropped anchor at Pattle Island just northeast of Robert Island. Ignoring the SNV in the area, the two Chinese sub-chasers *274* and *271* proceeded to marry up with fishing vessels *402* and *403* and proceed to Drummond Island, located off the southeast corner of Robert Island. On arrival, the Chinese immediately started to build up defenses on the island. Later on the 17th armed fishing vessel *No. 705* brought two further platoons of militia and proceeded to reinforce the defenses on Duncan and Palm Island.

At 0312 hours on January 18, 1974, the radar operator on *No. 271* detected HQ-*16* moving westwards, it continued until it was outside the 20-mile range of the Chinese radar. The Chinese suspected that the Vietnamese were making a flanking movement to take Drummond Island from the south. To meet this bluff, No. *274* moved at high speed towards HQ-*4* but HQ-*4* only detected *274* when it closed to within 200 meters. Alarmed at this sudden movement, it immediately switched on its floodlights. The Chinese retaliated with the same, and for a while, both vessels were lit up like Christmas trees. It was eyeball to eyeball, but the Vietnamese forces blinked first, and HQ-*4* decided to retire to Pattle Island. At dawn, around 0600 hours, HQ-*16* suddenly reappeared at Robert Island. The Chinese on *274* were alarmed. Outnumbered, they radioed for reinforcements and the CNS *271* decided to join the confrontation. While Fishing Vessel *402* was assisting No. *705* in moving stores to Duncan and Palm Island, Fishing Vessel *407* was sent with orders to sneak west and come round behind Robert Island but was detected by HQ-*16*, which blocked the movement. A game of cat and mouse soon developed, but in the sheltered water of the archipelago, due to the shallow draughts, the smaller fishing boat won the day and continued to outmaneuver the larger Vietnamese naval ship, until HQ-*16* decided it had enough and tried to ram *407*, but only managed to deliver a glancing blow to its port side. Its starboard anchor smashed into the fishing vessel's wheelhouse and became entangled with fishing boat

407. The alarmed Chinese sailors rushed onto the deck with small arms and grenades ready to shoot, while the larger Vietnamese warship tried to use its main gun, but could not depress it low enough and decided to reverse out of the confrontation. As dusk settled, the two sides decided to retire, but were still ready for a fight on the next day. In the morning, the SVN was joined by RVNS *Trán Bình Trong (HQ-5)*,[16] the ex-US Coast-Guard cutter *Castle-Rock (WAVP-383)*, while the PLAN saw the arrival of minesweepers No. *396* and *389*.

On the night of the 18th, the Chinese made a breakthrough; the Southern Fleet cypher section broke the SVN naval code and intercepted a message from Saigon ordering the SVN to retake Duncan Island using force if necessary. HQ-*10* and HQ-*16* were to take on the Chinese Navy while HQ-*4* and HQ-*5* along with a naval landing force was to eliminate the fishing vessels and the militia. H-hour was to be 0625 hours on the 19th. With this information in hand, the Chinese Navy was ready when the Vietnamese struck.

At 0727 hours, the PLAN ships in line abreast at the demarcation line detected rubber dinghies around the waters of Duncan Island and immediately deduced that a Vietnamese landing force had been launched. Before long the suspicion was confirmed by sounds of gunfire between the Chinese militia and the Vietnamese landing force. While the land battle was going on, the naval force maneuvered to a new position and split itself into two groups: CNS *389* and *396* and HQ-*10* and HQ-*16* were west of Duncan Island, while in the north HQ-*4* and HQ-*5* were challenging PLAN *271* and *274* on the south side. Both sides were playing a dangerous game of "chicken," until HQ-*16* smashed into PLAN *396*. Tension was at boiling point, and a Vietnamese sailor on HQ-*4* accidently discharged the HMG he was manning. The Chinese sailors on No. *274* saw—to their astonishment—an SVN officer storm out of the bridge and hit the unfortunate SVN sailor. This confrontation continued until 1023 hours when the SVN decided that live rounds should be used. Soon CNS *396* was being shelled by the Vietnamese and No. *274* saw HQ-*5* coming at them on full speed with all guns blazing. The

Chinese naval tactics at that time were to close with the enemy and focus their attack on one vessel first, before turning on others. In response, No. *396* and *386* focused both their fire on HQ-*10* while No. *271* and *274* attacked HQ-*4*. The SVN tactics were to use their superior long-range guns and radar to fight a standoff battle. The Chinese Type-*6604* and *6610* vessels were of World War II-Soviet open bridge design and both the Chinese naval commanders were very vulnerable at close range. Sometime during the chaos an SVN 40 mm shell hit the open bridge and killed Captain Commissar Feng Songbo and Deputy Captain Zhou Xitong of No. *274*. Fighting at this close range was akin to Napoleonic naval battles, and the Chinese sailors fought with all available weapons including hand grenades, RPGs, and LMGs, to bring additional fire on the Vietnamese. No. *274*, which was hit by 127 mm shell five times, lost its navigational controls but retained the use of its main and secondary weapons. In return HQ-*4* lost all its radar, communication and control systems. With HQ-*4* almost out of the picture the PLAN focused its attack on HQ-*5*. The first salvo seriously crippled its commander and HQ-*5* retired southwards.

The northern battle played out in an almost identical manner, PLAN *396* rapidly closed with the SVN and scored hits on HQ-*16* with its 85 mm gun. Damaged, HQ-*16* retired northwards to Pattle Island. HQ-*10* was the next target, and it too had its bridge destroyed. Without effective leadership they turned and ran. CNS *386* was also hit numerous times by the SVN and a fire broke out amidships; losing rudder control it smashed into HQ-*10*. To save the ship, it was ordered to be beached at Duncan Island, with CNS *396* acting as a shield. At about 1100 hours, HQ-*16* attempted to rejoin the battle but suddenly turned west and departed, most likely due to orders from Saigon. The Vietnamese withdrew because, just before noon, Chinese naval reinforcements arrived. CNS *281* and *282*, sub-chasers (Type-*37 Hainan*-class, 400 tons, length: 59 m (192 feet)), proceeded to finished off HQ-*10*. At about 1452 hours HQ-*10* sank after its ammunition stores exploded.

The next day saw the arrival of Chinese jets. They did a couple of bomb runs and made a few strafing passes over the three islands. Soon afterwards, a naval landing force arrived led by CNS *232* (later renamed the CNS *Nanchong*) and fifteen other vessels with four companies of infantry. The Chinese landed on Money, Pattle, and Robert Island. The Vietnamese forces on the islands were either captured or were lucky enough to escape using sailboats and fishing junks before the Chinese reinforcements arrived. The surviving SVN vessels retreated to their naval base at Đà Nẵng. Tallying their losses, the SVN saw HQ-*10* sunk, HQ-*16* heavily damaged, and HQ-*5* and HQ-*4* suffer minor damage. Fifty-three Vietnamese sailors including Captain Nguỵ Văn Thà of HQ-*10* were killed and sixteen others were injured. After drifting for a day, ten Vietnamese sailors from HQ-*10* who had escaped on fishing boats were rescued by a passing Dutch Shell tanker, *Kopionella*, on January 20. On the 29th a passing Vietnamese fishing boat picked up another fifteen. The Chinese took forty-eight POWs, including an American "advisor" by the name of Gerald Kosh.[17] The POWs were all later released in Hong Kong through the International Red Cross. On the Chinese side, all Chinese ships were hit numerous times by the Vietnamese Navy, but luckily none of the vessels sank and they all managed to return to port safely, albeit some were being towed. The Chinese confirmed eighteen dead.

2.4.3 The Air Force

For most of the 1970s aircraft development was stifled by the never-ending political campaigns. The whole country had become political and this affected the PLA also, as it struggled with its own internal battles. In the midst of this chaos, 1971 saw a failed coup by Marshal Lin Biao. He tried to escape in a CAAC Trident but crashed and died in Mongolia, apparently due to shortage of fuel. The PLAAF played a minor role in the 1979 Sino-Vietnam War with some CAP, logistics, and AA defense on the Chinese side of the Sino-Vietnam border.

2.5 1980s

2.5.1 The Army

Despite the conclusion of the 1979 Sino-Vietnam War, harassing artillery fire by the Vietnamese forces continued along the border area, and small troop clashes gave China many problems. To settle the score, China and Vietnam fought numerous battles in the mountain range that straddles the Sino-Vietnam border. Frequent raids by Vietnamese commandos and artillery ambushes infuriated China and soon these skirmishes grew bigger, resulting in a company-size clash between the PLA and PAVN on Luojiaping Mountain in Yunnan Province. In 1981 another clash occurred on the peaks of Koulin Mountain and later a similar battle occurred on Balihe East Hill, cumulating in a fifty-seven-day battle on Faka Mountain in Guangxi Province. This was a tough battle involving soldiers from the 2/9th Regiment of the 3rd Infantry Division against elements of the PAVN's 52nd Regiment, 337th Division. In 1984 the Chinese initiated a series of actions[18] to capture key ground across a series of hills that straddled the border area. The capture of the high ground enabled the PLA to dominate the surrounding area and push the Vietnamese forces out of artillery range of the Chinese border. These battles occurred mostly in the border areas of Chinese Yunnan Province and Ha Giang Province, Vietnam from April 1984 to 1991. These battles are collectively known as the "second punitive action" by the Chinese. As in Korea, the Chinese used every opportunity to gain combat experience, constantly rotating PLA units to the border war zones. Peace did not come until the end of the decade, when in 1991, the two warring nations eventually settled on a border line.

As in the 1979 war, these battles with Vietnam in the 1980s exposed major deficiencies within the PLA; reform was much needed. First was the cull of deadwood by cutting down the PLA's size. From six million in 1980 the PLA slimmed down to 4.5 million by 1984. However, the Chairman of the CMC, Deng Xiaoping, was still unhappy and he announced a further reduction of the PLA headcount by one million. To achieve this cut, the eleven military districts were reduced to seven; 117 military academies were reduced to 103, cutting 224,000 men. The Army was hit hardest by the downsizing, losing 23.2% of its personnel; the Air Force lost 19.6%. By the end of 1987, the PLA was only three million strong, the smallest it had yet been.

The Kosovo War of the late 1990s and the 1991 Gulf War gave the PLA generals a wake-up call on the capability of modern weapons in action. Comparatively the Chinese PLA was seen as both oversized and obsolete. Focusing on quality, not quantity, a further cut of 500,000 was made during the five years between 1995 and 2000. The ground forces continued to be reduced more than the Navy and Air Force, with cuts of 18.6%, 12.6%, and 11.4% respectively. High-tech weaponry needed educated soldiers, and in the first decade of the 21st century the PLA strove to place more university graduates in its ranks and made a push to strengthen its officer and NCOs corps along the lines of a Western army. Equipment-wise, the PLA went on a shopping spree, but with the military embargo by the West still in place, Ukraine, Russia, France and Israel became the main destinations for these Chinese arms buyers. Soon many of these imported arms were cloned, much to the displeasure of the arms sellers. Later on some improvements were made and soon the Chinese were making weaponry of their own.

The PLA was also becoming more international. China is now an active member in many of the UN's peacekeeping missions and plays a key role in international anti-piracy patrols in the Gulf of Aden and elsewhere.

The Daxing Mountain Forest Fire of 1987 and the Great Three Rivers Flood of 1988 saw over 90,000 PAP and PLA troops including airborne forces, PLAAF, local reserves and militias assisting in rescue and recovery missions.

The 1989 Tiananmen Square Protest was a controversial internal security mission that blighted the reputation of the PLA. Blatant insubordination occurred and loyalties were questioned. Post-protest purges occurred at many levels of the PLA. Reorganization of the security force provided more defined roles and highlighted the need for specialist equipment.

2.5.2 The Navy

In the spring of 1988, China and Vietnam fought a brief naval battle over what was known as Johnson South Reef or Chiguajiao (in Vietnamese: Đá Gạc Ma). It started on March 14, 1988 and was over in matter of days. These uninhabited reefs had been an area of contest throughout history, and their ownership is a very complicated matter, beyond the scope of this book, but the precursor to this incident was actually due to a UNESCO program. China, a member of UNESCO, was under instruction of the UN research body to build five observation points as part of the World Ocean Circulation Experiment (WOCE). The aim of WOCE was to build some 200 observation points around the world with the aim of monitoring the world's ocean sea surface topography. As it happened two of the five were to be located in the Paracel Islands and Spratly Islands. After the survey made in January by the PLAN, it was deemed that No. 74 marine observation station was best located in Yongshu Reef, or in English, Fiery Cross Reef, which is due west of Johnson South Reef. Both the Chinese and the Vietnamese were active in the area with fishing boats. Many of these were accompanied by armed militias on account of the frequent clashes that broke out between the Chinese and Vietnamese fleets. To support the increasingly large fishing fleet in the area, both sides started to construct staging or logistics posts on reefs or islands in the area. A clash was inevitable. On March 13, the CNS *Nanchong* with pennant number 502 and CNS *Kaiyuan* (503), both *Jiangnan*-class frigates, under the command of Commander Chen Weiwen and accompanied by a Type 053K guided missile frigate, CNS *Yingtan*, were on a patrolling and post-building mission in the South Seas.

The Chinese were alerted to heightened Vietnamese activities in the area and as such beefed up their numbers with up to fifteen vessels that were in the vicinity. On the morning of the 13th CNS *Kaiyuan* was ordered to detach from the flotilla and proceed to another reef, and CNS *Nanchong* proceeded to check on Johnson South Reef. At 1400 hours local time, a small boat was lowered with six sailors and dispatched, but the *Nanchong* then spotted on its radar a Vietnamese transport ship, HQ-604, heading toward Johnson Reef. At the same time, landing-craft HQ-505 was heading toward Collins Reef in a simultaneous two-pronged intrusion upon the disputed reef. The rowing boat was immediately recalled. The Chinese were able to observe that both Vietnamese vessels were crammed full of construction materials—obviously they had the same intention as the Chinese. On the night of the 13th, both sides were eyeballing each other with some trepidation. Chen recalled the CNS *Yingtan* (531), and directed frigate CNS *Xiangtan* (556) to support CNS *Nanchong*. To beat the Vietnamese vessels to the reef, Chen ordered a small force to land on the reef under cover of darkness—by the time the Vietnamese Navy tried to land on the morning of the 14th, they were shocked to see that Chinese forces were already there.

At approximately 0730 hours on Johnson South Reef, Vietnamese Navy Corporal Nguyen Van Lanh and Sub-Lieutenant Tran Van Phuong attempted to raise the Vietnamese flag on the reef. Chinese sailor Du Xianghou intervened and the result was a confrontation. In the confusion a shot was fired by a nervous Vietnamese sailor and Chinese sailor Yang Zhiliang was hit in the arm and fell down. What happened next was not entirely clear; some literature says that HQ-*604* opened fire first and PLAN counterattacked, some says CNS *Nanchong* started with its 37 mm gun on HQ-*604*. Whoever began the fight, the result was that HQ-*604* was set ablaze, and began to sink after only eight minutes. At the same time, just as the battle was about to start, CNS *Yingtan*'s main guns malfunctioned and she was only able to engage HQ-*505* with secondary armaments and thus could not deliver a knockout blow. After HQ-*604* sunk, CNS *Nanchong* turned to HQ-*505* and began directing all its fire on this Vietnamese vessel.

Meanwhile at Qiong Jiao (Lansdowne Reef in English), some 7 km from Johnson South Reef, at approximately 0915 hours, the CNS *Xiangtan* discovered nine Vietnamese sailors from transport HQ-*605* had already landed. The Chinese captain was at first unsure what to do and asked Chen whether to shoot or not. But in the ensuing firefight, Vietnamese vessel HQ-*605* was sunk and CNS *Xiangtan* then turned its guns onto HQ-*505*. With three against one, HQ-*505* was doomed. Unable to escape, the Vietnamese captain decided to beach the vessel at Collins Reef (Guihan Jiao, Vietnamese: Đảo Cô Lin) only some 1.7 km from Johnson South Reef.

Overall the Vietnamese Navy suffered sixty-four dead (other Vietnamese sources claimed forty while others said it was seventy-four), eleven wounded and forty captured (the Chinese claimed only nine prisoners). The Chinese losses were six dead and eighteen wounded, but some cite no deaths and only one wounded. Whatever the toll, the result was that two Vietnamese armed naval transports were sunk and one captured. As a result of this brief battle, the Vietnamese Navy withdrew from Johnson Reef entirely. However, the Vietnamese forces did not leave totally empty handed, as they succeeded in taking other reefs in the area, including / Collins and Landsdowne Reef.

2.5.3 The Air Force

In 1978, China turned its back on a Communist-planned economy with an economic liberation program termed "Restructuring and Openness." The PLA benefited from the increased wealth from commerce and soon was able to acquire new technologies from the Western powers and the Soviet Union. In 1984, PLAAF brought twenty-four UH-60L Blackhawks from the United States, and a Tu-154M transporter in 1985, as well as Super Puma helicopters from France in 1986. Border skirmishes with Vietnam continued well into the 1980s. Whilst these were largely ground wars, on March 28, 1984 the PLAAF's SAM unit 50th Battalion engaged and damaged a Vietnamese MiG-21P that intruded into Chinese airspace. Then, on October 5, 1987, PLAAF 3rd Regiment 97th Air Defense Battalion successfully shot down a Vietnamese MiG-21P reconnaissance plane.

2.6 The Modern Era: 1990s and Beyond

2.6.1 The Army

In 1991 the PLA made its first overseas deployment as part of the UN blue beret force, to Cambodia. Subsequent UN deployments included Namibia, Haiti, Congo, Liberia, Sudan, Timor, Darfur and Lebanon. In 1997 and 1999, the PLA took over military defense of Hong Kong from Britain and Macau from Portugal.

In 2003, it was announced that there would be a further reduction of the PLA by 200,000. The officer corps was hit the hardest, with 170,000 men but in one fell swoop. By the end of 2005 the PLA's total force rested at 2.3 million, down from 2.5 million in 1999, with the ground forces taking most of the cuts—19% down from precut levels. The ground force was now the smallest of the three services. To further slim down the military in 2006, jobs with the PLA were reclassified as non-civil service posts, thus ending the "iron rice bowl" concept of work for life. All PLA members were transferred to contract base employment, allowing "deadwood" and those that "past their sell by date" to be removed, preventing the possibility of the PLA ever again ending up at three to four million. The officer corps was streamlined and NCOs and volunteer soldiers fulfill an increasing number of roles. More jobs, mainly administrative non-combat duties, were assigned as non-military posts, making them open to civilians. To further raise the standard of the military, all recruits would now undergo psychological.

In 2008, China was hit by two great natural disasters. The snowstorms in January and the colossal earthquake in Sichuan (8.0 on the Richter scale) tested the modern PAP and PLA in all areas, especially civil aid missions, logistics, medical services, and mobilization. In 2010, the PLA committed 210,000 men to the Yushu earthquake in Qinghai. Since 2011, the PLA and PAP have committed 370,000 men in aid to civil authorities with an additional 870,000 men from the reserves.

2.6.2 The Navy

From the 1990s onward, life for the PLAN was relatively peaceful. The year 2008 marked a milestone with the PLAN undertaking its first overseas deployment, participating in international anti-piracy escort duties off the coast of Gulf of Aden. The 2011 crisis in Libya saw the PLAN's first ever deployment to the Mediterranean. CNS *Xuzhou* "(徐州)", a Type 054 *Jiangkai*-II-class missile frigate "(江凯 II 级)" from the ongoing seventh anti-piracy task force was diverted to Libyan coast to provide support and protection for the ongoing evacuation mission.

2.6.3 The Air Force

The modernization of the PLAAF truly began in earnest as the Soviet Union fell apart with an order for twenty-four fourth-generation Sukhoi Su-27SK Flanker-Bs and Su-27UBKs (NATO: Flanker-C) in 1992. Others such as Mil-17 (NATO: HIP) helicopters, IL-76MD (NATO: Candid-B) jet transporter were added to the fleet. In 2011, the crisis in Libya saw the PLAAF's first ever operation into the Mediterranean Sea, when four IL-76s carried out the rescue of 287 Chinese workers.

Notes

1   Although all units in the PVA belonged to the PLA, the PVA was separately constituted in order to prevent an official war with the United States.

2   In late November 1950 the 38th Army did a night march on fit kit that covered 72.5 km in 14 hours over rugged terrain to cut off the US 2nd infantry Division.

3   90% of 26th Army Group became casualties of frost bite.

4   There were 1,600 classified documents, which today can be read in the Library of Congress. It is also published by the Hoover Insitute as *The Politics of the Red Army*.

5   Five gunboats of which three were the CNS *Liberation*, *Vanguard* and *Struggle*, one landing ship, ten landing craft, and eight transports.

6   During the Cultural Revolution period the PLA was a rankless army. There were only appointments and titles.

7   From 1974–79, China counted 3,535 incursions by the Vietnamese into Chinese territory. Between August 1978 and February 1979 alone these caused the deaths of 300-plus Chinese.

8   The "Treaty of Friendship and Cooperation" between the Soviet Union and the Socialist Republic of Vietnam was a military treaty signed in Moscow in November 1978, which promised Soviet military aid to Vietnam. Appointing the USSR Ministry of Defense, General Gennady Ivanovich Obaturov led a team of twenty advisors to Vietnam.

9   28th, 42nd, 43rd, 54th, 55th, 121st, 125th, 126th, 127th, and 164th Division.

10   11th, 12th, 14th, 31st, 32nd, 37th, and 39th Division.

11   The PLA deployed its own version of Navajo Code Talkers by using natives of Wenzhou (溫州) as radioman. Their special dialect meant the Vietnamese were incapable of deciphering the Chinese transmission.

12   The Soviet aid to Vietnam during the Sino-Vietnam War amounted to one airlift of 20 MiG-21 fighters, 400 APCs and tanks, fifty BM-21 MBRLs, 100 AA guns, a number of SA-7 Missiles plus 8,000-odd RPG-7s. The Soviets also provided an

airlift—transferring an entire division from Cambodia to the defense of Lang Son. Direct military support was limited to a sixty-eight-man Signals Detachment to support the Vietnamese, on account of the poor communications between the front line and Hanoi.

13 Xisha Islands to the Chinese or Hoàng Sa Islands in Vietnamese.

14 HQ-*16* was an Ex-Barnegat-class seaplane tender, Displacement: 1,766 tons (standard), Length: 310 feet (95 m).

15 Ex-Edsall-class destroyer escort USS, DE-334. Displacement: 1,253 tons standard, Length: 93 m (306 feet).

16 HQ-*5* was the same class as HQ-*16*.

17 A former US Army captain, then US Embassy Saigon Liaison Officer

18 Battle of Lao Shan and Battle of Zheyin Mountain but in Vietnam as it is collectively known as Battle of Yi Xuyen.

CHAPTER 3

THE CHINESE PLA TODAY

Visitors to China may be confused by the number of people they see wearing military-looking uniforms. The problem of identifying who is wearing what, who and what is the PLA is confusing to many visitors to China. To understand the PLA, it is just as important to understand what the PLA is *not*. The confusion is increased by the fact that many government officials, including the judiciary and even health inspectors, wear military-style uniforms.

The PLA is the principal instrument of the State, an indispensable institution that plays a key part in the foundation and development of the People's Republic of China. In the early years of the republic there was no national or standardized police force and organized fire-fighting service, so that the PLA often stepped in to fulfil these non-military but essential tasks. Surplus PLA soldiers or whole units were assigned to different duties as and when the state required. Later many of these transfers were made permanent and the PLA units were rebadged as police, fire fighters, border guards, judges etc.

The PLA, like many armed forces, is steeped in history and traditions. These traditions may sound strange to readers who serve or have served in Western armies, but they are the fundamentals of the Chinese PLA and its philosophy:

1. The Party's Leadership of the PLA is absolute. The People's Army absolutely obeys the leadership and commands of the CCP.
2. Ten Military Principles: These are ten military principles established by Mao in the revolutionary and anti-Japanese war

period. Regarded as important as the "Ten Commandments" in the Holy Bible, these principles list what the conduct of a PLA solider should entail. To help the many illiterate soldiers commit them to memory, they were arranged in a song to be sung on the march.

   a. Eliminate isolated and small pockets of enemy first before concentrating forces to fight the big enemy.

   b. Capture small towns, villages and minor cities first before capturing the large urban areas.

   c. Eliminating and destroying the enemy's fighting capacity is the main aim, do not focus on holding territory and urban centers.

   d. Concentrate forces to achieve an overwhelming advantage in numbers to achieve total decimation of the enemy.

   e. Only fight battles for which you are well prepared.

   f. Promote bravery, self-sacrifice, and the ability to bear and endure hardship.

   g. A war of movement is preferable to static warfare; use mobility to decimate the enemy and at the same time take special attention to assaulting prepared positions to capture the enemy's vital grounds and urban centers.

   h. When fighting to capture urban areas, first go for the weakly defended cities, then if conditions allow go for defended cities leaving the heavily fortified cities to last, and only take these when all the necessary conditions to achieve victory are present.

   i. Whenever possible capture enemy weapons and supplies and use them against the enemy.

   j. Use the time between battles to rest and reorganize the army.

3. The Three Democratic Principles: people's democracy, economic democracy, and military democracy.

4. Three grand rules and eight points of order: Mao established these in the early days of the revolution as guiding principles of behavior for the Chinese Red Army.

    a. The three grand rules are:
        i. All actions must be as a result of orders.
        ii. Don't take anything from the people, not even a needle and thread.
        iii. All captured materials must be handed over to authority.
    b. The eight points of order are:
        i. Speak to the people in good manner and friendly tone of voice.
        ii. All trade must be carried out fairly.
        iii. All borrowed items must be returned.
        iv. Broken items must be compensated.
        v. Do not beat or scold people.
        vi. Do not damage the crops.
        vii. Do not molest women.
        viii. Do not ill-treat POWs.
5. Three Principles of the PLA:
    a. Execute military operations.
    b. Serve the general public.
    c. Develop civil development efforts.

The PLA standard, as in all armies around the world, is an object of reverence. As the PLA is the overall body for the entire armed forces of the People's Republic of China it is represented by a single standard, which serves as a ceremonial color for all units. It is based on the national flag, but instead of the four smaller gold stars it has the Chinese characters for the numerals "8" (八) and "1" (一), which stand for August 1, the date in 1927 on which the PLA was founded. The color/standard is fringed with gold tassels, and mounted on a red and gold pole. However, each branch of the PLA has its own standard. The Army's standard is the same as the PLA standard except with the lower 40% colored green. The Navy's standard is similar to the Army's, but with the lower part of the green replaced by three blue and two white horizontal stripes of equal width, while the Air Force replaces the blue-and-white striped portion of the Navy Standard with a solid light blue block.

The military anthem of the PLA is also known as the *March of the Chinese People's Liberation Army*, and was originally a patriotic song popular during the war with Japan. It was only made official in 1988 by the CMC.

Lyrics to the Anthem of the PLA

Forward! Forward! Forward!
Our army soars towards the Sun,
Stepping on the earth of the Motherland,
Carrying the hope of our people,
We are an invincible power!
We are the sons and brothers of the workers,
We are the arms of the People!
Fearless and unyielding, to fight bravely
Until we exterminate all counter-revolutionaries.
The banner of Mao Zedong flutters high!
Listen! The wind is roaring and the bugle is blowing;
Listen! How thunderously our revolutionary song roars!
Comrades, march forth united to the battlefields of liberation;
Comrades, march forth united to the frontiers of Motherland.
Forward! Forward!
Our army soars to the Sun;
Marching towards the final victory
And the liberation of all our land!

Another particular tradition of the PLA is the National Day Military Parade. From 1949 until 1959 these parades were an annual affair held on October 1, China's National Day. These parades were a useful barometer on the development of the PLA, its latest weaponry and who was "in" and "out" in Chinese politics. However during the Cultural Revolution, these parades were suspended for twenty-five years, until 1984 when Deng Xiaoping resurrected the tradition. To avoid unnecessary expenditure, these parades were then only held once every ten years with the last one held in 2015, the 70th anniversary of the end of World War Two. The changes in the style of salute and greetings in the parade are a good indication of the political climate of the times.

1949
Parade Commander: Long Life to the People's Republic of China!
Parade: Hurrah! Hurrah! Hurrah!

| Parade Commander: | Good Health to all Comrades! |
| Parade: | Good Health to Comrade Commander! |

1955

Parade Commander:	Long Life to the People's Republic of China!
	Long Life to the Chinese Communist Party!
	Long Life to Chairman Mao!
Parade:	Hurrah! Hurrah! Hurrah!

1984, 1999 and 2009

Parade Inspector:	Greetings Comrades!
Parade:	Greetings Leader!
Parade Inspector:	Comrades, [You have] worked hard!
Parade:	[We] Serve the People!

Like all armies, the PLA faces organizational changes. The PLA Railway Corps (1950–84) is now part of history. In addition to moving troops, the PLA Railway Corps once played a key role in the development of China. The Railway Corps built thousands of bridges, tunnels, and roads, and had over the years laid millions of kilometers of railway tracks[1] as part of civil construction. Disbanded in 1984, it was absorbed into the Ministry of Railways, and later as part of the national reform, the railway building part of the ministry was privatized into many companies. Some became rather successful and were listed on the stock market. For example, the former 2nd Division, PLA Railway Corps, with an illustrious history in China's Civil War, the Korean War and the Sino-Vietnam War, on transfer to the Ministry of Railways in 1984, was renamed as the 12th Engineering Department Ministry of Railway based in Taiyuan, Shanxi Province in northern China. In 1998 it was privatized and renamed the "China Railway 12th Engineering Group." As China undertook a mass privatization of state assets, many of these new corporations, from construction, pharmaceutical to consumer goods such as TVs and refrigerators, had their origin in the PLA.

Another unique Chinese military institution is the Xinjiang Production and Construction Corps or more commonly just known as the "Corps" in China. Technically it is not a part of the PLA, but is in fact an economic paramilitary organization with a unique role to "develop and protect Xinjiang Uygur Autonomous Region," a far-flung semi-desert region with a strong Islamic heritage. In 1949, the PLA units based in this inhospitable region began growing their own food in order to lighten the load on the local population, and soon the food production expanded to include daily items like soap and daily utensils like pots and pans. By 1954 the food production part was expanded to thirty-four PLA horticultural farms and eight cattle ranches. In October that year, the transformation was made official. The entire PLA First Field Army and the 22nd Independent Regiment, some 175,000 personnel, were transferred out of the PLA to an agriculture/forestry developmental role with a mission to "develop and defend the large areas of the Western desert area," better known as Xinjiang. Today the "Corps" is responsible for a wide variety of civilian duties including manufacturing, transport, education, and cultural, financial, and environmental development focusing on reclaiming the desert and transforming it into a green oasis. The Corps has also built towns and cities and provided land and work for disbanded military units. The existence of the Corps is unique to China, but the closest comparison that exists in the West is the British East India Company and its role in "developing" India. The development of Xinjiang, like India, was outsourced to a semi-official party. In addition to farms and factories, the Corps operates its own police and PAP elements, plus education, healthcare, and judiciary functions. Today the Corps has dual reporting channels, one to the Central Government and the other to the local Xinjiang Provincial Government. With 930,000 staff, the Corps is probably the largest company in the world, and living within the Corps' jurisdiction are 2.3 million people. These 930,000 staff are organized into fourteen divisions (of which one is a construction/ building division) or agriculture development zones and 185 regimental farms (including eleven construction and engineering regiments), 4,391 factories/businesses with a sizable militia capacity. These all play a key role in pacifying the region, socially and economically. Under the Corps is a private company known officially as the China Xinjiang Development Group Company that by and large operates all its commercial functions. Keeping to their military heritage, the senior managers of the Corps are still known by their military appointed titles such as Divisional Commander.

Another historic element of the PLA is the PLA Infrastructure Engineering Corps. As the name suggests its main function was infrastructure construction,[2] however it was also responsible for the protection of gold and other mineral assets, hydropower, reservoirs and water resources. After disbandment, its jobs and functions were siphoned off to other units. For example, the task of protecting gold and mineral assets as well as other infrastructure now belongs to the People's Armed Police.

The relation between the PLA and industry is a subject that many Western observers find difficult to understand. Today China has some eleven key defense groups that conduct research and design and produce weapons for the PLA; however, fifty years ago the PLA and defense industries were virtually as one. During the period of reform, the two systems evolved separately so that the relationship that now exists is primarily that between a "buyer" (the PLA), and the "seller" (the civilian defense industries). The PLA and commerce is also an area of contention. In the beginning the PLA were just soldiers, but in the 1970s and 1980s, to supplement income and unit funds, the central government encouraged the PLA to operate businesses, first mostly in farms and food services but later to diversify into anything that makes money, including hotels, taxi services, etc. Unfortunately, greed, corruption, and illegal activities marred the combat effectiveness of the military, and in 1988 the PLA was ordered to divest itself of all commercial enterprises except for some key ones vital to national defense. These are still subordinate to the PLA's headquarters and units. In 2016, in a new round of reforms, the PLA and the PAP were ordered to completely divest from all commercial ventures within three years.

Whereas the PLA has rid itself of commercial linkage, one area of reform that is still outstanding is that of the police—or as they are known, the China Public Security. Chinese police still control or have large interest in all the private security firms—armored security escort for banks, airport passenger screening, site security/security guards etc., all "belong" to companies that have links to the police. Non-Chinese companies are not allowed to enter into the private security business in China, therefore Western security companies like G4S have a very limited role there. The issue of military corruption remains a bugbear of the PLA, and has become headline news. Partly due to soaring housing prices over the last decade, the General Logistics Department (GLD) which controls the military housing budget has always been marked by the military auditor. In 2006 the head of GLD, Vice-Admiral Wang Shouye was caught along with his co-conspirators (three brigadiers, seven senior colonels). On March 31, 2014, the GLD was caught again. The former deputy of the GLD, Lieutenant General Gu Junshan, was indicted for serious corruption and abuse of power. Sentencing is still pending and the whole country is eagerly waiting for news of how the new President, Xi Jinping, plans to stem the corruption in the PLA.

3.1 National Defense Structure

On the founding of the People's Republic of China (PRC), the nation's highest authority on military affairs was the Central Government People's Revolutionary Military Committee (RMC). When the Ministry of National Defense National Security Council (NSC) was created in 1954, the President of the PRC was the nominal head of the nation's armed forces and served as the president of the NSC, at the same time the Chinese Communist Party (CCP) also ran a parallel NSC within the Party structure. During the chaotic times of the Cultural Revolution the head of China's military was shifted to the CCP entirely and was placed under the Chinese Communist Central Military Council Administrative Group (CCAG) and later renamed the Chinese Communist Central Military Administration Board (CCAB). In 1975 the NSC was disbanded but the control of the military still rested with the CCP which was now under the Chinese Communist Central Military Standing Committee (CMSC). This remained the situation until 1982 when the current structure was established, and the control of the Chinese PLA shifted back to the state. The daily workings of the PLA are now controlled by the People's Republic of China's Central Military Commission (CMC) reporting to the standing committee of the Central Committee of the CCP, better known as the Politburo, while the defense of

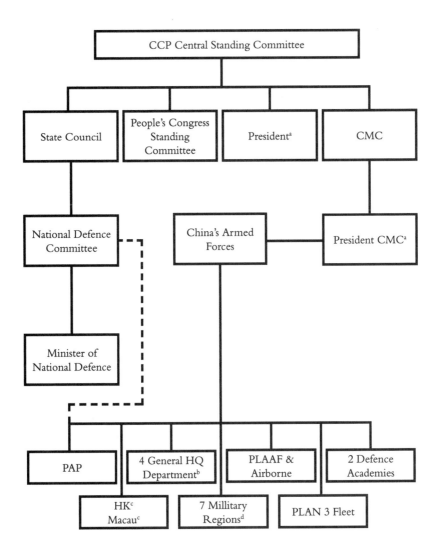

CCP Central Standing Committee

State Council

People's Congress Standing Committee

President[a]

CMC

National Defence Committee

China's Armed Forces

President CMC[a]

Minister of National Defence

PAP

4 General HQ Department[b]

PLAAF & Airborne

2 Defence Academies

HK[c] Macau[c]

7 Millitary Regions[d]

PLAN 3 Fleet

[a] Usually the same person; currently Mr. Xi Jinping
[b] Disbanded in 2016 and all functions absorbed into 15 departments under the CMC
[c] Administrative only, operationally under Guangzhou MR
[d] Reorganized as 5 War Zones in 2016

China, as stipulated by the nation's constitution, rests with the Laws of National Defense of China, which is the responsibility of the Central Committee of the CCP, National People's Congress Standing Committee, President of China, State Council and the CMC.

3.1.1 National Security Council

One of the outcomes of China's much-discussed Third Plenum, held in November 2013, was the recreation of the once defunct Chinese National Security Committee. The Chinese press claimed that the purpose of the new Chinese NSC was to better coordinate the total activities of the state in relation to security whilst coordinating foreign affairs, national defense, the police, the judiciary and the intelligence community, together with other elements of the state and to promote greater information-sharing between several branches of the PRC's government.

It is not clear what specific relationship the new NSC will have with the Central Military Committee (CMC), but as Xi Jinping, the current President, acts as chairman of both the NSC and the CMC, and several members of the CMC also hold positions within the NSC, their actions are coordinated. With tensions rising over China's territorial disputes with India, Japan, and some Southeast Asian nations, increased information-sharing and coordinated decision-making between Beijing and the rank and file of the PLA could be the deciding factor between a diplomatic incident and an accidental military skirmish.

3.1.2 PLA Command Structure

Today, the Central Military Commission (CMC) holds supreme control over the PLA. All members of the commission are Communist Party members. The PLA reports directly to the CMC, as do all the branches. These include:

PLA Navy (PLAN) and its three fleets

PLA Air Force (PLAAF) and its airborne forces: Rapid Reaction Force (RRF)

PLA Second Artillery and its bases

General Staff Department (GSD)*

General Political Department (GPD)*

General Logistics Department (GLD)*

General Armament Department (GAD)*

---

* Disbanded January 2016 (see p. 249).

Academy of Military Science (AMS)
National Defense University (NDU)
National University of Defense Technology (NUDT)
Seven Military Regions (MR) (Shenyang, Beijing, Lanzhou, Jinan, Nanjing, Guangzhou, Chengdu) and two Special Administration Region Garrisons (Hong Kong, Macau)
People's Armed Police (PAP—also reports to the State Council)

3.1.3 The Four General Headquarters Departments*

The command and control of the PLA begins with the CMC, which sets policies and directions, which are then executed by the four General Headquarters Departments (GHD) of the PLA. The General Staff Department (GSD) is responsible for operations, intelligence, electronic warfare, communications, military affairs, training, mobilization, meteorological surveys, cartographic functions, and foreign affairs. The GSD also acts as the service headquarters for the Army, Navy and Air Force. Through the four General Headquarter Departments, the orders are passed through to regional and operational headquarters.

Next in line is the General Political Department (GPD). The GPD is responsible for the political and ideological reliability and training of the PLA, including morale. It also takes care of public relations and publicity (dance troupes, museums, media, sports), and perhaps most importantly the GPD is also responsible for personnel matters (like personal dossiers and promotions), party discipline, internal security, and legal affairs. The GPD is in the direct control of political officers, better known as commissars. In Chinese it is known as *zhengwei* in at battalion level and above, and political instructors (*zhidao yuan*) at companye level and below in PLA/PAP units. Although there is no direct equivalent in the West, they act as the equivalent of military chaplains, education/training officers, and pay/finance officers. At all levels of the PLA, the principal commanders (or primary staff officers) and their respective political officers usually share the same rank, just as they share responsibility for the performance of their units. Through this system of political officers,

---

* See p. 249.

the Chinese Communist Party (CCP) ensures the absolute loyalty of the PLA to the Party.

Third on the list is the General Logistics Department (GLD). The GLD is responsible for military finances, military supplies, including POL to all branches of the PLA, military health services, transportation, barracks/ military infrastructure construction, and auditing. The GLD also supervises PLA-operated factories and PLA farms. (The PLA produces much of its own food—from animals to grains, vegetables and fruits—to supplement unit mess funds.)

Fourth and last is the General Headquarters Department (GHD). The GHD is responsible for all the weapons and equipment of the PLA. It also conducts maintenance and repair as well as research and development, including the procurement of major weapons, equipment, and ammunition.

3.1.4 Senior Military Academies

Reporting to the CMC are several key military academies. The Academy of Military Sciences (AMS) is primarily a research center for military strategy, operations, and tactics; military systems; military history; and cooperation with foreign armed forces. The National Defense University (NDU) trains senior PLA and PAP officers, usually those at divisional and corps level; at the same time, it also provides training to provincial-level senior civil servants. The National University of Defense Technology (NUDT) trains senior scientists, engineers, and commanders of technical units (such as maintenance and repair units and PLA-operated scientific or technical research institutes). In addition, it also operates introductory-level courses for technically oriented officer cadets who are destined for technical roles in the PLA.

3.1.5 Military Regions and Local Commands

Administratively the Chinese military is divided into military regions (MR).* The organization of these regions as well as the makeup of these areas has never been static and over the years there have been

* See p. 249.

a number of changes. In the 1950s, China was divided into thirteen Military Regions (MR), but by the mid-1980s two were eliminated from the list. This cull continues and before the end of the decade, two more were removed, giving a final total of seven. The Chinese MR is named after the city in which the MR headquarters is located. The territory of each MR is large, often encompassing a number of provinces. Within each MR there are a number of military districts (MD) and also city garrisons. Each MR contains a mix of all the services, and these units—whether Army, Navy or Air Force—are operationally grouped into "Army Group" (Jituan Jun) formations. Sometimes there are stand-alone independent divisions or brigades that are not part of any Army Group. In addition, each MR has its own logistics network and rear-echelon support troops, as well as local provincial military commands and reserve formations such as the militia. The head of each MR is usually a lieutenant general, but can even be a full general. He is supported by several deputies as well as a political commissar and his deputies. These deputies may come from each of the four key General Headquarters Departments. To coordinate the work of each of the General Headquarter Departments, a chief of staff is appointed to oversee and coordinate all staff work. In normal time, movements of units, however small, must first be ordered from the CMC and normally this order will be executed through the GSD, but in times of war or emergency, a war zone will be declared and with it a new command headquarters will be formed and the movement of these units will be decided by the war zone or emergency zone headquarters.

Each Military District is responsible for a single province and that bears the province or region name. The MD commander is responsible for the local and reserve forces in his province, and preparation for mobilization in times of emergency. Each MD is essentially a mini MR and within it are all the same departments as the MR. An MD commander is usually a major general, and his work also encompasses military-civil liaison such that he will have regular meetings with local government officials and PAP forces in the area.

Under each MD are a number of military sub-districts (MSD). In all respects, these MSDs are essentially miniature MDs. In addition to missions assigned to them by higher authorities, one of the key functions of the MSD is to organize the annual conscription campaign.

Under each MSD are a number of People's Armed Forces Departments (PAFD) which exist at county, city and even sometimes at large state-owned factory level. The PAFD's task is fulfilling conscription levels within the area they control, as well as demobilization and resettlement of former soldiers into the communities. Operational-wise, these PAFDs organize and coordinate all military activities including training in their area.

From 1984 to 1996 the PAFD wore a different uniform from that of the PLA, but in 1996 they were brought back into the PLA structure and now wear the same uniforms as regular PLA soldiers. The return of the PAFD to the PLA structure was in response to complaints of rampant corruption, abuse, and mismanagement of the conscription system. Essentially, wealthy families could "pay off" corrupt members of the PAFD to avoid military service, or sometimes offers were made to ensure conscripts were placed in "soft" postings, near their family home etc.

The guarding of large cities falls under the responsibility of the Garrison Command (GC). Their function includes maintaining military discipline and guarding military installations. The garrison headquarter troops have authority over military personnel only, and can sometimes be seen patrolling main streets in large cities like Beijing or setting up impromptu vehicle checkpoints. They are distinguished by their smart appearance, tall stature (1.8 m or above) and usually by their color-coded armbands (red stands for Army, navy blue is for Navy, sky blue is for the Air Force) with yellow lettering (*Jiu Cha*) on it. In addition, they wear a white helmet with red-stenciled letters "Jiu Cha" in Chinese on one side and the Chinese word for "Garrison Command" on the other. To complete the uniform, the GC soldier would wear a white Sam Browne belts with regulation pistol and spare magazine holder. In times of crisis, garrison troops can be assigned to operational duties as part of a larger formation.

The cities of Beijing, Tianjin, Chongqing and Shanghai, as well as Hong Kong and Macau, all have separate garrison command organizations. In addition to what is stated above, maintaining strict military discipline and guard duties, within their ORBAT are operational military units tasked to defend the cities/localities against external attack. In parallel to the PLA, the PAP also has a similar organization for enforcing unit and individual discipline. They too wear a similar white helmet and wear an arm badge that contains the word *Jiu Cha*.

3.2 The PLA Structure

The Chinese armed forces are a key part of the overall Chinese Security Apparatus along with the Chinese civilian police (under the Ministry of Public Security, MPS), and the Bureau of National Security (in charge of domestic and international intelligence gathering, but under the control of the Ministry of State Security, MSS). The Chinese armed forces consist of the People's Liberation Army (PLA) and its three sub-branches, Army, Navy and Air Force, the People's Armed Police (PAP) as well as the Chinese militia. The former two organizations, MPS and MSS, are civilian organizations reporting to the State Council headed by the Prime Minister. The Chinese armed forces report to a different chain of command, with the Central Military Commission (CMC) at its apex. The CMC is headed by the all-powerful Chairman, which under normal circumstances is an office held by the President of the PRC.

The regular and reserve Forces of the PLA are responsible for countering possible external threats while the PAP's primary role is internal security with a secondary supporting role to the PLA in times of national crisis. The militia, like the PLA, has the primary duty of external defense but also assists in maintaining domestic security if the situation demands. The PAP and militia also report to the State Council, especially in domestic matters working in conjunction with the police.

The PLA is a term that encompasses the regular and reserve troops of the Chinese Army, PLA Navy (PLAN), PLA Air Force (PLAAF), and strategic missile forces (formerly known as Second Artillery, and from January 2016 known as "Rocket Force"). The current size of the PLA is around 2.3 million, with about 1.6 million in the Army, 255,000 in the PLAN, 400,000 in the Air Force and 100,000 in the Second Artillery. The reserve for all four services is estimated to be about 800,000 strong. Special Forces were added to the ORBAT in the early 1990s for each of the services, and new additions to the force are "high technology" units that focus on electronic warfare, cyber warfare, information warfare, and psychological warfare.

The PLA is divided into main forces, or better known as the Field Army, which is dispatched throughout the country, and local forces such as coastal defense and border/frontier guards who are specific for local defense. The PLA ground forces are formed into combined-arms groups known as "Group Forces," or Jituan Jun in Chinese, their closest equivalent in the West being a full army corps. The rest of the PLA structure is pretty standard. It consists of: division, brigade, regiment, battalion, company, platoon, and squad.

3.2.1 PLA Reserve Units/Force

Before the formation of the PLA reserve in 1983 there was only the regular force and the militia. Like the Territorial Army/Army Reserve of the UK, or the National Guard in the United States, the Chinese PLA Reservists are essentially civilians in uniforms. Many have technical expertise, like a background in medicine or electronics. Retired/demobbed PLA regulars are also encouraged to join the PLA reserve units. The PLA reserve is classified into divisions, brigades etc, and they serve as infantrymen, artillery, AAA, engineers, signals, NBC, armored, field hospital etc. During peacetime, the reserve forces are under a dual leadership management: reporting to the military district and to the operational commands which they belong to but also following directives from the local government and local CCP cell. The use of the reserve force is increasingly common, especially in times of national domestic crisis such as the Sichuan earthquake in 2008.

3.2.2 The Militia

The Chinese militia has a long and illustrious role in the history of China. The militia played a key role in supporting the PLA in many of the epic battles of the 20th century; from the Chinese civil war in the 1940s to the Sino-Vietnam War of the 1980s, it is safe to say that without the militia in support, the PLA would not have won! In the Great Leap Forward Campaign (1958–61), under the slogan "Everyone a soldier," the militia was greatly expanded but without increasing the overall resource allocation. The militia was competing with the PLA for supplies, and that created tensions between the two forces. The rapid expansion also drew in unsuitable personnel—some so-called militia commanders were no better than local warlords and bandits. Weapon controls were lax such that guns were often used for crimes. The situation was not brought under control until the early 1960s. In 1987 the militia was reclassified into "primary militia" and "ordinary militia." The former was organized into quick reaction forces (QRF) for local emergencies. Women are also eligible for enlistment in the militia, but are normally allocated to ordinary militia.

The militia is a vast organization. According to the 2004 defense white paper; primary military membership alone is as large as 10 million. According to Chinese law, all male citizens between eighteen and thirty-five who are not already serving in the armed services shall be regimented into militia units. What this means is essentially almost every able-bodied male citizen is expected to serve. In practice, however, entry into the militia is a very selective process and only a small proportion of the population are active members. Militia can be found in almost every city government, district, county, village, business, and factory, organized into regiments and battalions down to platoon and sections. The annual commitment is a minimum of thirty days for officers and senior NCOs, and fifteen days for basic rank and file. While some militia units are organized effectively, in some places the unit is merely names on a list and the actual training conducted is highly questionable. Like the reform of the PLA, the militia is also being streamlined with the emphasis being placed on quality rather than quantity.

The militia assists the PLA by performing local security and logistics in times of emergency. The militia operates static AAA defenses and they conduct NBC decontamination, rapid repairs, and engineering work. In recent years the Chinese press has reported the existences of mysterious "urban" militia units within the PLA. No more open information can be found concerning these "units," but they are essentially private citizens with special skills such as communications, languages, computer skills, etc, who are helping the PLA and police to maintain public security.

3.2.3 The People's Armed Police (PAP)—The Cousin of the PLA

Although the PAP is a relatively new organization with just over thirty years of history, back in 1949, still within the PLA structure, there was a paramilitary organization called the PLA Public Security Army (*Gongan Jun*). The *Gongan Jun* conducted duties not dissimilar to those expected of the PAP today. After many twists and turns, the powers that be never quite made up their minds whether it should be part of the police or army, and the PAP had many name changes: the Chinese PLA Internal Guard Troops, People's Public Security Troops, PLA Public Security Troops, 16th Department of the Ministry of Public Security and associated armed police, PLA General Staff Department Garrison Unit, and Associated Public Security Troops are just some of the tongue twisters that came out before the name became established as the People's Armed Police (PAP) in 1983.

The PAP is a paramilitary force which was formed from the PLA border guards and PLA internal security units as well as some elements of the police. The PAP is estimated to be 1.5 million strong, with internal security comprising almost half of the total force. The PAP is organized into contingents for each province and city in which they perform a variety of tasks, from border security (including passport checking in airports and ports), forest security and forest fire fighting, hydro power security, urban firefighting, gold and strategic minerals security, VIP protection, anti-terrorist SWAT teams and sometimes road construction and transportation of specialized goods. A notable elite PAP commando force, the Snow Leopard Commando Unit (SLCU), is often in the limelight.

The PAP wears different uniforms to the PLA but often in the same brown/green shade, and it has a similar rank structure as the PLA which can be confusing. Although recruits for PLA and PAP are enlisted at the same induction period, the PAP has its own training institution separate from the PLA.

3.2.4 The Recruitment Process and Training of Conscript Soldiers

China operates a selective conscription system that requires selected citizens to serve the PLA or PAP for no less than two years. Conscription is carried out once a year and each year the number of new recruits needed

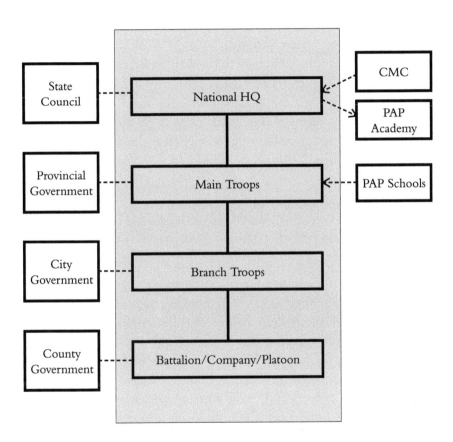

PAP Structure

State Council — National HQ — CMC, PAP Academy

Provincial Government — Main Troops — PAP Schools

City Government — Branch Troops

County Government — Battalion/Company/Platoon

is determined by the GSD and GPD. These manpower demands are then issued to each MR with quotas for each MSD to fulfill. Quota numbers include both PLA and PAP. In November of each year, potential new recruits are notified and then undergo physical and political tests. If they pass the tests, they are issued with uniforms and a travel order to report to the training regiments in groups. Units receiving new soldiers will have established reception committees to help them settle in. Division and brigade commanders and political officers are responsible for basic training which is conducted according to set standards. Selected officers and NCOs from the division pool are drafted to conduct recruit training. Recruits are grouped into squads and each one is headed by a JNCO. These squads are grouped into platoons and platoons into companies. Basic training lasts about three months and is generally held over the coldest time in the winter months.

At the end of training, the new soldiers are given insignia and rank and take the "Soldier's Oath." The soldier raises his/her right arm clenched in a fist but not so that the hand is above the head and, while looking at the PLA flag or Army badge, reads out the Soldier's Oath. The PLA oath has gone through a number of changes; the latest, 12th, edition promulgated in June 2010 can be translated as:

> I am a member of the PLA. I promise that I will follow the leadership of the CCP, serve the people wholeheartedly, obey orders, strictly observe discipline, fight heroically, fear no sacrifice, work hard, practice hard to master combat skills, be ready for combat at all times, under no circumstances will I betray the PLA and will defend the motherland until my death.

After basic training, soldiers are assigned to their permanent units for additional training. Specialist and technical training can include driving, radio operation, artillery firing, chemical defense, etc. Previously those recruits with special ability were quickly identified and selected to become potential junior NCOs, but as the PLA is moving towards a professional force, this practice is being abandoned and JNCOs are selected from volunteers and those who sign on as professional soldiers. Whilst serving as conscripts, these new soldiers are not allowed to get marry and must stay in the barracks throughout the period of their two-year service.

First-year soldiers are called Private (*Lie Bing*), in the second year they are promoted to Private First Class (*Shang Deng Bing*). Pay is dependent on rank and years in service, with a supplement given to those serving in difficult conditions such as desert regions or snowy mountaintops. Conscripts normally serve for two years, and by November of the second year, those who do not want to sign on as professional soldiers will be demobilized and return home. Some demobbed soldiers may be required to continue serving in the reserves or militia.

3.2.5 The PLA NCOs

Until 1999, the PLA followed the Soviet system of NCO recruitment and their role in the army. In 1999, China decided to move the PLA towards a professional army closer to the Western model e.g. the British Army or US Army. The decision to cut conscription time to two years was accompanied by a concurrent decision to increase the number of NCOs and give them greater responsibilities. NCOs are selected from capable volunteers from the end of the conscription period. Some NCOs are brought into the PLA directly from civilian life because of their specialist technical knowledge or skills.

NCOs are divided into six grades and may stay on active duty for thirty or more years up to the age of fifty-five. SNCO ranks and lengths of service for each grade are categorized as below:

- Junior Sergeant is divided into two grades: Grade 1 NCO and Grade 2 NCO, both requiring a minimum service of three years.
- Intermediate Sergeant is also divided into two grades: Grade 3 NCO and Grade 4 NCO, both requiring a minimum service of four years.
- Senior Sergeant is also divided into two grades: Grade 5 NCO, with a minimum of five years of service, and Grade 6 NCO, requiring a minimum nine-year contract.

Newly selected candidate SNCO candidates take an exam in January and those accepted are required to report to PLA schools for two or more years of training. Prospective NCO candidates must submit a written application and be recommended by his/her unit and the party/political officer. Grade 1 and 2 NCOs are approved at the regimental level. At the end of the contract, should the NCOs wish to extend his/her service they must undergo the same recruitment NCO processes.

Promotions are approved at division or brigade level for Grade 3 and 4 SNCOs, and at Army level for Grades 5 and 6 SNCOs, who are encouraged to continue their professional education through either correspondence courses or attendance at military or civilian institutions of higher learning. Grading of the performance of NCOs is uniquely Chinese, for besides recommendation by their superior/officers, they are also evaluated by the soldiers in their unit, and therefore opinions of the ordinary soldiers do count.

NCOs may marry, though due to a shortage of married quarters many married NCOs are required to live in barracks and their spouses are allowed to visit the barracks once a year, staying at quarters inside the garrison for up to forty-five days. Obviously, long-term separation between husbands and wives is not ideal, and disapproving voices are getting more and more vocal. The PLA has responded with more housing for service families. SNCO families are authorized to live in barracks when approval is given.

The PLA expects its non-commissioned officers to be capable and take on more responsibilities. The PLA is moving to replace supply/logistics officers with SNCOs. SNCOs are increasingly expected to command operations, organize training, and manage subordinates.

3.2.6 The PLA Officers

The PLA's officers are distinguished by their rank, post, and job category. Category-wise this can be classified as operational officer, political officer, logistics officer, armaments officer, and technical officer. For the most part, once officers are categorized they do not get transferred out of their specialties unless being promoted to general-grade officers.

Like all branches of the PLA, the officers enter into five possible career tracks: military (or command officer), political, logistics, equipment, and technical. Military officers serve as unit commanders and staff officers are responsible for operations, intelligence, training, unit organization, administration, and communication. Political officers serve as unit commissars and staff officers in political departments. They are responsible for unit personnel records, public relations, political and party work, civil—military relationships, and security and cultural activities. Logistics and equipment officers serve as unit directors and staff officers in their respective departments. Logistics officers are responsible for transportation, finances, quartermaster's stores, POL, housing/barracks facilities and medical care while equipment officers are responsible for managing the development, acquisition, maintenance, and repair of all equipment and weapons systems. They also serve as representatives in civilian research institutes and factories that develop and produce weapons systems and equipment. Finally, technical officers serve primarily as engineers, weapons system and equipment maintenance and repair officers, computer technicians, academics, and doctors. Today a high percentage of college graduates who join the PLAAF as officers serve in this track.

Officers are further categorized into three grade levels and ten ranks, similar to the Western structure. On average, an officer is promoted approximately every four years on condition they have passed the required exams. During the Cultural Revolution, military ranking was abolished and there were only two categories: "soldiers" and "officers." During this period, soldiers and officers were often referred to by the post they held, such as "Comrade Company Commander" or "Comrade Squad Commander."

Today all arms of the PLA are currently organized into fifteen grades/appointments and ten rank structures. While ranks are easy to understand, colonel, captains etc., appointments are essentially jobs one might hold, such as regimental commander or battalion 2ic. To understand the PLA, we need to understand that in China, throughout its five thousand years of history, one's job or appointment has always been the key, and not rank. In fact, the concept of rank was a Western idea that was only reluctantly accepted in the PLA in the 1950s, when it was essentially being remodeled after the Soviet Red Army. Today, the concept of rank and its associated insignia is primarily a visual guide to one's seniority, but the appointment or job truly reflects the person's status. For example, the simple fact is that the housing assigned to an officer is determined by the job held and not by rank, and promotion in job appointments determines how one moves up the career ladder. Therefore, a major holding a position as regimental 2iC holds more influence and better "status" than a major holding a job as a battalion commander. In daily conversation the Chinese still prefer to address each other as "Comrade Regimental Commander" rather than as "Comrade Colonel."

Another unique feature of the PLA in contrast to Western armies is that in the PLAAF, indeed throughout the entire PLA, the promotion of officers and enlisted personnel, at least in the field grades until at very senior level, is decentralized and determined by party committees within the unit itself. These selection committees operate at the corps level but permeate as far down as regimental level. This also explains why most personnel remain within the same unit or at least in the same division for most of their career.

Officers new to the PLA are increasingly being recruited from university graduates, with civilian colleges and universities targeted as sources of recruitment. Of course those who were lucky enough to be admitted as cadets to PLA military universities have a beeline to the PLA ahead of civilian candidates. Last but not least are personnel selected from the enlisted ranks to become officers. This last category of "promotion from rank and file" had been the traditional source of officers for the PLA, but as modern warfare puts increasing demands on technical skills, increasingly more officers with higher levels of education are needed.

The PLA, like many Western armies, also sponsors promising students through universities with a scholarship scheme known as "national defense students." While attending colleges, these students are managed by the "Reserve Officers Selection and Training Officers" located in the various schools. All national defense students are required to attend military training during university vacations, and on graduation all students on PLA scholarships are required to serve the PLA. Secondary or high school graduates continue to be the main source of officers for the PLA, and sending off their son/daughters as cadets to military academies is an increasing popular option for many Chinese families. Increasingly the PLA is seen as a secure job with prospects. Applicants for military academies must be under twenty years old, unmarried, and physically and politically qualified. Tuition fees are paid by the government and cadets are paid modest sums while attending the academy.

Another key reform of the PLA is that since 2006 the PLA has not been part of the civil service and employments are based on contracts. How long can one stay in the PLA? For officers, the service period is governed by the rank they attained. For platoon leaders the minimum service period is eight years, as it is for company 2iCs, but for a company commander the minimum period is twelve years. Battalion second in commands require a minimum service period of fourteen years, which rises to sixteen years for battalion commanders. Officers serving in leadership capacities in regimental formations or above serve a minimum of twenty years. Technical grade officers have a different set of service requirements. Junior technical officer service contracts are a minimum of twelve years, while middle grade technical officers are required to serve a minimum of sixteen years, extending to twenty years for senior grade officers.

3.2.7 PLA Academies

There are approximately thirty-five military academies throughout China that allow civilians to gain entry to the PLA and also at the same time receive an education. School fees are paid by the PLA and the cadets get a salary. No wonder it is a popular option with many parents, especially those from rural areas where job opportunities are not as numerous as in big cities like Shanghai and Beijing. Cadets usually attend a four-year undergraduate degree course, and upon graduating are immediately commissioned as second lieutenants and enter the PLA. In addition to college-level education, these institutes provide basic military training to prepare cadets for assignments to operational units immediately after graduation. Academies are subordinate to the various services they belong to but ultimately their operation is overseen by the various General Headquarters Departments in Beijing.

GSD-supervised academies focus on military skills such as infantry craft, armor, and artillery, while GLD-supervised academies focus on logistics, GPD academies train future political officers, and GAD academies train technical specialists. Some PLA institutions also offer advanced degree courses, and the PLA can also send officers to civilian universities in China and overseas for further education. A much smaller number of intermediate-level academies, referred to as "command academies," train mid-level officers serving in battalion- and regimental-level posts. Like many staff colleges in the West who host students from friendly allied nations, the PLA's Nanjing Army Command Academy also has a Foreign Training Department, which is attended by officers from many different countries.

The top of the PLA's professional military education pyramid is the National Defense University and National Defense Science and Technology University. The importance of these two institutes is confirmed by the fact that they report directly to the CMC. Students to the NDU are senior PLA commanders, staff officers, and researchers, while senior civilian officials from government organizations above provincial level can also attend. Courses include the three-month "National Defense Course" for officers awaiting promotion, and refresher courses for officers assigned to new posts.

NUDT students are senior scientists, engineers, and commanders of technical units who attend senior-level classes as well as undergraduates just out of high school. NUDT students are mostly from (or about to enter) the armaments system or are technicians.

3.2.8 Uniformed PLA Civilians

Within the PLA are uniformed civilians who despite wearing some form of uniform are not part of the formal PLA and do not hold any military ranks. Many are instructors and research staff within the military education system. PLA civilians are categorized as specialist technical cadre, on-specialist technical cadre, and office or administrative personnel. PLA civilians may become officers after completing the required training, and likewise PLA officers who have reached retirement age may become PLA civilians and stay on within the military system.

3.2.9 National Defense Education

Like many countries, China also has its own national defense awareness campaign. The National Defense Education Act governs the rules and laws of defense education in China. Military education comes in many shapes and forms, from specialist publications, physical education, games, competitions, TV and radio shows, art and museum visits. Every third Saturday of September is set aside as National Defense Education Day, and schoolchildren throughout the nation participate in some form of national defense education. This can be a simple visit to a military museum, while others can be more informative like visiting an actual military base. In Britain schoolchildren are encouraged to join the various cadet forces organized by the army, navy and air force. In China, the national defense education carries out similar activities for the Chinese schoolchildren under the all-encompassing National Defense Education Office (NDEO), which coordinates military training in schools and sets the syllabus.

In China this form of military training focuses on patriotic education and basic knowledge of national defense with a bit of fun shooting and marching thrown in. This differs from the military training held in Taiwan schools where the emphasis is on developing suitable candidates for officer cadets in the reserves or regular army. In Chinese tertiary education establishments there are the University People's Armed Forces Corps (UPAFC). These mysterious establishments are responsible for organizing military training in the respective universities/colleges. They assist in promoting national defense education and in the annual draft including draft registration, promoting civil—military cooperation and maintaining the university cadet corps arsenals. Controlling these many corps throughout the country is the National Tertiary Education Military Education Committee (NTMEC), which is part of the Ministry of Education. Within the PLA's National Defense Academy there is also an office (the Student Military Education Teaching Coordination Center, or SMETCC) that coordinates the work carried out by National Defense Education in the various educational establishments. Military camps usually take place in nearby PLA camps before the start of regular academic classes and may last a number of weeks. Shooting, first aid, NBC, drill, and basic field craft, etc., are usually incorporated in these camps.

3.3 Uniforms and Combat Equipment

3.3.1 PLA Uniforms

Prior to 1949, the PLA was essentially still a guerrilla army equipped with a variety of captured weapons and uniforms. Often a soldier would just wear the old Nationalist Army uniform with the badge removed and replaced by a red star and a printed cloth over left breast pocket with the words "Chinese People's Liberation Army" (*Zhongguo Renmin Jiefang Jun*). If lucky he might get a sandy yellow four-pocket cotton-padded tunic. The uniform would come with a Mao cap with an attached Ba Yi (ノ\一) Red Star with yellow border.

The first uniform code of the PLA was issued in January 1950 and named the Model 50 Military Uniform. The PLA of 1950 already had land, sea, and air capability, and so, for the first time, there were separate uniforms for the Army, Navy and Air Force—all green for the Army, a deep blue for the Navy in the winter and whites for summer, and a green top and blue trousers for the Air Force—and cap badges. The Model 50 was the official uniform for the PLA from January 4, 1950 to September 30, 1955. It was this uniform that the PLA wore when they went into Korea, with all insignias and badges, including the red star, removed.

The introduction of the Model 55 uniform formed a part of the great reform of the PLA, which also included a military pay-structure and scale, and a professional army career system as well as a system of awards and decorations. The 1950s coincide with the Sino-Soviet honeymoon period, and as such the PLA went through "Sovietization" with Soviet weapons and Soviet-style uniforms. This included collar badges with arms identification and military rankings with Soviet-style shoulder boards. For the first time different types of uniforms were also introduced: working and ceremonial dress, winter and summer dress, and even combat dress with subdued badges. During this period the PLA also incorporated into its uniforms elements of Western military outlook, such as Soviet-style Sam Browne belts for officers. In the winter, all ranks wore *ushanka* furry hats with large overcoats. Sometimes officers retained their peaked cap and the enlisted ranks a side cap. Members of the armor corps adopted Soviet-style cavalry boots with matching cavalry trousers. In 1960, there was a minor revision to the Model 55 uniform; military ranks were to be placed on the collar tabs instead of the Soviet-style shoulder boards. As Sino-Soviet relations soured, the 1960 revision also began to gradually remove obvious elements of Soviet styling in the uniforms. For example, the badge for the transport corps was originally a Soviet GAZ truck; the new badge was transformed to a Chinese-made "Liberation" truck.

1955 and the 1987 The Chinese PLA's First Military Rank Structure

In 1955, the Chinese PLA went through a period of "Sovietization" and adopted a Soviet-style ranking structure. There were eight categories of troops: command, political, technical, logistics, medical, veterinary, and judiciary. The nineteen ranks split into six different grades:

Marshals	Senior Marshal (1)*	Marshal (10)		
Generals	General (10)	Lieutenant General (57)	Major General (177)	Brigadier (1360)
Field Officers	Senior Colonel	Colonel	Lieutenant Colonel	Major
Junior Officers	Senior Captain	Captain	Lieutenant	Sub-Lieutenant
NCOs	Sergeant	Corporal	Lance Corporal	
Privates	Private First Class	Private		

* This was given to Mao, but he refused to assume it and the rank was left unclaimed.

One feature of the Soviet-style ranking structure was that it is top heavy with officers' ranks and with a very thin NCO structure. The rank structure was abolished in 1965 only to be re-established in 1987. The current structure is a 1994 modification of the 1987 model, and is more in line with Western armies, putting greater emphasis on the NCO structure and a flatter pyramid.

Generals	General (abolished 1994)	Lieutenant General	Major General	Brigadier
Field Officers	Senior Colonel	Colonel	Lieutenant Colonel	Major
Junior Officers	Captain	Lieutenant	Sub-Lieutenant	
NCOs	Sergeant	Corporal	Lance Corporal	
Privates	Private First Class	Private		

The re-introduction of ranks was made in 1988 by Deng Xiaoping. On the same day he created seventeen general-grade officers and 1,435 other lesser-ranked generals, 180,000-plus field officers and 450,000 junior officers, giving the PLA some 631,000 officers, with the officer corps constituting about 21% of the entire PLA.

After ranks were abolished in the 1960s, the PLA was left wearing Model 55 uniforms with no badges or ranks. But the political climate in China was changing and China went into a period of internal chaos with the advent of the Great Cultural Revolution. The Cultural Revolution created an era when political thinking dominated and therefore the result for the PLA was the creation of the Model 65 uniform. One striking feature of this new uniform was that it had no insignia of any kind. The only identifying feature was a cap badge—simplified to just a five-pointed red star. On the jacket, the famous Mao jacket, the only "decoration" was a simple red collar tab. The only way to distinguish between officers and ranks was that officers had four pockets while the rank-and-file only had two top breast pockets.

Towards the end of the Cultural Revolution, in 1974, Mao issued one of his last edicts to the PLA. He authorized changes to the bland

Model 65 uniform, and with these new changes the PLA went into the era of the Model 74 uniform. The Army retained the sample plain green Mao suit, but the Air Force now wore green jackets with blue pants. The greatest changes occurred in the Navy with the reintroduction of navy whites and blues and peaked caps. The enlisted ranks returned to Soviet-style sailor suits and caps that included a headband with the word "Chinese People's Liberation Army Navy."

In 1978, China reopened its door to the Western powers and introduced a series of economic reforms. After the bitter experience of the 1979 war with Vietnam, a rankless army was no longer considered practical, and in 1980 the CMC announced the reintroduction of military ranks into the PLA. As a temporary measure before the full-scale introduction of military ranking, a stopgap measure for only three years (1985–88) introduced the Model 85 uniforms. In the Model 85 the greatest difference was the reintroduction of colors (green for Army, navy blue for the PLAN and sky-blue for the PLAAF). Shoulder epaulettes were also added with collar tabs and different metal pins for each of the three services. The Chinese characters "8.1" came back in the middle of the red star on the cap badge as well as gold rims with added wings for the Air Force and an anchor in the background for the Navy (almost returning to the Model 55 look). Winter and summer dress was included, and for the first time in many years, skirts were worn by female PLA soldiers.

After a hiatus of twenty-three years, the CMC formally reintroduced military ranking back into the PLA and PAP in 1987. Known as Model 87, for the first time an elaborate NCO system was introduced with four classes of JNCOs as well as SNCOs. Ranks were displayed on the shoulders using slides over epaulets and Soviet-style shoulder boards for officers' dress uniforms. All ranks now wore peaked caps and in extreme cold weather *ushanka*. For the first time the Model 87 uniform included a unique design for the National Honor Guard, PLA Band and Entertainment Regiment. Members of the PLA honor guard, both male and female, had a very elaborate uniform for each of the three services in their unique colors, with cavalry boots and pinstriped trousers with a large gold aiguillette hanging from the left shoulder. The Military Band and the Entertainment Regiment had a similar uniform code but with their own unique epaulets.

Military Band and Entertainment Regiment

Song and dance troupes have played a prominent role in the Chinese military, a tradition that came from Russia, where artists were drafted or trained within the army system with the sole purpose of entertaining the soldiers. They receive rudimentary military training and are expected to perform right on the front line, often sharing the same trench or foxhole with regular combat troops. President Xi Jinping's wife, Madam Peng Liyuan, launched her career as a singer in the PLA song and dance troupe. Many of today's top-performing artists started in the PLA and only recently the song and dance troupe of the SAC topped the charts with a folk song, *China Dream*. However, the topic of PLA performers is being questioned as a form of show-biz glitter and thought by some to be dragging the army into a quagmire of commercialism. At a recent party meeting, a call was tabled for non-fighting elements of the PLA to be cut. In 2006, a naval commander was given a suspended death sentence for corruption—he was found to have five mistresses from the song and dance troupe. In September 2013, the son of two prominent PLA performers was sentenced to ten years in jail for rape in a widely publicized trail. Performers and uniformed civilians in the PLA have no ranks but only senior/junior grading, and the press often addresses in error artists with rank, calling Madam Peng "General."

The Model 97 uniform was a short-term experiment with a new style that was created for the PLA Hong Kong Garrison. At that time there was a hope to extend the Model 97 uniform to the rest of the army in 2000, but due to high costs only a limited number of the PLA were able to wear it. Therefore, until the arrival of Model 07 the rest of the troops had to make do with the Model 87 uniforms. To extend the life of the Model 87, minor modifications were made in 1999, 2004 and 2005 to the uniform code to incorporate a new summer dress and working dress as a stopgap measure until the introduction of the current Model 07 uniform code. The most prominent feature of the Model 97 uniform was the introduction of berets; and for NCOs chevrons replaced bars on shoulder rank slides and the formation shoulder patch. To complete the new look, the Model 97 uniform included metal collar pins and breast pins denoting the three services as well as a US-style plastic name badge.

The Model 07 uniform was unveiled in late June 2007 during the celebration ceremony for the tenth anniversary of transfer of sovereignty over Hong Kong. These new uniforms were set to replace the Model 87 and Model 97 uniforms which were in use by PLA garrison troops in Hong Kong and Macau. The immediate reaction to the Model 07 was that they are closer to a Western-style uniform than the old Soviet style. For the first time, the uniforms have cuff insignia in the form of stripes, worn not just by the PLA's honor guard but by all NCOs and junior and senior officers except the general officers.

Compared to the previous "olive green" service uniforms that were in service with the PLA ground forces since the mid-1980s, the new Model 07* uniforms feature a colder "pine green" color, combined with better quality fabric and better tailoring to give a more stylish and yet professional appearance. Each PLA servicemen has a winter combat and training uniform made of woolen material and a summer combat and training uniform made of poly/cotton twill fabric. Both uniforms consist of a coat, trousers, a soft cap and black leather boots. All rank insignias are on green backgrounds. The old standing-collar winter service uniform was abandoned in favor of an open-collar design. As a part of the introduction of this new uniform there is a new cap badge, a service cap for female soldiers and officers and a simplified ranking structure for the NCO corps. There is also a British-style pullover with the introduction of a rank grade for cadets. Overall, the uniform is much more colorful, with a liberal expansion of the use of formation shoulder patches (thirty-seven different badges available), metal breast pins, cloth breast patches, nametags, national flag patches, and ribbons.

---

* Modifications to the Model 07 uniform were made as part of the 2016 reform; designs of badges were changed but uniform design remains unchanged.

3.3.2 PAP Uniforms

Throughout the years, the PAP followed a similar pattern of uniform changes to the PLA, albeit with minor changes and variations. During the 1960s in the midst of the Cultural Revolution, the then-PAP wore the same Model 65 uniform, with the same cap badge, as the PLA. In 1974 and again in 1983 a new cap badge was introduced. In 1983 a new PAP shoulder pin was introduced; otherwise there was no difference between the PAP and the PLA uniform. Like the PLA, ranks first reappeared in the PAP structure in 1987 with the introduction of the Model 87 uniforms. A new cap badge, rank slides and a large PAP formation shoulder patch are the major points of differentiation. A new NCO rank structure came into being in 1993 expanding the previous six grades of NCOs to twelve grades, but this was once again reduced to seven grades in 1997. Other minor modifications to the Model 87 were made in 2001, 2004 and 2005, and in 2007 a new PAP uniform code was also introduced.

For many observers, it is hard to distinguish between PLA and PAP uniforms, so much so that often in Western media the labels are wrong. A helpful distinguishing feature is the pinstripe down the side of the pants on all PAP dress uniform. The PLA almost never has color pinstripes on the trousers except for the Honor Guard, Military Band, and Entertainment Regiment.

Deciphering PLA "decorations"

On the latest Model 07 uniforms worn by officers, there are often rows of on the left breast of the dress jacket. Whereas in Western armies these ribbons are often miniature symbols of military awards, decorations of service and personal accomplishments, in China these ribbons depict the career of the soldiers through the positions he/she has served in. They are divided into platoon, company level (OC and 2iC), battalion (CO and 2iC), regiment (CO and 2iC), etc. up to appointments at the level of the Central Military

Commission (CMC). One set of ribbons denotes the time served in that position, and there are six different types of "time served" ribbons. Each of these has a different number of vertical stripes, with each stripe depicting years served, from one to ten years.

The second type of ribbon is the appointment ribbon. This denotes the position held by the officer in question. If the candidate has more than one row of ribbons, the bottom row signifies the most basic appointment and in army terms this usually means a platoon- or company-level appointment.

The next level up is appointment to battalion level and the third bar is regimental appointment. Fourth is for divisional while fifth is corps level. The sixth is MR-level positions, and last but not least, if the person has seven rows of ribbon, this signifies that he/she is serving at the highest level of the PLA—a general holding a position at the CMC.

3.3.3 Combat Equipment

For many years, the PLA personal combat equipment remained virtually unchanged since the 1950s. Chest rigs for ammunition have always been popular. For banana-shaped AK magazines, these can be either three- or four-cell-long banana-shaped pouches with assorted smaller pouches. Soldiers and those with the Type-56 semi-auto rifle (the Chinese version of the Soviet SKS rifle) had similar chest rigs but with ten smaller-sized ammo clip pouches holding up to 200 rounds. Squad gunners with drum magazines have a separate over-the-shoulder web holder and other equipment such as water bottles, gas mask holders, a haversack for personal kit, and a separate grenade pouch holding up to four stick grenades slung over the shoulders, all tied down with the brown leather belt. For long-distance combat, a backpack without a carrying frame, more commonly known to Western culture as a Vietnam/Chicom rucksack, completes the set. For officers a leather pistol holder and leather ammo holder are commonly seen attached to the leather waist belt.

This situation did not change until the arrival of the Type-91 Personal Combat Gear (PCG). The personal combat gear now had an integrated belt and chest pouch ensemble which is similar to the late 1980s US Army Integrated Individual Fighting System (IIFS). As part of the Model 07 uniform, the PLA also introduced the Type-07 PCG. Outfitting the PLA takes time, and so far only front-line Type A units have been fully kitted. Many units, especially those in reserve, second-line Type B formations, and recruits/conscript training battalions, still use a mix of old and new PCG. The Type-07 PCG resembles the US MOLLE with a vest-like tactical assault panel (TAP) which replaced traditional yoke- and belt-style PCG. In addition to the Type-07 PCG are US-style pouch attachment ladder system (PALS) for pouch attachments, and the tactical vest can be reinforced with ballistic armor plates as well as an attached groin protector. To complete the Type-07 PCG the PLA soldier also carries a gas mask, water bottle (a Camel Bak© type water carrier has been seen in elite units), a NATO-style foldable entrenching tool, first aid kit, and a bayonet.

Today the PLA is being equipped with the new "Fritz" reinforced anti-ballistic helmet QGF–03, but the older GK–80 steel helmet is still in use, especially in Type B second-line units. For regular day-to-day work, the PLA solider may wear the camouflage pattern soft forage cap or in a more formal setting, dress uniform with peaked cap or beret. Type A units will be equipped with the QBZ-95 assault rifle and Type-07 PCG, a large load-carrying pack that resembles any modern mountaineering rucksack, and Model 07 combat boots. Type B units use the Type-81 assault rifle, which is usually matched with the Type-91 PGC.

In the 1979 Sino-Vietnam War, the PLA was still marching into Vietnam in plain green uniforms. In the mid-1980s, camouflage uniforms made their first appearance—a reversible camouflage suit, with US woodland style camouflage on the primary side and duck hunter spot look-a-like camouflage on the inner side. For almost twenty years the PLA used the US woodland look-a-like camouflage pattern for its three services until the introduction of the new Model 07 uniforms. Then for the first time there were introduced four basic camouflage patterns with each in a four-color scheme. The universal pattern (or urban) is the most commonly seen camouflage pattern. There is also a desert pattern, a winter pattern and a woodland pattern that was issued to Second Artillery Corps in dense forested regions. Finally, an ocean camouflage is gradually being issued to naval special units and marines.

Notes

1 Includes the Beijing Metro Line 1 and 2,9,344 km or 30% of railroad built between 1954 and 1983.

2 Beijing International Airport, Second Ring Road, Beijing, 2nd Automotive Works, Baoshan Steel Works, Daqing Oil Field, Nanjing Railway Bridge, Sanxia Dam, 30,000-plus km of optic cable, Taishan Nuclear Power Station, and 2,200 Project Hope Charity Schools, to name a few.

CHAPTER 4

KEY ARMS

4.1 PLA Ground Force Tactical Organization

It is said that no successful organization can ever stand still, and the PLA is no different. It is constantly changing. In 1949, the PLA was largely an infantry-based army with over seventy corps-size units, but over the years it was reduced to thirty-five and then twenty-four by 1988. Today the PLA ground force is just eighteen all-arms "Group Army" corps (GA, or *Juntuan*). The GA system is the direct descendent of the numbered army corps of the post-Korean War 1955–85 period, the Field Army system of the early PLA 1946–54, the Eighth Route Army period, 1937 –45, and the Red Army period, 1927–30. The structure of the GA varies but, by and large, it was organized in a standard Soviet model of "threes": three divisions form a corps, three regiments form a division, etc. and with a strict demarcation between arms. Now it is totally an all-arms concept, with an independently maneuvering all-arms strike force tailored to either threat/tasks or a geographic area.

4.1.1 Current Tactical Organization: Battalion and below

Like Western forces, the PLA is made up of similar building blocks, section/squad, platoon, company, battalion, regiment, brigade, division and corps. However, today the PLA is moving toward a battlegroup concept that is generally based around a battalion, and toward a three-level command structure of corps, brigade and battalion. The divisional structure remains for administration in many military regions containing brigades instead of regiments to accommodate the battlegroup concept. The idea behind the brigade and battlegroups is to "adapt to information warfare and to enable more rapid decision-making on the battlefield." In the PLA, the primary difference between a regiment and a brigade is that the brigade is capable of independent operations whereas a regiment is directly subordinate to the division, as it does not have the headquarters staff to carry out independent operations.

The PLA squad consists of nine to twelve men depending on tasks and organizations. A standard PLA infantry squad is nine strong, organized as follows:

Squad leader (*Banzhang*)	JNCO	Type-81/Type-95 assault rifle
Light machine gunner	Private	Type-81 LMG/Type-95 LSW
Assistant light machine gunner	Private	Type-81/Type-95 assault rifle
RPG gunner	Private	Type 69-1 40 mm RPG/ PF-98 120 mm
Assistant RPG gunner	Private	Type-81/Type-95 assault rifle
Three riflemen	Privates	Type-81/Type-95 assault rifle
Sniper	Private	Type-85 (Improved Dragunov SVD rifle) or QBU-88 sniper rifle

However, in mechanized infantry units, the rifle squad is ten strong. Organized into two fire teams, one headed by the squad commander, the other by the assistant squad commander, usually a JNCO in command of a LSW and a grenadier as well as two riflemen. Each fire team leader is equipped with a small radio. They are expected to carry the new bull-pup design Typ-95 assault rifle (official name QBZ-95 5.8 mm assault rifle—QBZ is short for Light Infantry Weapon, Rifle, Automatic) and 500 rounds of ammunition (300 rounds for self and 200 rounds for LSW gunner), a multipurpose bayonet and six WY-91 grenades. The grenadier is similarly equipped, but the Type-95 assault rifle has attached to it an under-slung 35 mm grenade launcher. The grenadier is expected to carry 300 rounds of 5.8 mm ammunition, fifteen extra 35 mm grenades and two WY-91 grenades. The LSW gunner is equipped with the Type-95 LSW (Light Infantry Weapon, Rifle, Squad use, QBB-95 5.8 mm LSW), 745 rounds of 5.8 mm ammunition stored in three 75-round drum magazines, four 30-round straight magazines and 400 rounds in bandoliers. The rest of the squad carries an extra 600 rounds of ammunition for the LSW. In addition, the LSW gunner has his multipurpose bayonet and two WY-91 grenades.

The support weapon squad is eight strong, equipped with a crew-served GPMG, the 5.8 mm Type-88 machine gun (QJY88), one QLZ-87 35 mm AGL, and a PF-98 120 mm antitank missile. Each soldier is also equipped with his personal weapon, a Type-95 short assault rifle and WY-91 grenades.

The PLA infantry company consists of eight officers and 184 other ranks split into one company headquarters and three rifle platoons with one fire support platoon. The platoon is in turn comprised of platoon headquarters with a platoon leader, usually a lieutenant or second lieutenant, and his radio operator. The platoon leader and radio operator is equipped with a short Type-95 assault rifle (a 609 mm vs. 745 mm standard barrel length), 300 rounds of ammunition, multipurpose bayonet, WY-91 grenades, and binoculars. The support weapon platoon has one officer and forty-two other ranks. It has a two-person platoon headquarters and four squads. Squad one is equipped with two QJZ-89 12.7 mm heavy machine guns (some may have QJZ-77 or 85) each with 800 rounds of ammunition, and each gun is served by a squad leader or assistant squad leader in command, gunner, assistant gunner, armor and rifleman with the Type-95 assault rifle for close protection.

It was reported in 2002 that some units have an additional fire-support platoon with the Type-75 14.7 mm AA HMG or the newer Type-02 14.7 mm AA HMG. In addition to the heavy machine gun squad, the support weapons platoon has two light mortar squads. Each squad contains ten men with two PP-93 60 mm light mortars and each tube is equipped with 120 rounds of mortar bombs, served by a crew of four with one rifleman for close protection. Finally, there is also an antitank missile squad with two HJ-9 (Red Arrow, *Hong Jian*) missile launchers, each with twelve missiles, served by two crews of four and a rifleman for protection for each launcher.

The PLA infantry company headquarter has eighteen soldiers and four officers. The officers are company commanders usually holding the rank of captain, an assistant company commander, political instructor (*Zhidaoyuan*) and a supply/logistics officer or SNCO (*Si wuzhang*) who are in charge of administrative matters. Within the company HQ there are also two radio operators, two medics, six snipers, each equipped with the QBU-88 5.8 mm sniper rifle, and finally one squad of cooks commanded by an NCO with eight privates as cooks. All except the snipers are equipped with the Type-95 shortened assault rifle. In technical or mechanized units, the company headquarters has additional technical support staff responsible for upkeep, maintenance, and training.

In a PLA infantry battalion there are normally three infantry companies, one mortar support company, one weapons support company, one recce platoon, and one medical platoon, giving a total of 625 other ranks and forty-five officers. Starting at the headquarters there is the battalion commander, normally a major, and his deputy political officer and supply officers. In addition, there are three radio operators, two admin clerks, seven security guards and a section of cooks giving a total of five officers and twenty other ranks.

The mortar support company consists of three platoons and a company headquarters. Each platoon has two tubes of PP-87 8 mm mortar with a range of 5.7 km, each with ninety bombs. The platoon is commanded by an officer, his radio operator, and twenty soldiers. The mortar company is commanded by a captain, who is assisted by his deputy. In addition, there are the political officer and supply officer, two radio operators, four technical NCOs as well as half a squad of cooks. Like the mortar support company, the antitank company is similarly organized with three platoons, each with four HJ-9 antitank launchers. The standard missile capacity is seventy-two rounds, although some B class units may still be equipped with recoilless rifles. The recce platoon has one officer and twenty-one men, and medical platoons normally have three doctors and seventeen medics. As the situation dictates, an antiaircraft platoon can be added consisting of one officer and twenty-eight men equipped with twelve QW-1 or 2 (Vanguard) MANPAD shoulder-launched AA missiles. The latter are reported to be a Chinese- developed shoulder-fired AA missile based on captured Russian SA-6 and US Stinger systems.

4.1.2 Current Tactical Organization: Regiment and Above

Brigades in PLA terminology are true combined-arms formations that can independently execute decisions. Since 1998, regiments have been increasingly converted to brigades and now it is commonly regarded as one entity, with the terms brigade and regiment often used interchangeably. Brigade level has become more prominent in the PLA as many divisions have been reduced in size and new brigades formed. A senior colonel normally commands a brigade.

A PLA motorized infantry brigade comprises some 4,500 to 5,000 troops in three or sometimes four (four-battalion brigades are mostly in the northern MR facing the Russians) motorized infantry battalions with three motor rifle companies, one fire support company and one tank battalion with thirty-two tanks. Some units may still be equipped with the antiquated T-59 MBT, though with upgraded reactive armor, which is known as the T-59D, or the other extreme, the latest T-98 or 99 MBT. In some units that are trained for amphibious operations—the 1st Amphibious Mechanized Infantry Division of 1st Group Army of the Nanjing MR and the 124th Amphibious Mechanized Infantry Division of the 42nd Group Army from Guangzhou MR are just two examples— the MBT used by these specialist units are the ZTS-63A amphibious tank which is an upgraded T-63 (a Chinese-designed tank based on the Soviet PT-67). In areas of lesser threats like southern China, light tanks such as the T-62, T-63 and ZTS-63A may be used. Organization-wise, the PLA tank companies normally have two tanks in the Company HQ and three platoons of four tanks each, making a total of fourteen tanks per company.

Each motor rifle battalion is equipped with over thirty ZSL-92 6x6 APCs (known also as the WZ-551). In support there is an artillery regiment with its radar, survey and communications function attached to the regimental HQ. The regiment consists of one field artillery battalion with eighteen guns. These can be either the latest Type-86 or the older Type-83 122 mm field artillery (some units are being equipped with

152 mm howitzers and the field artillery battalion is reduced in size to company on account of the increased firepower). One battalion of MBRL are equipped with eighteen truck-mounted Type-82 30-barrel 130 mm MBRLs and one battalion with four companies of mixed AA guns and missiles. A typical configuration of the AA battalion is two companies equipped with six Type-74 37 mm AA guns, and one company of PGZ-95 or Type-87 25 mm AA guns. A company of twelve units use shoulder-launched AA missiles; currently it will be either HN-6 (known in the West as the FN-6 Flying Cross Bow but in the PLA as the *Hong Ying* (Red Tassel)) or one of the Vanguard shoulder-launched MANPAD missiles.

The regiment also has a strong antitank force of company strength. "A" level units are all-missile AT units, but "B" level units may still have a mix of AT guns (two platoons of towed 100 mm Type-85 AT guns) and missiles. The missile platoons may have HJ-8 or HJ-9 antitank missiles mounted on jeeps, although some units may still have the Chinese-made HJ-73C, which is an improved version of the Soviet (NATO: Sagger) type AT-3 missile with SACLOS and anti-ERA capacity. Additional supporting arms include a battalion of engineers with flamethrowers, explosives and mining, building and bridging capabilities, as well as the means to conduct NBC decontamination for the entire brigade. The communications/electronic warfare battalion and the logistics battalion take care of the maintenance of all vehicles and weaponry. The engineers have their own unique vehicles, including the GSL-430 light jeep-mounted MCLC and FPH-02 man-portable flamethrower and the FHJ-84 62 mm twin-barrel man-portable reusable incendiary rocket/smoke screen launcher. Finally, to complete the list are the support units attached to the brigade HQ. This includes a reconnaissance company, a medical team, a transportation company, a training team, and an assortment of clerks and radio operators.

Units previously equipped with ZSL-92 6x6 IFVs are also gradually being upgraded. Some units' ZSL-92s have been replaced by the ZBD-09 8x8 IFV. For fully mechanized units, they are spoilt for choice.

Older units have the venerable Type-85 (improved Type 63 APC with extra road wheels) or 89 APC (Type-89 APC is an improved Type-85 with HMG mounted turret). Other may have the Type-86 IFVs (Type-86 IFV is a PLA copy of BMP1) but increasingly the ZBD-97 (also known as ZBD 04), a total IFV, is replacing the older IFV/APC. Units in Nanjing and Guangzhou MR were first to receive the ZBD-97 and they were first seen by the public in the 2009 sixtieth National Day parade. Instead of towed 122 mm artillery, the PLA is moving to SPGs such as the Type-89 122 mm SPG, and towed 100 mm ATGs in the antitank company are gradually being replaced with the PTL-02 6x6 100 mm SPATG.

As the emphasis is increasingly placed on independent brigades, the difference between a modern PLA brigade and a division is less clear. Operationally, brigades appear to have become equivalent to divisions and many former divisions have been downsized into brigades, though as a means to confuse they still retain the old divisional names.

In the early 1950s, The PLA maneuver divisions were organized along the Soviet model. Most Soviet maneuver divisions, either tank or infantry, were organized in "threes." For example, a motorized rifle division had three subordinate infantry regiments supported by a tank regiment; a tank division had three tank regiments, supported by a regiment of infantry. Full-strength PLA infantry and tank divisions followed that structure until the 1990s and substituted the word armored (*zhuangjia*) for tank (*tanke*) division to signify the move to an all-arms unit. In an all-arms brigade there are usually some air defense assets, for example a Yi Tian (sky dependent), WZ-551 6x6 wheeled AFV on which is mounted a Tian Yan-90 (Celestial Swallow) short-range surface-to-air missile. A Yi Tian air defense battalion consists of a battalion headquarters and three self-supporting air defense companies. The battalion headquarters consists of a ZSL-92 armored command vehicle and a 4x4 truck with a folding mast-mounted IRIS-80 radar. The air defense company headquarters consists of a single ZSL-92 ACV mounting a surveillance radar, six ZSL-92 air defense vehicles, two 4x4 resupply and two 4x4 maintenance trucks. Each company could be split into two self-supporting groups. Whether the company is organized into two vehicle platoons or squads is unknown.

The PLA classifies each unit's state of readiness and strength as either Type A (*Jia*) or B (*Yi*). Type A divisions with heavier armaments are found mostly in the Northern MR. They are approximately 18,000 strong with three infantry brigades, each with five battalions, one tank regiment supported by an artillery regiment and an AA regiment. Type A units are usually fully manned or up to 80%-plus of stated TO&E (Table of Organization and Equipment) levels and can be deployed with little or no additional training. Type B divisions are normally found in southern China. They are a much smaller and lighter unit with only 9,000 to 10,000 men, with 60%–80% TO&E and would most likely require additional training to meet operational requirements. As with Type A divisions they also have three brigades, but each is only four battalions strong and each battalion has only four companies—three infantry companies and a support company. Some Type B divisions have no attached tank regiment. In the past there existed an even lower-level unit known as Type C (*bing*) formations but in recent years they have been rarely mentioned in the press and it can be assumed that the reorganization of the PLA has done away with this level of classification.

The true spearhead of the PLA is the Type A all-arms group army with anything from 50,000–70,000 troops. The Type A all-arms group army can have divisions or even brigades as maneuvering units in either two or three divisions, either two tank divisions with one infantry brigade or the other way around. Some group army forces may have air assets such as transport and/or attack helicopters attached. The Type B Group Army is 30,000 to 40,000 strong with a battalion less per brigade and each battalion has one less company. It has a much weaker force support capacity and has no attached tank regiment. In addition to the supporting arms asset each Group Army also has five regimental-sized rear-echelon units. These are training regiments and training depot, military hospital, quartermaster's stores, and uniquely to the PLA, the PLA farms. The group army is usually commanded by a major general.

The PLA's New Armored Mechanized Infantry All-Arms Division

The PLA's 112th Mechanized Infantry Division was the first unit to adopt this new structure. The announcement was made in a TV report in 2006. The new division is organized and equipped to fight as an independent battle group in mountainous or urban terrain. It is given equipment much lighter in weight and firepower than those of traditional PLA divisions tasked to defend the nation against aggressors equipped with main battle tanks. Its theaters of operation are Xinjiang and Tibet where the division's lighter vehicles and support weapons can operate in areas where the communications infrastructure can be described as poor at best.

In this new set up, there are three mechanized infantry companies to the battalion and three battalions to the brigade, with three brigades in the division giving a total of 351 Type 86 IFVs. The Type 86 IFV, a Chinese version of the BMP-1, has been updated by replacing the 73 mm low-velocity gun turret with the new Chinese one-man "universal turret" containing a 30 mm chain gun. These are supported by an artillery brigade of seventy-two PLZ-89 122 mm self-propelled guns and a tank battalion of T-96 main battle tanks. Type 89 armored command vehicles are provided throughout the division down to the company level. Intelligence and electronic warfare assets are held at the divisional level in a battalion and distributed when required.

The new mechanized infantry brigade has four mechanized infantry battalions, one armored battalion, one fire support battalion, one engineer battalion and one communication battalion. Each mechanized infantry battalion has three mechanized infantry companies. Each has three platoons with every company having thirteen infantry fighting vehicles; four in each platoon and one headquarters vehicle.

Each armored brigade has three armored battalions for a total of ninety-nine main battle tanks, one mechanized infantry battalion, one artillery battalion with eighteen self-propelled guns, and one air defense battalion of eighteen AAA guns. Each armored battalion has three armored companies and the three platoons within the company have eleven main battle tanks; three in each platoon and two headquarters vehicles. There are no tanks at the battalion or brigade headquarters. A complete armored brigade contains 2,200 soldiers.

The support company of the battalion consists of one 100 mm mortar company with ten vehicles, with one mortar per vehicle, a fire control vehicle, and an automatic grenade launcher (AGL) platoon in two vehicles with two AGLs each. There is also an antitank platoon in two vehicles which share three antitank guided missile systems, normally the HJ-8. There are a total of eighteen Type 89 series armored vehicles in each brigade providing fifty-four antitank guided missile systems in the division.

The wheeled units are equipped with the ZSL-92 family of vehicles. In 1990 it was the Type 90 (WZ-551A) IFV, which was equipped with a turreted 25 mm automatic cannon, but in 1992 came the Type 92 (WZ-551B), altogether a cheaper APC with the semi-open turret. Also the PLZ-98 with the 100 mm assault gun served the brigade's antitank role.

The division headquarters comprises an engineer battalion, an electronic warfare battalion, a chemical defense battalion, the division headquarters, an air defense troop and a guard company for HQ protection. Logistics is provided by corps assets attached to the battle groups as required.

Within each mechanized infantry battalion there is an air defense platoon of three vehicles with four HQ-6 man portable air defense system (MANPAD) missile launchers per Type 89 APC vehicle, for a total of twelve. A division has twenty-seven air defense vehicles and has 108 HQ-6 MANPADS available at any time. They come under operational control of the air defense brigade commander.

The divisional air defense brigade consists of one battalion of twenty-four towed 57 mm AA guns and one battalion of eighteen towed twin 37 mm anti-aircraft guns. It is also has an air defense platoon of six Type 95 self-propelled combination AAA/SAM vehicles and one of light surface-to-air missiles which are attached to the artillery brigade.

The Type 95 SPAAG/SAM system uses the same hull as the PLZ-89 122 mm SPG, with a turret mounting four 25 mm automatic cannon, and can be fitted with four QW-2 IR-homing, short-range surface-to-air missiles. This is the Chinese equivalent of the Russian Igla-1 (SA-16 NATO: Gimlet).

If heavier forces are required, more punch can be added, and the 6th Armored Division is a good example of a new style "heavy" division. It has a similar structure to the mechanized infantry division but with added firepower in the form of an independent supporting artillery brigade (72 152 mm Type 83 or the new PLZ-45 155 mm SPG. The latter can use the Chinese version of the Russian KBP laser-guided round giving added range and accuracy). For antitank work, it has the 16th Antitank Regiment in support, which contains six PTZ-89 120 mm SPGs and eighteen Type 89 HJ-8 antitank guided missile tank destroyers. To protect from ground-attack aircraft or helicopters there is an air defense brigade that consists of a battalion of twenty-four 57 mm towed anti-aircraft guns and another battalion of six HQ-7 SAM systems, the Chinese clone of the French Crotale SAM. To date the PLA still depends on towed AAA despite having vehicles available to replace them.

4.2 PLA's Army Aviation Unit—the Army's own air force

The formation of the PLA's Army Aviation Unit (AAU) was approved by the Central Military Commission (CMC) in 1986 and the first regiment was formed in January 1988. At that time, the PLA army aviation unit consisted mainly of the PLAAF's helicopter force transferred to the AAU and a handful of Mi-4 scout helicopters from the border patrol force. PLA's AAU is a strategic asset and thus reports directly to the General Staff Department (GSD). The function of the AAU is to deploy helicopters and light aircraft to support ground operations, performing antitank operations, special force insertion and electronic countermeasure operations. Except for two Y-8 (Cloned Soviet An-12) transports, all aircraft in the AAU are rotary wing. This includes a small number of S-70C Sikorsky helicopters, Gazelle helicopters and eight Super Pumas for VIP transport which were purchased in the 1980s. The main fleet is domestically licensed and produced helicopters and they are: Z-8 transports (*Zhi*, "Vertical," Chinese for helicopter: vertical lift flying machine); the Chinese-licensed and -produced French Aérospatiale SA 321 Super Frelon heavy transport helicopter, the Harbin Z-9 (a license-built version of the French Eurocopter Dauphin) and the Z-9W gunship antitank helicopter (*Wu*, armed) and Mi-17 helicopters. For training the PLA had been using the Mi-4 and Mi-6 for many years until the advent of the Z-11, itself a licensed copy of the French AS-350B Squirrel 7. In 2012 at the Zhuhai air show, the PLA's latest attack helicopters, the Z-10, and the lighter, smaller Z-19W scout and reconnaissance helicopter were officially introduced to the public, even though the existence of both had been known for some time.

With the ever-increasing number of helicopters coming into the PLA, in 2012 up to six out of the ten aviation regiments were converted into brigade status with one acting as a training brigade. China claims to have 500 helicopters in its AAU, which is organized into eight army aviation brigades (AAB) with an aviation brigade allocated to one of each of the ground armies.

An aviation brigade consists of a mix of troop transport, ground attack and scout helicopters. Each role within the brigade is performed by a dedicated squadron with up to six squadrons within a brigade. Each ground attack squadron is equipped with twelve Z-10W attack helicopters.

With the rapid expansion of army aviation each MR is now assigned helicopter brigades. The PLA's Hong Kong and Macau garrisons are covered by an army aviation regiment with Z-9 and PLAAF Z8-KH for search and rescue. Each army aviation brigade typically controls one to three aviation regiments and supplementary reserve units. There are ten regular and nine reserve aviation regiments plus a training regiment in support.

Army Aviation			
Army Group	Regiment	Base	Aircraft
		Shenyang MR	
39	9 AAB	Liaoning-Liaoyang 辽宁-辽阳	Mi-171, Mi-171E, Z-8B, Z-9W, Z-9WA, Z-10A, Z-19
		Beijing MR	
38	8 AAB (Army Aviation Brigade)	Hebei-Baoding 河北-保定	Mi171, Mi-171E, Z-8B, Z-9W, Z-9WA, Z-9(EW), Z-10A, Z-19
Training Base	2nd Regiment	Shanxi-Houma 山西-侯马	Z-11
Training Base	3rd Regiment	Shanxi-Linfen 山西-临汾	Z-11, HC-120
65	4th Regiment	Beijing-Tongzhou 北京通州	Y-7, Y-8, Mi-171, Mi-171E, Mi-171E Salon, Mi-17-V7 Salon, Z-9WA, Z-10A, Z-19
Army Aviation Academy		Beijing-Tongzhou 北京通州	Mi-8, Z-9, Alouette 3, Mi-8
Training Base	4th Regiment	Wenshui	Z-11, HC-120
		Lanzhou MR	
	3 AAB	Xinjiang-Wujiaqu 新疆-五家渠	Mi-171, Mi171-1V, Mi-17-V7/V5, Z-9WA
		Jinan MR	
26	7 AAB	Shandong- Liaocheng 山东-聊城	Mi-17-V5, Z-8A, Z-9W, Z-9WA
54	1 AAB	Henan-Xinxiang 河南-新乡	Mi-17, Mi-17-V5, Z-9W, Z-9WA, Z-10A, Z-19
		Nanjing MR	
31	10 AAB	Henan-Luocheng 湖南-罗城	Mi-171E, Z-9G
1	5 AAB	Nanjing City 南京市	Z-8B, Mi-171, Z-9A, Z-9W, Z-9WA, Z-10
		Guangzhou MR	
42	6 AAB	Guangdong-Sanshui 广东-三水	Mi-171, Z-8, Z-9W, Z-9WA, Z-10A

(Continued)

		Chengdu MR	
13	2AAB	Chengdu City-Feng Huang Shan 成都市-凤凰山	Mi-171, Mi-171E, Mi-171 Salon, Mi17-V7, S-70C, Z-9WA, Z-19
13	2 AAB	Chengdu City-Taipingsi 成都市-太平寺	Mi-171, Mi-17 Salon, Mi-17-V5, Z-9WA
13	2 AAB	Tibet Lhasha-Dongguan 西藏拉萨-城关	Mi-171, Mi-171 Salon, Mi17-V5, S-70C, Z-9WA, Z-19
Training Base	1st Regiment	Sichuan-Yibin 四川-宜宾	Z-9, Mi-8

4.3 The PLA's Teeth—Armor

In 1949 the PLA tank force was equipped with captured Japanese tanks and US tanks supplied to the Nationalist Army. Each tank company had only seven tanks (each platoon had two tanks plus one for the company commander). A tank battalion could only muster twenty-three tanks with three companies, and a tank regiment had only two or three tank battalions. The total PLA tank force was only 375 tanks, mostly the Japanese Type-97, US Stuart light tanks and LVT Amphibious Water Buffalos.

In September 1950 Mao wrote to Stalin to ask for Soviet aid to build a Chinese tank force. In his letter, Mao asked for 468 tanks and SP guns, 2,000 supporting trucks and vehicles, plus enough associated equipment to equip three tank repair factories. This letter also included a "want-list" for nineteen other armament projects as well as 123 experts and advisors to support the above projects. True to their word, by the end of November, the Soviets delivered ten regiments worth of tanks and vehicles consisting mainly of T-34/85s (300), JS-2s (60), and SU-122s (40). Between 1951 and 1954 another fifty-seven regiments worth of tanks and AFVs were added, and by 1955 the PLA could boast an all Soviet-style tank force of 3,030. With Soviet aid, by 1959 China was able to produce its own tank, a copy of the T-54A named the T-59. Despite more than ten years of production by the 1970s, the building of the armor force was slowed on account of disruption by the Cultural Revolution. A third of the PLA's tank regiments had just forty or fifty tanks and the whole PLA was short by 2,200 tanks. Each tank division had 266 T-59 tanks and between twenty and thirty T-63 light tanks. For the motor rifle divisions, the tank regiment was equipped with eighty T-59 MBTs, but the PLA was a very unbalanced force with virtually no other type of APC. APCs came late to the PLA, and by 1980 there were 10,000 T-59s but only 2,000 APCs and even fewer SPGs and only around 700 recovery tanks. In the 1979 Sino-Vietnam War, the PLA could only muster one armored MBRL battalion for the campaign. The 1969 border wars with the Soviet Union spurred the PLA into meeting the Soviet tank threat with a reform of its tank force and an increase in its antitank capacity.

By the mid-1980s the PLA's tank divisions were beginning to be classified into Type A and Type B, and the ORBAT was split into Northern units and Southern units. Northern units were deployed to meet the Soviet threat. It was a traditional tank heavy force with as many as six regiments per division for Type A units. In 1985 independent tank regiments were all regrouped into army groups. On paper a tank battalion has forty to forty-one tanks and a tank regiment is equipped with 150 MBTs, but the actual tank force is very much smaller. A battalion has only thirty-one tanks (thirty tanks spread over three companies with one tank for the battalion HQ). A regiment only had ninety-three and a tank division had 290 tanks which included eleven light tanks from the divisional recce company. Compared with the Soviet tank division of the same era with 324–334 tanks, on paper at least it is highly questionable whether this force could resist a head-to-head encounter with a Soviet tank division.

In the 1950s there were as many as six tank schools in China. No. 1 Tank Academy was the earliest, first established in Beijing but later moved to Shanxi Province, and was disbanded in 1969. The No. 2 Tank School focused on technical matters and this establishment merged with the No.6 Tank School to be what is known as PLA Armored Corps Technical Academy today. No. 3 Tank School was located in Beijing and was originally established for tank and AFV crews, and the No. 4 was essentially the same as No. 3 and No. 6 but also included driver training for both AFVs and motor vehicles. Duplication of resources meant that both were disbanded in the 1960s.

To illustrate the history of the PLA armor force, a brief history of the 2nd Armored Division of the 12th Army Group based in Nanjing MR can serve as a microcosm. Like all Chinese armor formations, it had a humble origin with a few captured tanks. It was founded on 1949, on the foundation of the People's Republic, though at first the 2nd Tank Division was known as the East China Armored Vehicle Regiment. The unit's ORBAT consisted of two battalions with a total of six companies. They had thirty US M-3A tanks, ten ex-Japanese Type-97s and twenty-fur armored cars of various types along with 1,460 personnel. During this period Tank Number 102, a captured Japanese Type 97, was awarded the honorary title of "Zhu De" after the marshal of the PLA, for its combat performance. It is currently on display at the Military Museum in Beijing. Later the formation was renamed the 1st Armored Vehicle Regiment on July 1, 1949 and incorporated a new amphibious tank battalion of captured US LVT Buffalos; soon it was upgraded to divisional status by incorporating 2nd Instructor (Training) Regiment of the 24th Army. The division consisted of the 1st Armored Vehicle Regiment (with three battalions), Amphibious Tank Regiment and a New Armor Regiment (two battalions) consisting of a grand total of 149 tanks, ninety-five miscellaneous armored vehicles and 162 soft vehicles. The formation was renamed the PLA 2nd Armored Division in 1950. The Amphibious Regiment also took on an additional 90 LVT Buffalos. In November 1950 the ORBAT of the 2nd Armored Division was as follows:

- Division HQ
- 3rd and 4th Tank Regiment
- Motorized Infantry Regiment (former 258th Regiment)
- Mobile Artillery Regiment (former 306th Regiment)

During the Korean War Period, two Soviet tank regiments arrived in China and transferred their equipment to the 2nd Tank Division en masse. Both the 3rd and 4th Tank Regiments received thirty T-34 tanks, six JS-2 heavy tanks, four JSU 122 mm self-propelled guns and two T-34 armored recovery variants each. The Mobile Artillery Regiment received one battalion of twelve JSU-122s and two battalions of twelve 76 mm field guns, and soon they were dispatched to the Korean front. In Korea the 2nd Tank Division was not employed as a whole unit, but rather split out to serve as infantry support units performing fire support. The 3rd Tank Regiment, AAA Regiment and the Engineering Regiment entered Korea on May 30, 1951 and saw action by June as a support element for the 39th and 43rd Armies. They claimed two tank kills and one damaged but were almost wiped out by UN forces. The 3rd Tank Regiment left Korea in 1952 and was replaced by the 4th Tank Regiment. The 4th Tank Regiment was assigned to support the 23rd and 38th Armies. Tank Number 215, a T-34, claimed five tank kills and one damaged. In addition it was also credited with destroying twenty-six bunkers, nine artillery pieces and one truck. As a result, Tank 215 was honored as a "People's Hero Tank" and is currently on display at the Tank Museum in Beijing. In order to give real combat experience to all, later on both the motorized infantry regiment and mobile artillery regiment of the 2nd Division were deployed to Korea on February 15, 1953, and served as mobile defense units to guard China's supply route into Korea. All in all the Chinese sent 320 tanks to Korea and recorded 246 engagements, destroying 146 US-made tanks and damaging thirty-five others. In May 1953, they were ordered to the front to support the 23rd and 24th Armies during the Battle of Seoul. The AAA Regiment returned back to China in 1954, and the mobile artillery regiment in December 1954. On the conclusion of the Korean War, the Motorized Infantry Regiment took on elements of thirteen companies from the 12th, 20th, and 57th Armies to reconstitute its former strength, and the whole division was placed under the command of the Jinan Military Region in 1955. By 1958 the 2nd Armored Division had under its command the 3rd and 4th Tank Regiments (minus their JS-2 and JSU-122 companies) all equipped with the T-34/85. The Mechanized Infantry Regiment (former Motorized Infantry Regiment) had three infantry battalions and a T-34 tank battalion, a tank training battalion, and a motorized artillery regiment with three battalions of 122 mm artillery as its core fighting assets.

In July 1963, the 3rd Tank Regiment started to receive eighty T-59 tanks. With the deterioration of Sino-Soviet relations in the late 1960s, China was planning to fight an all-out war with the Soviets and required a massive buildup of strength, and many experienced cadres were transferred out to be used as the basis of new units in a rapid military buildup. In 1969 the 3rd and 4th Tank and the Motorized Artillery Regiments were renamed the 5th, 6th and 7th Tank Regiments. The 7th Tank Regiment received its eighty T-59 tanks during February 1971 in two batches.

In February 1976, No. 1 and 2 Companies of the Tank Battalion and Mechanized Infantry Regiment were transferred to form the basis of the new Armored Troop and Political Cadre School of the Central Military Commission. At the same time No. 3 Company was assigned to form the Armor Technical College. The 2nd Division was transferred from Jinan to Nanjing MR in 1978 and dispatched 110 officers and 1,579 troops to the 1979 Sino-Vietnam War. In 1985 Deng Xiaoping announced that one million troops were being decommissioned as part of the PLA reform. The Group Army system was being set up and 2nd Armored Division was allocated to 12th Group Army. The 2nd Division faced cuts once again in 1988 under the 500,000 force reduction program ordered by President Jiang Zemin. The equipment of the armored infantry regiment was distributed to other surviving regiments. In June 1989 seventy-six personnel from the 2nd Company, Recce Battalion and Communication Battalion were airlifted into Beijing to quell civil unrest, and the rest of the division was assigned "police" duties in and around the Xuzhou area. Today, still part of the Nanjing MR and under the command of the 12th Group Army, the 2nd Armored Division is equipped with the T-96G MBT.

4.4 China's Special Force and Airborne Troops

Although the PLA's first true special force unit only became formal in the late 1980s, the PLA has a tradition of stealth operations. Prior to 1988, the PLA would select more capable soldiers for selective missions but never formalized these into any special force (SF) units. In the Korean War and the 1979 Sino-Vietnam War, the PLA deployed numerous special force commandos and conducted numerous raids behind enemy lines in sabotage actions, kidnappings, and LRRPs. In the Sino-Vietnam War, Vietnam deployed numerous (what the Chinese would call) spies (*Te gong*) in small teams, from ones and twos to half a dozen or so SF soldiers to infiltrate into rear areas of the PLA and create havoc by undertaking sabotage and direct action raids. The PLA organized special teams of troops to counter these raids and also to conduct raids deep into Vietnamese rear areas. This vicious head-to-head contest between Vietnamese SF and Chinese SF is widely known in China but has not been reported in the Western media.

The PLA initially formed its rapid reaction unit (RRU, *Kuaisu Fanying Budui*) in the Guangzhou MR and it soon proliferated to every MR in China. A shift in military doctrine from "people's war" to "local war under high-tech conditions" was already in progress, and this shift was accelerated by senior officers of the PLA who had observed the 1991 Gulf War, a conflict fought with high-tech weaponry and strategic use of SF—they knew the PLA needed to evolve rapidly to catch up. Today the PLA's SF is more akin to British Royal Marine Commandos and US Rangers rather than the UK's Special Air Service (SAS) and US SEALs. Chinese SFs are focused on special reconnaissance and direct action missions; in addition, they may also have Counter Terrorist (CT) and security force roles in airborne operations.

The PLA's SF is organized into regiment-sized units with 1,000-plus personnel, supplied with the best equipment the PLA can field. Chinese SFs, like their counterparts around the world, appear to emphasize superior physical fitness and small-arms proficiency. All PLA SF units are trained in martial arts and airborne operations, with elements of each unit having specialized training in one or more of the following areas: UAVs, amphibious operations, demolitions, communications, computers, and foreign languages. The Chinese PLA Ground Force, PLAN and PAP all have their own indigenous SFs. Prior to the Gulf Anti-Piracy Patrol, when Chinese PLAN SFs were first deployed, the Chinese SFs had only been seen in action publicly in the numerous international SF competitions that the PLA/PAP had entered, all with very impressive results. All SFs in the world have their special insignia; while the British SAS may have its beige beret and the US SF has its green beret, the Chinese SF is awarded the coveted black beret.

Chinese SFs are equipped with some weapons that are not normally seen in regular PLA units. These include: the QSW-67 7.62 mm silencer pistol, the QSW-06 5.8 mm silencer pistol, the QCW-05 silencer sub-machine gun, a crossbow, tranquilizer dart gun, and the unique QSB-91 7.62 mm pistol dagger.

Today the PLA has eleven SF groups, known to the Chinese as TZBD, a short form of special force. Each PLA MR has its own SF group, each with its own name and insignia. In addition, SF units are also based in Xinjiang Sub-Military Region, Tibetan Sub-Military Region and the PLA Navy. Some known SF units are:

- Beijing MR—"Excalibur of the East" SF claims to have a force of 3,000 and is reported to have sea, land, air capacity.
- Jinan MR—"Black Beret" SF and "Eagle" SF. Eagle SF specializes in sea, land, air reconnaissance operations; nothing is known about its counterpart Black Beret SF.
- Shenyang MR—"North East Tiger" SF is a submarine specialist SF with an emphasis on underwater direct action operations.
- Nanjing MR—"Flying Dragon" SF was founded in 1992 and claims to have a strong CT role. In a notable exercise conducted in 1997 in the full view of the media, the Flying Dragon SF conducted an airplane hostage rescue combining UAV, helicopter strike force, and hostage rescue teams.
- Guangzhou MR—"Sword of Southern China" SF was founded in 1988 and claims to have a force of 4,000 troops with extensive sea, land, air capability. The SF unit was cross-trained with PLAN and PLAAF specialists in amphibious operations. Four hundred members of this SF force are said to be trained pilots and boat/marine vessel operators.
- Chengdu MR—"South West Cheetah" SF. Southwest China is an area of high mountain plateaus and forestry, and as such the SF

troops of this MR are skilled mountaineers and have strong cold weather operational capability.

- Lanzhou MR—"Sirius" SF. Lanzhou, because it is close to Yanan, has been traditionally a PLA stronghold, even back in the 1940s anti-Japanese campaign. The founding father of Chinese SF, General Peng Xuefeng created a force which was known as the Xue Feng (Snowy Maple) Regiment. It is also called by the nickname "Tiger" or "Night Tiger Regiment" on account of its fighting skills and stealthy movement. This tradition continued to the year 2000 when Sirius SF Group was formed from the nucleus of No. 8 Special Tactic Company of the Xue Feng (184th) Regiment. Each member of the SF is required to be cross-trained in a number of skills and be proficient in at least six types of weapon, and all need to be parachute qualified, skilled mountaineers, swimmers, drivers, and proficient in hand-to-hand combat.

- Second Artillery's Special Force—Besides the army's SF, the SAC are a separate branch within the PLA which has its own SF. Its existence was only revealed in 2011 in the official media, showing SAC's recruit selection camp, where among a shortlisted fifty members, only three were selected for further training. This unit was formed only in 2005, nicknamed "Sharp Edge," and has a different badge from the Army's SF.

4.4.1 China's Blue Beret Airborne Force

In 1950, the PLAAF had its own ground force with the establishment of the 1st Ground Combat Brigade (*Luzhan Diyi Lv*) in Shanghai. This brigade was formed from elements of the 89th Division of the 30th Army. Later on the brigade's headquarters moved to Kaifeng in Henan Province and was upgraded to divisional status. In its lifetime the unit has had several name changes, the 1st Parachute Division, then the 1st Airborne Division to name a couple. In May 1961 it was renamed for the 15th Army as a means to honor the 15th Army's illustrious battle record in the Korean War. Lacking its own aircraft the PLA planners lobbied for their own transport and in October 1964 they got their wish: a PLAAF transport regiment was created to support the airborne force and by 1969 it also had its own helicopter regiment. The 13th Transport Division of the PLAAF is now permanently assigned to support the airborne army with an airlift regiment with about 25–30 aircraft assigned to support each of the three divisions. However even if the entire PLAAF lift capacity is committed to the airborne army, it can only lift one division of men with their equipment. Until the new Chinese indigenous heavy lift aircraft is ready, the Chinese airborne army has to make do with help from civilian aircraft and utility transports. Within the airborne army there is a QRF force. This is an enlarged regiment of paratroopers with light armored vehicles and they can deploy anywhere within China in under twenty-four hours.

Being elite does not mean you are safe from cuts. The unit went through several phases of culls, notably in 1975 and 1985 when paratroops were seen as old fashioned. In the 1990s, a change of military concept from "people's war" to "local war under high tech conditions" resulted in a boost of the RRU concept and the airborne force was rewarded with an all-over increase of 25% in the 15th Army's strength.

In 1993 the unit was transferred from Guangzhou MR's command to be under the strategic reserve placed under the direct control of the CMC. Organizationally, China's airborne troops are part of the PLAAF, and the current organization, 15th Airborne Army, is the primary national-level rapid reaction unit in the PLA with 95829 as the unit code. Nicknamed "The Sword of the Blue Sky," the 15th Airborne Army was reformed in 2001 with the HQ relocated in Xiaogan near Wuhan City in Hubei Province, which is in the center of China, probably to facilitate rapid deployment to all corners of the nation.

Today, the 15th Airborne Army is composed of three airborne divisions: the 43rd Division, the national first-grade Quick Reaction Force (QRF) located in Kaifeng City, Henan Province with the 127th Honor Regiment, 128th MR and 129th Airborne MR Regiments. The 44th Division is the corps reserve and also doubles as the Airborne Corps Training School. Under the 44th Division are the 130th (airborne infantry) and 131st (airborne artillery) Regiments. The final leg of the 15th

Airborne Army is the 45th Division which is the priority QFR, which is on constant standby.

The 45th Airborne Division is made up of the 132nd (airborne mechanized infantry), 133rd (airborne mechanized infantry), and 134th (airborne mechanized infantry) Regiments. Each division is about 10,000 strong and the Army is supported with integrated artillery, air defense, reconnaissance, engineering, chemical defense, communications, and logistics units. Each airborne regiment has three airborne battalions and each battalion constitutes three spearhead companies. Each company consists of three platoons, each equipped with a 3-ton air-portable ZBD-03 IFV. With an additional vehicle for the company OC, one airborne spearhead company will have ten ZBD-03 IFVs. Multiplying the company set-up with three and adding two IFVs for the battalion HQ, one for the OC and one for the 2iC, one battalion will have thirty-two ZBD-03 IFVs.

Paratroopers are recruited throughout China by special recruiting teams. The new recruits are generally between the ages of eighteen and twenty and most are junior high school graduates. Recruits enlist for a minimum of four years and may stay for up to six years. Those who want to stay in the army as a career soldier must be selected as NCO or officer material. Junior officers assigned to the parachute force receive their basic officer commission at the military academy and then are transferred to the parachute depot for airborne training. A notable deployment of the PLA's airborne force was during the 2008 Sichuan earthquake that included an operational jump by fifteen pathfinders to survey the damage.

PLA Hero, HUANG Jiguang's (黄继光) Company—a unique Chinese military tradition

Each nation's military has its own traditions, and this is also true for the PLA. One unique tradition of the Chinese airborne force concerns a PLA hero from the Korean War.

Huang Jiguang (1931–52) was a PVA battalion runner serving with 9th Company, 135th Regiment, 45th Division. He made the ultimate sacrifice in the battle of Triangle Hill (in China this battle is known as Shanggan Hill) in October 1952 where he was part of an assault team to silence a machine-gun pillbox. Despite lobbing many grenades the pillbox continued to pour out fire, suppressing the advancing Chinese. After running out of grenades, Huang dashed forward and used his body to block the gun port of the pillbox. This momentarily blinded the gunner inside the pillbox, allowing the rest of the assault team to close in and blow up the pillbox with satchel charges. This act of self-sacrifice allowed the eventual capture of the 597 high point, an important landmark of the area. Huang was posthumously awarded the "Special Class Hero" award by the Chinese and the accolade of "DPRK Hero" by the North Koreans for his deeds.

Today the 45th Division is part of the 15th Airborne Corps and the 133th Regiment is now a mechanized airborne infantry regiment. The 6th Company, in which Huang once served, has been given the honorific title "Huang Jiguang" Company. To keep the memory of this PLA hero alive, one unique tradition is that Huang's name is still read out during the morning and evening roll call. In the spirit of comradeship the entire company will answer in unison "Present!" The squad in which Huang once served still maintains an extra bed space in the name of Huang with a neatly folded blanket as well as a set of PCGs hanging on the bed frame. The only difference between Huang's bed and the rest of the squad's is that the uniform and PCG for Huang is of the old style he would have used in the 1950s, while the others are all equipped with the Model 07 uniform and PCG.

Like the Soviets, who like to grant special units with "Guard" title as battle honor, the Chinese PLA follows a similar tradition and encourages esprit de corps by granting special units with honorific titles. Within the 15th Airborne Corps there are two other titled units: the "8th Company of Shanggan Hill"—the 8th Company of the 134th Regiment; and "The Third Red Company"— the 3rd Company of the 130th Regiment, the company in which

Liu Qinghua, the Commandant of the PLAN in the 1980s served. Besides these honor titles, other notable honorific titles include the "Hero Regiment of Tashan"—the 367th Regiment, 123rd Division, which commemorates an especially hard-fought battle during the Chinese civil war, and "The Iron Army"—127th Division 54th "Red" Corps, which gained this honorific title back in the 1920s during the Northern Expedition.

4.5 PAP's SF Force—Snow Leopard Commando Force

The Snow Leopard Commando Unit (SLCU) is the premier PAP counterterrorist strike force under the command of the Beijing PAP garrison special operation command. Founded in 2002, as a result of 9/11, the existence of the unit was only revealed to the public in 2006 as part of the overall security effort for the 2008 Beijing Olympics. Officially the "Snow Leopard" is part of the 3rd Regiment, 13th Detachment of the Beijing Garrison PAP. The story is that originally the unit was named "Snow Wolf" but was renamed after it participated in the 2007 military exercise held under the Shanghai Cooperation Organization in Russia, when it was unofficially named by the Russian press as "Snow Leopard," and the name stuck. Although based in Beijing, SLCU has a national role; it should not be confused with the Beijing Police SWAT team which has a local Beijing-only role.

Not much is known about this force. The SLCU consists of four squadrons assigned with very specific responsibilities: the 9th and 10th Squadrons are CT specialists, the 11th specializes in bomb disposal, and the 12th Squadron is a sniper force. Occasionally the SLCU gets unexpected exposure in the international media. In 2003 selected individuals from the Beijing PAP SF Battalion, 5th Detachment were assigned to Iraq for VIP and embassy protection, and in 2006 another detachment from the Beijing PAP SF was assigned to Kabul for similar duties. To ensure as many members of the PAP SF teams as possible got combat experience, a unit rotation plan between various PAP SF teams was initiated as soon as the first detachment landed. It was reported in the Chinese press that a detachment from the SLCU was again assigned to Kabul in 2008 and 2009.

4.6 The PLA Air Force

4.6.1 Organization and Staffing

In its formative years the Chinese PLA was heavily influenced by the Soviet Union, and during much of the 1950s the PLA not only dressed in Soviet-style uniforms, but its soldiers paraded with Soviet-style ranks and titles, and even the organization of the PLA Army, Navy and Air Force took on a Soviet bearing. The Soviet armed forces consisted of the Ground Forces, Naval Forces, the Strategic Rocket Force, Public Security Army and, oddly as a standalone entity, the Air Defense Force, known as *Protivo Vozdushnaya Oborona Strany, PVO Strany* (*Anti-Air Defense of the Nation*). The PLA of the 1950s was no different, with Army, Navy, Air Force, and—as a separate service between August 11, 1955 and July 26, 1957—the People's Liberation Air Defense Army (PLADA). The formation of the PLADA was motivated by the serious air threat posed by the Nationalist Chinese and United States Air Force in the early years of the Republic. The PLADA was formed from the PLA Air Defense Command (PLADC) that was comprised of two AAA divisions, sixteen AAA regiments, one searchlight regiment, two radar battalions, and one air-observation battalion, all to be split into four air defense zones that covered the entire country.

After many years of stagnation brought about by the Cultural Revolution and political turmoil, the Chinese armed forces began to modernize. In the 1970s China bought Spey engines from Britain and in 1985 bought S-70C-2 Black-Hawk helicopters from the United States. Gazelle SA 342L1 helicopters from France were later added to the list. Limited by financial constraints, these purchases were small and it was not until the 1990s that the PLAAF began to purchase hi-tech weapons in greater numbers. From Russia, China brought Su-27 fighters which were its first true modern weaponry for many years; for SAMs China procured the SA-10. With new equipment in place the PLAAF also went through significant organizational changes, among which were two radical developments: they re-designated the Radar Branch as a Specialty Force and combined the three airborne brigades into a single grouping to create the 15th Airborne Corps and subjugated this force to the Central Command as the nation's Rapid Reaction Force.

Today the PLAAF consists of Central Air Force Headquarters, and within the seven military regions each has its own regional headquarters. Beneath that are corps and divisional commands followed by brigades and regiments. Currently the air force has four branches: aviation, SAM, AAA and airborne troops, augmented by five specialty forces. They are communications, radar, ECMs, chemical defenses, and technical reconnaissance. For administration purposes it is split into four departments: HQ, political, logistics, and equipment. In support, the PLAAF runs its own education, research, testing and training establishments.

For a long time, Chinese aircrew training was carried out in the Soviet way, but in keeping with the trend to modernize, more Western-style training is being introduced. To improve standards, in 1986 the PLAAF introduced grading for all its pilots, navigators, gunners, and other aircrew as well as their instructors. This consists of "special," "first," "second," and "third" grade, depending on test results. The system used from initial training all the way through to operational squadron life is not only to drive continuous improvement but also to enforce an esprit de corps.

Gone are the mixes of aviation schools, and today there are just four Air Force universities. The Air Force Engineering University was founded in 1999 and Aviation University in 2004. Later the PLAAF overhauled the Xuzhou Air Force College into the PLAAF Logistics University and the Guilin Air Force College into the combined Antiaircraft and Airborne University. Cadets entering these institutions embark on a four-year degree course as well as a military commission for fast-track entry into the PLAAF. Modern weaponry needs smarter soldiers and the PLA is no different. First the practice of recruiting officers from the rank and file was terminated. However, this clearly did not lead to an overall improvement of its staff, so that as recently as 2000, only 20% of

PLAAF pilot candidates had a college/university education. Repeated drills and regimented procedures went a long way to compensate for the deficiency in education. To attract more qualified candidates, today officers can enter into the PLA via three means: a nationwide university scholarship program known as the "Defense Student Program," via the Reserve Officer Program, or direct from the civilian world that mainly attracts graduates with engineering/technical degrees. Air Force University courses for pilots usually last only thirty months, and on graduation the flight graduates move to one of the seven flight colleges for actual flight training. Flight Schools 1 and 2 are for bombers, transport pilots/navigators, as well as communication specialists, while 3, 4, 5, 6, and 13 specialize in fighter and ground attack pilot/navigator and weapons training. Flight School 4 has a specialist cell that can conduct training in English, that is where foreign pilots are assigned. These flight school courses last in general eighteen months.

While the USAAF conducts all its basic training for enlisted personnel in one central location such as the Lackland AFB, the PLAAF and indeed the PLA as a whole do not train recruits in a single location, instead they receive their basic training at their operational units or the technical centers where they will eventually serve. The recruits will be under the care of a training cadre while doing their Basic; usually a sub-unit assigned for recruit training duties. After the Basic, these recruits are assigned "jobs" within the unit and will receive further on-the-job training. Technical officers continue to play a hands-on role in aircraft and weapon maintenance, assisted by specialist NCOs. Airmen on the other hand are given rudimentary training while serving their two-year conscript duties and are essentially on probation to see if they have the qualities to either go into an NCO specialist role or be commissioned.

With the emergence of the NCO Corps in 1988, NCO education is conducted in specialist schools that focus on technical and specialty occupational training. This training can occur in special NCO schools or NCO programs at the Officers' Academy. Qualified personnel with secondary school graduation certificates can enroll in a two to three-year program where they can obtain a senior technical degree. Of the 398,000 PLAAF personnel, approximately two thirds are enlisted soldiers and of

Above left: The current cap badge of the PLA. Note the Red Star with the Chinese characters for "8" and "1" in the center, a reminder of the date, August 1, on which the PLA was founded. Below the star is Tiananmen Gate, the gate to the imperial palace, then as in now a symbol of the power. Accompanying it are the cog wheel depicting industry and wheat symbolizing agriculture.

Above right: This badge is worn by all members of the PLA above their top left breast pocket whilst on active duty in a national defense role.

Below: In the very early days, the PLA's armory was a mix of WWII leftovers and hand-me-downs. The Air Force flew American and Japanese planes. Thirty-nine P-51s were captured by the Communists and they served the PLAAF until 1953.

Above: Publicity photograph from the early 1950s showing PLAAF pilots in leather flying jackets discussing ground attack tactics. Note the MiG-15 in the background.

Below: A rare photo of the PLAN on parade. The PLAN sailors are wearing Model-1955 uniforms with a very distinct "Soviet" look.

Above: PLA's first armored force march past on the first National Day parade, with captured Type-95 Japanese tanks. *(China magazine)*

Below: Lorry-mounted infantry with Thompson sub-machine guns. The Chinese cloned the Thompson SMG, some were later chambered for 7.62 mm. These unique firearms are sought after by collectors. *(China magazine)*

Above: This shallow draft ex-Japanese river boat was originally a war prize given to the Nationalists but later defected to the Communists. It was saved from the wrecker's yard because of its accolade as "hero" vessel for its part in the 1951 Toumenshan sea battle, one of the many skirmishes between the Nationalist and the Communist Chinese in the 1950s.

Below: From 1950 until the late 1960s the main force of the PLAN was hundreds of high-speed torpedo boats, and the naval strategy at that time was known as "naval people's warfare" which was essentially hit-and-run guerrilla warfare. This P-4 torpedo boat was based on the Soviet K-123 hydroplane design and is armed with twin 14.5 mm HMG and two 17-inch/43 cm torpedoes.

PLAAF Tactics

MiG Top Cover

Heavy AAA

RF-84 ROCAF
Nationalist China

Top left: Before the arrival of high-altitude SAM like the SA-2 Guideline SAM, the only way for the PLAAF to catch the high-altitude spy planes was to use the "jump" ambush technique because the MiG-17 did not have the ability to maintain the level of altitude at which the RB-57 cruised.

PLAAF Interception Method

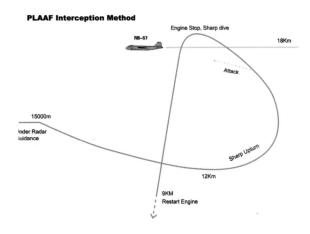

RB-57

Engine Stop, Sharp dive

18Km

Attack

15000m

Inder Radar
iuidance

Sharp Upturn

12Km

9KM
Restart Engine

Left adjacent: A typical PLAAF tactic against Nationalist reconnaissance planes was to use jets positioned as top cover and force down the ROCAF jet to a low level over the target areas to be ambushed by the waiting AA batteries.

Below: Two of the many dogfights between ROCAF and the PLAAF in the late 1950s to mid-1960s.

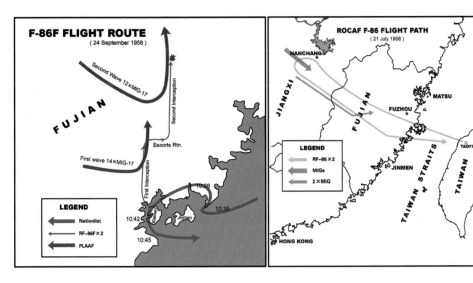

F-86F FLIGHT ROUTE
(24 September 1958)

Second Wave 12×MiG-17

FUJIAN

Second Interception

Escorts Rtn.

First wave 14×MiG-17

First Interception

10:38

10:35

10:42

Jinmen

10:45

LEGEND

Nationlist

RF-86F×2

PLAAF

ROCAF F-86 FLIGHT PATH
(21 July 1956)

NANCHANG

JIANGXI

FUJIAN

MATSU

FUZHOU

TAOYUAN

JINMEN

TAIWAN STRAITS

TAIWAN

LEGEND

RF-86×2

MIGs

2×MiG

HONG KONG

A set of training posters depicting the key skills that a PLA infantryman should have: digging, throwing grenades, swimming, using sachet charge, using bayonet and rifle.

Battle for Johnson South Reef: Vietnamese armed transporter HQ-*604* (Ex-RSVN *Keo Ngua*) or HQ-*605* (Ex-RSVN *Kim Qui*) under attack. *(China magazine)*

Pledge of loyalty to the CCP. The loyalty of the PLA to the CCP must be absolute. This poster appears in the PLA's garrison camp in Hong Kong—the four main characters says: "Loyal to the Party."

Left: 1980s PLA Type-66 152 mm howitzer deployed along the Sino-Vietnam border. Type-66 is a licensed copy of Soviet Union D-20 howitzer with a crew of nine.

Below: A fighting patrol moving out on a mission. Note the type of shoes the soldiers are wearing—canvas-top, rubber-soled plimsoll boots known as "liberation shoes." These are still popular in China and increasingly seen by the youth as fashion items. *(China magazine)*

Right: The skirmish at the Sino-Soviet border in the late 1960s was the closest China got to nuclear war with the USSR. Clashes on Zhengbao Island were the most serious of these border skirmishes.

Below: The 1980s border wars between China and Vietnam were fought over mountainous terrain. This picture shows the typical ground of the battle area. Compare with the 1979 war, this war was a pretty static war of trenches, artillery duels, and commando raids separated by some very deep valleys. (*China magazine*)

The 2008 earthquake in Sichuan China saw massive mobilization of both regular and reserve forces in their aid to civil powers role. Seen here are Mil-17 and US Blackhawk helicopters. The Blackhawks were a favourite of the Chinese on account of their superior performance in high altitudes. However the restriction placed by the United States after 1989 on parts and service means that these helicopters' service with the PLA will soon come to an end. The Chinese has developed its own improved version Z-20 and is expected to replace the Blackhawk force soon.

Above: Coastal defense was and remains a key job for coastal militia units, in the past many members were just fisherman or had jobs related to the sea. This PR poster drawn by Chinese artist Feng Youkang in August 1975 shows an all-female gun crew, militia unit 6386, Shanghai garrison. *(Stefan R. Landsberger collection)*

Below: Female militia members parading in the 1999 National Day parade in a "unique" specially designed uniform. The female soldiers are carrying Type-85 (7.62×25mm Tokarev) sub-machine guns.

Above: This photo shows students of Chengdu Polytechnic University on a swearing-in ceremony at the beginning of their 2009 student military training camp. The students are dressed in cast-off Model-87 camouflage and sneakers, while the lieutenant at the front wears the Model 07 uniform. *(China magazine)*

Below left: PLA soldiers in Model 07 camouflage uniform with Type-95 PCG and QBZ-95 rifle. The soldier at the front is a lieutenant.

Below right: PLA Standard Guard of the Hong Kong Garrison at the National Day parade in October 2011. They wear the Model 07 Honor Guard uniform, from left to right, Navy, Army and Air Force. In the PLA the Army is the senior service and thus always the standard carrier.

Above left and center: Front and rear view of new and old PCG. The new PCG seen here is the Model-95 version with integrated chest ammunition carrier and side pockets. Note the stick grenades on the side. The blanket and spare shoes bundle of the old-style PCG is replaced with a large rucksack. *(China magazine)*

Above right: A PAP version of the Model 07 pixelated camouflage uniform. The shoulder tab is that of a lieutenant general.

Below: The latest air-droppable IFV is the ZBD-03, armed with a 30 mm gun and coaxial 7.62 mm MG, and a launcher rail for the HJ-73C ATGM. Based on the Ukraine K/STW-17 BPS system, the ZBD-03 has four large parachute packs mounted on top of the vehicle, and for the drop it rides on a platform with eight large airbags to cushion the landing. It is reported in the Chinese press that the vehicle can be dropped off the drop zone in 10 mins 30 sec after touching down. This picture was taken on the 2009 National Day parade. *(China magazine)*

Above: This is a ZZH-07 wheeled armored command vehicle (ACV) in service with the PLA Hong Kong garrison. At 17.5 tons and 6.73 m long, this ACV is capable of 110 km/h on road and 8 km/h in water. In addition to both HF and VFH net, this ACV has video monitoring capability and searchlight (daylight and IR).

Below: This Chinese Humvee, better known as a "Warrior" (Mengshi 猛士) EQ2050ER, is manufactured by Dongfeng (East Wind) automotive works. This started as a reverse-engineered GM Humvee but is now fully localized using Chinese-manufactured parts. Besides the PLA, this is in service with the police and PAP.

Top: The Z-10, or Fierce Thunderbolt (Pi Li Huo 霹雳火), as it is known in Chinese media, the first attack helicopter developed by China. It is designed primarily for antitank missions but has secondary air-to-air capability as well. Above: The Z-19, a reconnaissance/attack helicopter developed in China for the PLAAF and the Army Air Force. The Z-19 is a twin-seat tandem updated modified version of the Z-9W. *(China magazine)*

Below left: WZ-141, an air-portable antitank destroyer, was developed in 1976 to answer the threat from the Soviets. Below right: The WZ-122 was a new type of MBT which was developed in March 1970, but eventually cancelled in 1974 due to financial and technical problems. *(China magazine)*

Above: PAP special force snipers in an annual national special force competition. Note the masks and collar tabs. These soldiers are carrying QBU-88 5.8x42 mm sniper rifles. *(China magazine)*

Below: Hong Qi-7 (Red Flag) is the PLA's short-range SAM for fixed location defense. Based on French Thales/Thomson CSF Crotale SAM mounted on either 4x4 or 6x6 vehicle it is the PLA's Mechanized Infantry Division's Air Defense System. Both soldiers wear the PLA woodland-style summer short-sleeve camouflage suit, working cap and PLA cap badge. Note that the soldier on the left down is wearing the PLA combat shoes, plimsoll-style training shoes. The canvas top is of camouflage pattern. *(China magazine)*

Above left: China operates both SU-30MKK and SU-30MK2. The SU-30MK2 is a maritime strike aircraft with better C4ISTAR (command, control, communications, computers, intelligence, surveillance, target acquisition and reconnaissance) abilities than the MKKs. *(China magazine)*

Above right: Shore guard duty PLAN lance corporal in Model 07 uniform. He is carrying a QBZ-95 rifle. His red arm band shows that he is "on duty."

Above: This is the current arm badge on the Model 07 uniform. The winged propeller is the obvious symbol for the PLAAF and this is for the Hong Kong Garrison.

Right: The PLAAF chest pin is a mark of the aviator's flying status and skills level. This is worn on the Model 07 uniform.

Above: Two vessels of the China Maritime Surveillance; both vessels are for service in the northern waters. *(China magazine)*

Below: A China Fishery Protection Vessel 312. Originally it was a costal oiler (NATO: Shengli-class), first launched in 1981, but now transferred to the Southern Fleet for fishery protection duties. *(China magazine)*

Above: On the left is SY-1 and to the right is a HIJ missile. SY-1 is an improvement of the Soviet P-15 Termite missile but with a solid fuel-powered and improved warhead. The HIJ is probably the HY-1J, a ship-to-ship variant for Type 051 DDG.

Above: The CJ-10 is a land-attack nuclear-capable cruise missile (LACM) currently in service with the PLA. The CJ-10 was first debuted during the October 1 military parade in 2009. *(China magazine)*

Above: DF-31 (US DOD: CSS-10) is a long-range, road-mobile, three stage, solid propellant intercontinental ballistic missile (ICBM). It is designed to carry a single 1-megaton nuclear warhead. There is a submarine-launched version known as JL-2. These are mounted on HY4430 semi-trailers towed by a ZX-TJ 2000 turbocharged diesel 8x8 tractor, being forced to travel on prepared surfaces. *(China magazine)*

Left: A Chinese PLAMC member in a respirator and carrying a QBZ-95 rifle. Note his unique arm badge. *(China magazine)*

Below: This J-10AY is in the livery of the PLA 8.1 acrobatic team. J-10A is a single-seat multirole fighter while the J-10SH is a twin-seater version for the Navy. As well as serving as training aircraft, the J-10S can also be used for the ground attack role where the rear seat pilot would act as the weapon systems operator.

Bottom: J-16 fighter/bomber is a new strike plane designed and manufactured in China based on the J-11BS but with longer range and upgraded avionics. The J-16 is comparable to American F-15E and the aircraft can be viewed as an upgraded version of SU-30MKK. *(China magazine)*

The Kamov Ka-28 (NATO reporting name "Helix") is an export version of the Ka-27, which saw service with the Soviet Navy. China has three Ka-27s and five Ka-28s to operate from their Russian-built Sovremenny destroyers. In addition, China ordered nine Ka-28 helicopters in 2009. *(China magazine)*

Above: According to Chinese media disclosure, by the end of 2015, all its T-99s were serving with the 38th Army Group. Why are so few in service? The main reason seems to be cost, plus according to an interview with an SNCO there had been problems, though there were all now "solved." The report gave the following numbers: 124 T-99A MBT and thirty-six battalions of T-96A, sixteen battalions of T-99, and thirty-one battalions of T-96 MBTs. *(China magazine)*

Below: PLA Type-86-I IFV conducting maintenance whilst on a joint Russian-Chinese exercise. The truck at top left indicates that these soldiers come from Shenyang MR and the Y on the back of the truck shows that the support unit is a reserve unit. *(China magazine)*

From top:
The ZHI-6 is a Chinese helicopter development based on the Z-5, itself a clone of the Russian Mi-4. A limited production run was made but soon terminated due to inferior performance. This is the only ZHI-6 helicopter left, which can be found in Beijing's National Aeronautical Museum.

Yanan No. 2 (延安二号) was a Chinese-made light observation helicopter in the 1970s. Three prototypes were made and today only one survives. It can be found in the Nanjing Aeronautical University's museum.

Known in China as the Type-051 destroyer (NATO: Lvda-class) missile destroyer based on the Soviet Kotlin-class destroyer. This is an upgraded Lvda known as Type 05DT, with HQ-7 SAM (copy of French Crotale) system. The HQ-7 became PLAN's standard short-range air-defense SAM in the 1990s with a typical configuration is one 8-cell launcher, with stores of reload missiles in multiples of eight. This vessel is probably CNS *Kaifeng 109* serving with the Northern Fleet.

The Submarine Rescue Vehicle (SRV) is a rarely seen force of the PLAN, and resembles the British/Australian LR5 Deep Submergence Rescue Vessel. In 2014 a publicity photo of an unidentified SRV and the "mother-ship" Submarine Support and Rescue Vessel (SSRV) was published in the Chinese press. This rescue sub has manipulator arm and also Submarine Escape and Rescue (SMER) capabilities. This SRV is believed to be operated by a crew of two and can accommodate approximately 16–17 people.
(All China magazine)

Above: The Diaoyu (Senkaku) Islands are a group of uninhabited islands in the East China Sea claimed by China (both People's Republic and the Republic/Nationalist) and Japan. *(China magazine)*

Below: The QSW-06 ("Minimal Sound Pistol, 2006") is a sound-suppressed semi-automatic pistol based on the QSZ-92 semi-automatic pistol and is designed to replace the aging QSW-67 silent pistol. QSW-06 is a polymer-framed, short recoil operated, semi-automatic pistol that is chambered for DCV05 5.8 X 21 mm subsonic rounds. The QSW-06 is also capable of firing the standard PLA pistol round, the DAP92 5.8 x 21 mm as well. The QSW-06 uses a double-column, double-feed twenty-round magazine. QSW-06 comes with a detachable suppressor that can be screwed onto the barrel. *(China magazine)*

Top right: The 8x8 ZBL-09 is the replacement for the ZBL-92 APC. The armor of the ZBL-09 provides all-round protection against 7.62 mm armor-piercing rounds. The ZBL-09 has a crew of three and capacity to carry seven to ten troops.

Right: The most distinct visual difference between the ZBL-90 and the ZBL-92 is that the former has a distinct gap between the first and second pair of wheels. The total number of ZBL-90 is small because it is inherently underpowered.

Below: The PLZ-05 is a 155 mm SPG developed to replace the Type-59/1 130 mm. It was officially unveiled at the Military Museum of the Chinese People's Revolution to mark the eightieth anniversary of the PLA in July 2007. It carries a 52-caliber barrel that can fire the WS-35 guided ammunition with a maximum reported range of 100 km *(Max Smith)*

From top:
The Type-022 missile boat is easily recognizable by her stealth feature and wave-piercing catamaran hulls. Today approximately eighty-three of these missile boats are currently in service it can either be armed with C801/802/803 Anti-ship missiles or Hongniao missile-2 long-range land attack cruise missiles. In addition it is also armed with a KBP AO-18 6-barrel 30 mm gun (AK-630) and the crew carries QW MANPAD for air defense.

Technically the MV *Xue Long* (雪龙, *Snow Dragon*) is a non-PLAN Chinese icebreaking research vessel owned by the Polar Research Institute of China, part of the State Oceanic Administration of China. Being a government-owned vessel it can be called upon to support the PLAN in a national emergency. Built in 1993 at Kherson Shipyard in Ukraine, it was converted from an Arctic cargo ship to a polar research and re-supply vessel in Shanghai by the mid-1990s. The vessel was extensively upgraded in 2007 and in 2013.

The J-15, also known as Flying Shark, is a carrier-based fighter. This photo shows the J-15 with its wings folded.

The LS-6 is a standoff precision-guided bomb against enemy fixed ground targets. With a wing kit and a GPS/INS guidance unit, the conventional low-drag aerial bomb is converted into a precision guided bomb with standoff attack ability. It features day/night and all-weather attack, multiple target capability, and standoff attack. *(China magazine)*

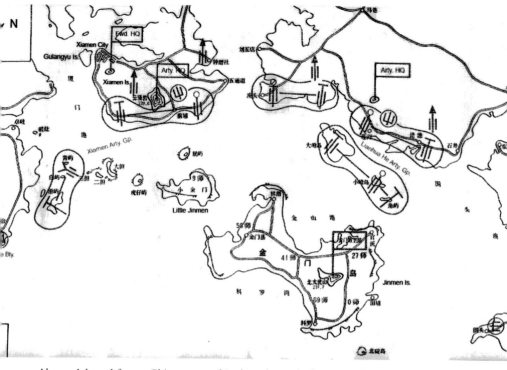

Above: Adapted from a Chinese map, this chart shows the location of key artillery batteries and main headquarters of the PLA engaged in the Jinmen artillery battle.

Below: U-2 wreckage number 56-669 as it appears today at the Military Museum of the Chinese People's Revolution, Beijing. This plane was shot down on January 10, 1965, southwest of Beijing by an S-75 Dvina (NATO: Guideline) missile.

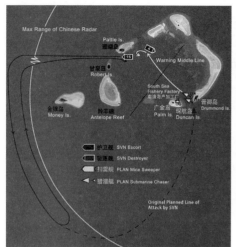

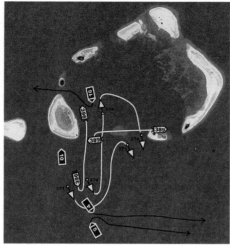

Top left: The opening phase of the Paracel Islands battle on January 18, 1974. Note the flanking move attempt by the South Vietnam Navy (SNV) and the demarcation line between the Chinese and Vietnamese at the initial phase.

Top right: The battle just before noon. The battle ended with SNV HQ-16 retiring from the battle, HQ-10 sinking and HQ-4 and HQ-5 escaping eastwards.

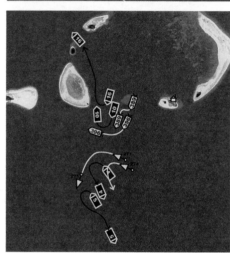

Left: The battle in the early morning of January 19. It shows two distinct battles, one on the north with HQ-16 and HQ-10 against CNS 389, 396 and slightly south of this battle is a separate skirmish, HQ-4 and HQ-5 against sub-chaser CNS 271 and 274.

2011 年 2 月 28 日，中宣部、解放军总政治部、共青团中央、中共黑龙江省委在人民大会堂联合举行邰忠利先进事迹报告会。邰忠利是黑龙江省边防某部战士，2009 年 8 月在

Above: Transitional Model 85 regulations introduced peaked caps for service dress uniforms for all ranks. The officers' cap had a red band and silver chin cords, while the enlisted men's cap had a green band and a black chinstrap.

Opposite, from right: Lei Fēng (雷锋, 1940–62), a PLA soldier characterized as a selfless and modest person who was devoted to the Communist Party, Chairman Mao Zedong, and the people of China; Tai Zhongli (邰忠利), a border guard on the Sino-Soviet border in Heilongjiang province, who lost his life saving a man who had fallen through ice in 2009; Huang Jiguang (黄继光, 1930–52), a PLA hero in the Korean War.

Above: The ZBD-04 or Type-04 is a Chinese IFV. It mounts a turret similar in design to that of the Russian BMP-3 with 100 mm gun and a 30 mm machine cannon, although the chassis is different, with a front-mounted engine, and rear troop compartment, a crew of three and seven passengers.

Above, top: CNS *Shichang* (pennant number 82), a training vessel from the Dalian Naval Academy. This vessel is named after Deng Shichang (邓世昌) an admiral from the 19th century.

Above, bottom: CNS *Zhenghe* (pennant number 81), a ship from the Dalian Naval Academy training ship. The ship is named after a famous Chinese admiral and navigator from the 14th–15th century, Zheng He (郑和). *(China magazine)*

Above: ZTZ-89 prototype tank testing in 1994—western desert area of China.

Below: On the turret from right to left, the square box is the anti-missile laser warning sensors, the pillar-type object is the GPS and next to it is the wind sensor. The commander and the gunner both have a thermal sight and the IR disrupters are on each side of the main gun. *(China magazine)*

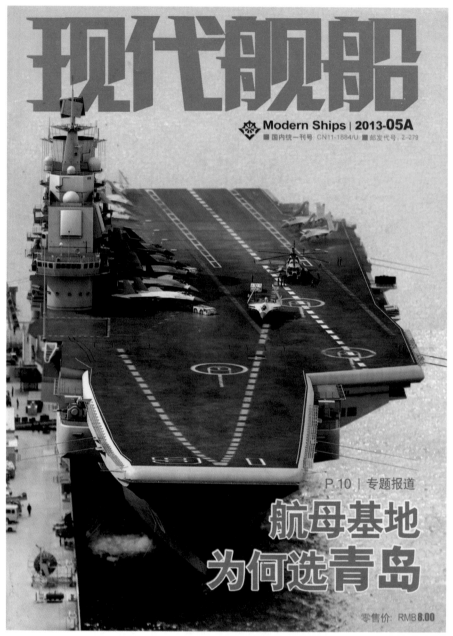

现代舰船

Modern Ships | 2013-05A

国内统一刊号：CN11-1884/U ■ 邮发代号：2-279

P.10 | 专题报道

航母基地
为何选青岛

零售价：RMB **8.00**

CNS *Liaoning* (pennant number 16) is the first aircraft carrier of the Chinese Navy. It was officially commissioned into PLAN on September 25, 2012. *(China magazine)* these some 50,000–60,000 are in their two-year conscripts' terms. To increase quality of enlisted personnel and attract more college/university graduates, the enlistment age has been raised to twenty-four (twenty-three for females) and to entice recruitment, qualified students-turned-soldiers are rewarded a one-off bonus of 24,000 RMB (Chinese Yuan, around US$3,900) to help pay for student loans or school fees.

While the ground forces have extensive experience in working with reserves and militia, for most of its history the PLAAF did not have a reserve element. It was as recently as 2004 that the PLAAF developed its own reserve force focused in the following areas: field station, flight support, SAM regiments, and radar battalions.

It is believed that the PLAAF today has a total of thirty-eight divisions, down from fifty in 1986. They are divided into twenty-nine fighter, three ground attack, three bomber, and three transport divisions. Most of these divisions have two regiments, although some—in locations that tend to face areas of high threat, namely the East China Sea and the South China Sea—have three. Just like the ground forces, there is a movement within the PLAAF to create smaller units. The PLAAF has already created "air brigades" in four of the seven military regions, and each brigade has several aviation flight groups.

As a general rule, Chinese pilots fly half as many hours as their US counterparts, but training hours are increasing. An aggressor squadron based on the USAF/USN has been formed, where senior pilots acting as the aggressors stage realistic combat duels with rotating student units. The first such aggressor unit, known as the 2nd Regiment or Blue Army, is based in the Flight Test and Training Center Canzhou-Cangxian AFB. It is reported that this Blue Army staffed by "special" class flyers operates J-8D (NATO: Finback), J-7E (Upgraded MiG-21) and JL-9s *Mountain Eagle* fighters. A second such unit, the 3rd Regiment, is reported to fly Su-30MMK and also J-10 *Vigorous Dragon*. Since then similar smaller units have been set up in each of the seven MRs, and the PLAAF also now sends detachments to Russia to train with the Russian Red Flag Composite Training Research Unit. A further enhancement of the PLAAF ability is the revamping of the 1958 Dingxin[1] desert field firing range site. Located in the Gobi Desert, it is reported to include a replica of a "Taiwan AFB" with all the panoply of military infrastructure. Since 2005 the PLAAF has staged its own versions of the USAF "Red Flag Exercises" known as the "Red Sword Exercises," that are held in Dingxin and are getting more and more complex. Exercises involving over 100 planes of different types are common. The PLAAF has also introduced its version of the US "Top Gun" program with the award of the prestigious "Golden Helmet" to the pilot who performs best in different combat scenarios.

4.6.2 The Hardware

Like the other parts of the PLA, the PLAAF was initially equipped with an all-Soviet arsenal, reflecting the nation's political alliance at that time. The switch from Soviet to Western sources began in the 1970s but was abruptly terminated in 1989 following the Tiananmen Square incident. Faced with vilification from almost every quarter, China once again turned to Russia and Ukraine, which were more ambivalent in their attitude. Modernization began in earnest as the Soviet Union fell apart with an order for the Sukhoi Su-27SK (NATO: Flanker) which led to a locally made version named J-11 and later a modernized version, the J-11B. Later the Chinese brought in the Su-30MKK (*Modernizirovannyi Kommercheskiy Kitayski*—"Modernized Commercial for China") (NATO: Flanker G). In a boost to the Chinese aviation industry, all deals conducted included a heavy element of technology transfer. Technology in both the J-11 deal and extensive cooperation with Western companies enabled the Chinese to develop their own aircraft like the J-10 *Vigorous Dragon* and later the J-20 *Mighty Dragon* fourth-generation long-range fighter. While the J-10 is the successor to the J-7—a modified upgraded MiG-21 (NATO: Fishbed) short-range interceptor—and the J-8 (NATO: Finback) high-altitude interceptor, the FH-7 *Flying Leopard* was conceived to replace the venerable Q-5 (NATO: Fantan) ground attack aircraft. China also developed its own AWACS using the only available large airframe they have, the Y-8 (NATO: Cub), a reverse engineered An-12, roughly comparable to the US C-130 Hercules.

The first true modern Chinese ECM plane was the Y-8CB ECM that flew in the year 2000; the next was a Y-8JB ELINT (ELectronic

INTelligence) that is also seen in service also with the PLANAF. The Y-8G is another platform currently seeing service with the 4th Independent Electronic Brigade in Shenyang, Yu Hung AFB, home to China's many electronic assets. Next is the Y-8T, the C3I (Command, Control, Communication, Intelligence) which will be used to coordinate air operation control where ground radar is lacking, such as over the ocean. The Y-8W Balance Beam (or KJ-200) AWACS is in service with both the PLAAF and the PLANF where the radar is mounted in a pressurized C3I compartment with the operator who can communicate with the fighters using datalink. The antenna assembly is much like the Swedish Ericsson PS-890, including the ram air-cooling system for transmit-receive modules. Like the Erieye, the Y-8W cannot provide coverage over the nose, but due to large aperture size this has an excellent broadside power-aperture rating and angular resolution. At least four fly from Wuxi, Shuofang AFB with the 76th Airborne Command and Control Regiment which also flies the Y-8T. The Y-8Q is believed to be an ASW similar to the P-3 Orion, but the deployment is unknown. The Y-8XZ is similar to the USAF EC-130E Commando Solo—psychological warfare. It broadcasts propaganda on TV and radio and also has a jamming role. Another is the Y-8E used for launching UAVs.

The Y-8 is showing its age and there is a new replacement in the system, the Y-9. The Y-9 has a more spacious cabin and improved cargo handling. If the Y-8 can be likened to a C-130 Hercules, the Y-9 will be equivalent to the C-130J Super Hercules. Another AWACS platform was built on the much bigger Il-76 (NATO: Candid) strategic lifter, named as KJ-2000 (NATO: Mainring) which is similar to the Beriev A-50 (NATO: Mainstay) AWACS. KJ is the first character from the Chinese language Pinyin spelling of Kong Jing, short for Kong Zhong Yu Jing, which means Airborne Early Warning. The current KJ-2000 AWACS is equipped with a domestic AESA (active electronically scanned array), also known as active phased array, radar. The radar was designed by the Research Institute of Electronic Technology (also more commonly known as the 14th Institute) at Nanjing. It is supposed to carry AESA antennae mounted in a fixed, non-rotating dome on top of the fuselage in a triangular pattern to give 360° coverage. It is claimed that it can track up to 100 targets within a 400 km range.

The KJ-2000 development program started after the cancellation of the A-50I deal with Israel and Russia in July 2000, due to strong US pressure and interference regarding the Israeli radar that was to be mounted. Originally a tri-nation deal, Russia would provide four Beriev A-50 Mainstay airframes, which were to be fitted with the Phalcon airborne early warning (AEW) radar and other C3I systems developed by Israeli Aircraft Industries Ltd (IAI). In May 1997, China, Israel and Russia reached an agreement to supply one such AWACS aircraft under the designation A-50I for US$250 million, with the option of three more for a total cost of US$1 billion. In October 1999, Russia delivered the first A-50 aircraft to Israel for the installation of the Phalcon AEW radar system. By May 2000 the Clinton Administration voiced strong objections and urged Israel to cancel the sale of the Phalcon, and after some intensive talks the Israeli government finally cancelled the deal with China in July 2000.

The fallout of the Phalcon deal was a major blow for China's military modernization program. China reacted to the setback by starting a domestic program to develop its own airborne early warning radar and relevant C3I systems. The Israeli Phalcon radar and other onboard electronic systems were retrieved from the unfinished A-50I and the airframe was handed to China via Russia in 2002. Modifications on the airframe began and eventually a total of four planes were produced, with one based on the A-50I airframe (which can be identified by its nose-mounted aerial refueling probe), and the other three being converted from existing IL-76MD transports in service with the PLAAF.

China then went on to develop a domestic AWACS and the first aircraft made its maiden flight in 2003. Today a total of four examples are being operated by the PLAAF 26th Air Division based in the eastern Zhejiang province near the Taiwan Strait. The story does not end there; as a means to compensate the Chinese for non-delivery of the aircraft, Israel returned all the money paid by the Chinese, believed to be some US$190 million. And to maintain a long-term good relationship with China, Israeli Prime Minister Ariel Sharon personally wrote an apology to President Jiang Zemin. Israel went out of its way to sweeten the compensation package by agreeing to all the terms of the contract, and an additional US$160 million was offered as a special gift, not in cash, but in kind through a hi-tech dairy farm with all the latest Israeli gadgets, located just outside Beijing. This not only helped to boost Chinese milk production but also acts as a showcase for Israeli high-tech farming products and expertise. For many years the Israeli Embassy in China has supported the project with a full-time agriculture/dairy expert at the Sino-Israel Dairy farm achieving year-on-year still the highest productivity/yield in China.

A perhaps surprising development has been the adaptation of two Boeing 737-3Q8s as C3I platforms for the 102nd Regiment at Beijing Nan Yuan AFB. The characteristic SATCOM "bumps" mounted behind the cockpits are evidence of their unusual role. This unit also flies two Lear jets, a 35A and 36A, as well as several Tu-154s (NATO: Careless) with ECM and ELINT sensors aboard.

Aside from the older Soviet Clone transport planes such as the Y-5 biplane (cloned An-2), Y-7 (cloned An-24), the Chinese are building the Y-20. The Y-20 "Ark" is a large military transport aircraft developed by Xian Aircraft Industrial Corporation and officially launched in 2006. The official codename of the aircraft is "Kunpeng," after the mythical bird of ancient China that can fly for thousands of kilometers. The Y-20 is similar to the Lyushin Il-76 transport aircraft in a general layout that incorporates a high-set wing, T-tail, rear cargo-loading assembly and heavy-duty retractable landing gear.

The other 1950-vintage Soviet aircraft adapted by the PLAAF is the Tu-16 (NATO: Badger) known as the H-6 in China. Today, the PRC is the only country in the world that still deploys the Tu-16/H-6 in operational service, in a wide range of roles from nuclear and tactical bomber, to naval missile bomber, tanker, reconnaissance/electronic warfare, engine test bed and cruise missile platform. About 120 serve in both the PLAAF and PLANAF. A nuclear bomb version of the H-6E has been in service since the 1980s and has been upgraded to the H-6H for the PLANAF which can carry two KD-63 radar or TV/data-link guided LACM (Land Attack Cruise Missile). The KD-63 cruise missile is derived from the HY-4 Sadsack, itself a turbojet derivative of the Kraken/Seersucker series. Chinese sources claim the radome covers the datalink antenna for the KD-63 missile system. With a range of some 200 km, it is a true standoff weapon. An improved version, the H-6M, carries four such missiles instead of two, and better electronics to match. The most modern version is the H-6K that utilizes new composite materials, better Chinese engines that give a combat radius of 6,500 km and can carry six CJ-20A LACMs, an air-launched version of the CJ-10 cruise missile with a range of 2,000 km or more. The Badger has been adapted for air-air refueling as the H-6U for the PLAAF and H-6DU for the PLANAF. Fitted with a hose and drogue refueling system, the tanker entered PLAAF and PLANAF service in the mid-1990s primarily intended to support the J-8D fighters deployed by both services. The PLA has reportedly ordered eight Russian Il-78 (NATO: Midas) refueling tankers as a supplement to its existing H-6 tanker fleet.

Initiated pilots still start their careers on the old but dependable CJ-6A. This is a single-engine propeller plane with tandem tricycle undercarriage and a low wing; it has the form and feel of a WWII fighter! Besides its role as a trainer, it can also carry small bombs and be armed with MGs if necessary. The CJ-6 (or *Chuji Jiaolianji* = Primary Trainer) is an all-original Chinese design that is commonly mistaken for a Yak-18A (Its predecessor, the Nanchang CJ-5, was a license-built version of the Yak-18.) If the student pilot passes his/her tests, the next step is probably to progress to the JL-8, a joint venture between Pakistan and China. This is a two-seat intermediate jet trainer and light attack aircraft with conventional controls. In Pakistan it is known as the K-8 Karakorum. Another new trainer, a replacement for the JJ-7 (MiG-21-style tandem trainer) is the JL-9, also known as the FTC-2000 *Mountain Eagle*, a two-seat fighter-trainer for PLAAF and the PLANAF (in naval service it is known as the JL-9G). The job of the JL-9 is to prepare Chinese pilots for the newest generation of fighter aircraft such as the Chengdu J-10 and Sukhoi-derived aircraft, such as the Sukhoi Su-27SK, Sukhoi Su-30MKK and Shenyang J-11. The JL-9 made its maiden flight on December 13, 2003, only two years after the start of the project, making it the shortest development time for an aircraft in Chinese aviation history. A parallel new trainer, the L-15 Falcon, is a Chinese supersonic training and light attack aircraft being developed by the Nanchang-based Hongdu Aviation Industry Corporation (HAIG) for both the Air Force and Navy as a lead-in fighter trainer (LIFT) such as J-10, J-11 and F-16 fighter jets and other third-generation craft. Whilst in service with the PLAAF the L-15 received the designation JL-10.

Ever since the 1950s, China has operated a fleet of UAVs. The CK-1 was a reverse-engineered Soviet La-17 target drone from the 1950s but by the 1960s the BUAA (Beijing University Aeronautics and Astronautics) came up with the WZ-5 reconnaissance drone (*wuren zhenchaji* pilotless reconnaissance plane) based on a US Ryan AQM-34N Firebee UAV that China was able to obtain after shooting down a few in the 1960s. Fast forward to the 2000s, Chinese scientists have progressed to developing their own UAV without the need to clone or reverse-engineer Western or Soviet technology. China introduced the BZK-005 UAV to the world, a high-altitude long-range UAV that is now in operation with the Special Strategic Reconnaissance Squadron directly reporting to the PLA General Staff Department based at Taizhou-Luqiao naval air base. It is also believed to be based at other AFBs as well. The BZK-005 is designed by Beijing University of Aeronautics and Astronautics and Harbin Aircraft Industry Group, and features a stealth-optimized fuselage and twin tailfins tilted outwards to reduce RCS. A large SATCOM antenna is thought to be installed inside the nose bulge, which provides live data transmission over thousands of kilometers. Within the small turret underneath the nose are the FLIR/CCD cameras.

Another notable UAV is the Xianglong, or Soaring Dragon, which flew in December 2009. Chinese sources credit it with a 7,500 kg takeoff weight and 3,800 km range. The forebody is bulged to accommodate a high-data-rate satcom antenna and a futuristic stealthy-looking Lijian Sharp Sword UAV that looks similar to a mini US B2 bomber.

4.6.3 PLAAF Restructuring

Like all parts of the PLA the PLAAF is undergoing massive reorganization. Alongside the current "divisions" and "regiments," the

PLAAF will establish brigades and AFBs as an organization structure within the current framework. Meanwhile those divisions that lost one regiment will regain it while the four brigades in all the AFB will act as the training, transition, and operational conversion units. The main purpose of this restructuring is to streamline the command structure and reduce redundancy, provide each zone with sufficient depth and to improve levels of war preparedness across the PLA while also reducing the size of the PLA. As of 2003, there were twenty-nine PLAAF divisions but four have been remodeled as AFBs. Parallel to these structural changes is the increasing transparency of the entire PLA. A few years ago, it was impossible to gain any open information on PLA units, their bases and even serial numbers since all images were censored. It is now possible to access images and information from a number of blogs and websites. The fact that images of the latest warplanes such as the J-20, J-31 etc. appear even before their maiden flight is something that couldn't be imagined a few years ago. What was once deemed as intentional leaking of images and information by arms manufacturers has become more of a public affair as the Chinese government becomes increasingly open. One reason is the confidence that the Chinese government has in its weapons and the other is to address international concerns.

4.6.4 PLAAF ORBAT

A major part of the PLAAF reorganization is the development of an MR Training Base concept to replace the traditional dedicated "training regiments." To boost combat power, many of these "training regiments" are being converted to operational combat units. Eventually, like the USAAF, flight training will eventually be done at a central base rather than each MR doing its own thing. Currently there are four major bases: Dalian AFB in Shengyang MR, Shanghai AFB in Nanjing MR, Urumqi AFB in Lanzhou MR, and Nanning AFB in Chengdu MR. Along with these changes on the training side, the operations side has also experienced similar changes. Traditional division and regiment structures are being revamped to independent brigade status. The air force division concept will gradually become a thing of the past.

Beijing MR			
Division	Regiment	Base	Aircraft
7 Fighter	19th, 20th, 21st	Hebei-Zhangjiakou Beijing-Yanqing County Hebei-Tangshan	J-11/ Su-27SK Su-27UBK, J-7B, JJ-7A, J-7G
15 Ground Attack	43rd, 44th, 45th	Shanxi-Datong-Huairen Shanxi-Xinzhou County Inner Mongolia-Bikeqi	J-7G/JJ-A or J-10A/ J-10S, Q-5J or FH-7A
24 Fighter	70th, 72nd	Hebei-Zunhua Hebei-Yangcun	J-10A, J-10S
	8.1 Demonstration Team	Hebei-Yangcun	J-10AY, J-10SY
MR Training Base		Hebei-Yangcun	Q-5B, Q-5C
34 Transport	100th, 101st, 102nd	Beijing-Shahe Xiqiao Hebei –Xingtai Beijing-Nan-Yuan	AS332L-1, EC-225 Y-5/Y-7, Boeing 737-300/700/800, 3Q8, Bombardier CRJ200, CRJ700, Y-7G, Tu154M/D, Lj-35A, Lj-36A BZK-005 (UAV), Puma
4 Flying College	1st, 2nd, 3rd, 4th	Hebei-Shijiazhuang	CJ-6A, JL-8, Jl-9, J-7, J-8, Y-5
6 Flying College	1st, 2nd, 3rd	Zhouzhou City Tianjin-Tangguantun Baoding City-Dingxing	CJ-6A, JL-8,
MR Training Base		Hebei-Tangshan	J-7II, JJ-7A
MR Training Base	203th	Bejing-Shahe Town	Y-5, Y-7H, Y-8

Chengdu MR			
Division	Regiment	Base	Aircraft
4 Transport	10th, 11th	Chengdu City-Qiong Lai	Y-7, Y-7H, Y-8C/F, Y-9, Mi-17V5
20 Transport	59th	Sichuan Luzhou-Lantian	Y-7

(Continued)

20 Fighter	60th, Unknown, 58th (EW)	Guiyang City-Leizhuang	Y-8XZ, J8FR, JJ-7A, Y-7, Y-8CB, Y-8G
33 Fighter	97th, 98th, 99th	Sichuan-Luzhou Chongqing City-Dazuc Chongqing-Baishiyi	J-7B, JJ-7A, J-11, Su-27SK, Su-27UBK
44 Fighter	130th, 131st, 132nd	Yunnan-Mengzi Yunnan-Luliang	J-11A, Su-27UBK, J-10A, J-10S, J-7, JJ-7A, J-7H
2Flying College	1st, 2nd, 3rd	Sichun-Jiajiang Chengdu City-Pengshan	CJ-6A, HJ-5, Y-7 HYJ-7, J-7G, JJ-7A

Jinan MR			
Division	*Regiment*	*Base*	*Aircraft*
5 Ground Attack	13th, 14th, 15th	Weifang-Weixian Zhucheng	Q-5L, Q-5J, JH-7A
12 Fighter	34th, 35th, 36th	Shandong-Wendeng Shandong-Gaomi Shandong-Weihai Shandong-Qihe	J-8B, JJ-7A/J-7E/G or J-10S/J-10A
19 Fighter	55th, 56th, 57th	Shandong-Jining Henan-Zhengzhou Jiangsu-Lianyungang/ Baitaibu Henan Shangqiu-Liangyuan Guantang	J-11B, Su-27UBK, Su-27SK, J-7B, JJ-7, JZ-8F
32 Fighter	94th, 95th, 96th	Jiangsu-Xuzhou Jiangsu-Lianyungang Shandong-Xintai	J-7B, JJ-7A, J-11B, Y-5, Y-7, Z-9B
Independent	1st Indep. Recce.	Shandong-Weihai Xintai	JZ-8F
?	Unknown	Shandong-Jining	H-6
?	Training	Shanxi-Zhangzhuang	JJ-6, JJ-7, J-7B
?	?	Shandong-Jinan	Y-5, Y-7

Nanjing MR			
Division	Regiment	Base	Aircraft
3 Fighter	7th, 8th, 9th	Anhui-Wuhu Zhejiang-Changxing	J-7E/G/JJ-7A or J-10A/ J-10S, JH-7A,
10 Bomber	28th, 29th, 77th	Anhui-Anqing North Nanjing City– Dajiaochang	H-6K, H-6H, Y-8G, Y-8CB, Y-8XZ, Y-7, KJ-2000, Y-8T
14 Fighter	40th, 41st, 42nd	Jiangxi-Zhangshu Jiangxi-Jiujiang Nanchang-Xiangtang Fujian-Wuyishan	J-7E, J-11B or Su-27UBK
26 Special	76th, 77th	Wuxi-Shoufang Nanjing City	KJ-2000, Y-8T, Kj-200, Mi-171 Salon, Y-5
28 Ground Attack	82nd, 83rd, 84th	Hangzhou-Jianqiao Jiaxing	JH-7A, J-7E, Q-5J or JH-7A, JJ-6
MR Training	3rd Indep., 93rd	Jiangsu-Suzhou	J-8FR, JJ-7A
MR Training	85th	Quzhou	J-11, Su-30MKK
MR Training	86th	Jiangsu-Rugao or Jiujiang-Lushan	J-7E, JJ-7
MR Training	87th	Shanghai-Chongming Island	J-8DH, JJ7A
13 Flying College	1st	Anhui-Bengbu	CJ-6A
	1st	Fujian-Liancheng	J-6 (UAV)
	5th	Fuzhou City	J-6 (UAV)
	4th	Jiangxi-Jinggangshan Jian	J-6 (UAV)
	3rd	Fujian-Wuyishan	J-6 (UAV)

Shenyang MR			
Division	Regiment	Base	Aircraft
1 Fighter	1st, 2nd, 3rd	Liaoning-Anshan Inner Mongolia-Chifeng	J-11B, Su-27UBK, J-10A, J-10S, J-8F, JJ-7A

(Continued)

Shenyang MR			
Division	*Regiment*	*Base*	*Aircraft*
11 Ground Attack	31st, 32nd, 33rd	Jilin-Gongzhuling Huaide Jilin-Siping Dalian City-Sanshipu Liaoning-Wafangdian Liaoning-Dandong	JH-7A, Q-5D/J
21 Fighter	61st, 62nd, 63rd	Heilongjiang- Qiqihar Heilongjiang Mudanjiang-Hailang Jilin-Yanji	J-8DJ-8H, J-8F, J-7E, J-7F
30 Fighter	88th, 89th, 90th, 91st	Dalian base Liaoning-Yingchengzi Liaoning-Pulandian Liaoning-Dandong Langtou	J-7E, J-11B, JJ-6
Direct Reporting	4th Indep. Recce	Shenyang-Yu Hong Tun	Y-8,
16 Fighter	47th, 48th	Shenyang-Yu Hung Tun Harbin-Shuang Yu Shu	JJ-7A, J-8R, J-8FR, Y-8C, Y-8CB, Y-8G, Y-5, Y-7, Z-9WA
1 Flying College	1st Brigade	Harbin City-Shuangchen (Lalin County) Harbin City-Wanggang	HYJ-7, Y-5, Y-7
3 Flying College	1st, 2nd, 3rd, 4th, 5th	Jinzhou-Xiaolingzi Jinzhou-North, Liaoyang Liaoning-Kaiyuan	CJ-6A, JL-8, JJ-5

Lanzhou MR			
Division	*Regiment*	*Base*	*Aircraft*
?	?	Lanzhou-Xiaguanying	Y-5, Y-7
6 Fighter	16th, 140th	Gansu-Lintao Yinchuan City	Su-27, Su-27UBK, J-11
36 Bomber	107th, 108th	Shaanxi-Lintong Shaanxi-Wugong	H-6E
37 Fighter	109th, 110th, 111th, 112th	Xinjiang-Changji Xinjiang-Urumqi-South Xinjiang-Korla	J-8F, JJ-7A, J-8G, J-8H, J-11B, J-11BS, JH-7A

(Continued)

Lanzhou MR			
Division	Regiment	Base	Aircraft
8 Flying Academy	4th	Xinjiang-Hami	JL-9
5 Flying College	3rd	Gansu-Wuwei	JL-9
MR Training Base	?	Gansu-Jiuquan	J-7, Y-8, JJ-7A
Air Navigator	1st Training	Shaanxi-Hu Xian	HJ-5, Y-7, Y-9
?	Indep. Aerial Survey	Shaanxi Hanzhong-Chenggu	Y-8H, An-30, Y-12-IV

Guangzhou MR			
Division	Regiment	Base	Aircraft
2 Fighter	4th, 5th, 6th	Guangxi-Liuzhou Guangxi-Guilin Foshan City Zhanjiang Suixi	J-11, Su-27UBK, J-8DH, J-10A, J-10S
8 Bomber	23th, 24th	Hunan-Shaodong Hunan-Leiyang	H-6K, H-6U, H-6H
9 Fighter	25th, 26th, 27th	Guangdong-Shaoguan Guangdong Shantou-Denghai Guangdong Huiyang Foshan City-Shadi	J-7D/E, J-10A, J-10S, J-8D, JJ-7A
13 Transport	37th, 38th, 39th, unknown	Henan-Kaifeng, Wuhan City-Yangluo	Y-8C, An-26, Tu-154, Y-8, IL-76MD, IL-76TD
18 Fighter	52th, 53rd, 54th	Changsha City-Datoupu Wuhan City-Shanpo Hubei Wudangshan (Lao He Kou)	J-7B, Su-30MKK
42 Fighter	124th, 125th, 126th	Guangxi Baise-Tianyang Guangxi Nanning-Wuxu	J-7B, J-7H, JJ-7A
Training Base	2nd Indep. Reconnaissance	Hubei Wudangshan (Lao He Kou)	J-7B, JJ-7
Hong Kong Garrison	Indep. Helicopter	Hong Kong-Shikong	Z-8KH, Z-9ZH
	Unknown	Guangzhou City	Y-7, Z-9

Central Command			
Academy	Regiment	Base	Aircraft
Aviation University Flight Instructor Training Base	4th Training	Anhui-Bengbu	JL-8
Flight Test and Training Centre (FTTC)	171 Brigade	Hebei-Cangzhou	J-8B, J-7E, JJ-7A, JL-9
	172 Brigade		Su-30MKK
Aviation University Flight Instructor Training Base	1st Training	Changchun City-Dafangshan	JL-8
Aviation University Basic Training Base	1st Air		CJ-6A
	Sky Wing Air Demonstration Team		CJ-6A
Aviation University Basic Training Base	1st Training	Changchun City-Datun	Y-5, CJ-6
Flight Test Evaluation FTE	AWACS Test	Gansu-Dingxin	KJ-2000
Tactical Training Centre TTC	175th Brigade		J-7B, J-7H, JJ-7A, J-8F, J-11B, JH-7A, Q-5, Y-8, Z-9
Aviation University Basic Training Base	3rd Training	Liaoning-Fuxin	CJ-6
Aviation University Basic Training Base	2nd Training	Harbin City-Shuangcheng	CJ-6
Aviation University Basic Training Base	4th Training	Jinzhou-Liushuibao	CJ-6
FTTC	170th Brigade	Hebei-Gucheng	J-10A, J-10S, JL-9
ETC		Xian City-Yanliang	
Aviation University Flight Instructor Training Base	3rd Training	Jiangsu-Yancheng	JL-8
Aviation University Flight Instructor Training Base	2nd Training	Shandong-Zibo	CJ-6

(Continued)

Central Command			
Academy	*Regiment*	*Base*	*Aircraft*
15th Airborne Army	43rd Division	Hebei-Kaifeng	Uses aircraft from 37th Regt
	6th Transport	Hubei-Xiaogan	Y-5, Y-7
	Helicopter Wing		Z-8KA, Z-9WZ
	6th Transport	Yinshan-Guangshui North	Y-5, Y-7, Y-8

4.6.5 PLAAF SAM Units

In 1991, during the period that Soviet Union was disintegrating, China's air defense capabilities were of debatable effectiveness. They were built around indigenous clones of the Soviet S-75 Dvina /SA-2 (NATO: Guideline) and indigenous fighter aircraft such as the J-8 (NATO: Finback), in addition to vast numbers of aging J-6 (NATO: Farmer) and J-7 (NATO: Fishbed) fighters. Radar capabilities centered on cloned 1950s Soviet equipment, some pre-Tiananmen Western imports and a stalled indigenous AEWAC program centered on a turboprop engine Tu-4 (NATO: Bull, clone of B-29 Superfortress) airframe. However back in the late 1950s China had had one of the world's most modern SAM systems and was instrumental in making the world's first SAM kills against Nationalist Chinese RB-57D spy planes.

The PLA's air defense capabilities are transforming from a legacy force with static and undeployable systems to a state-of-the-art force, highly deployable within the country and demonstrably expeditionary as it matures. While the SA-2 remains numerically significant, it has been modernized almost on a continuous basis. In the past, first-generation SA-2/HQ-1s (Hong Qi, Red Flag) used an AK-20K/TG02 propellant combination liquid fuel mix that is toxic and highly corrosive—requiring all personnel to wear protective gear. The latest model is the HQ-2B, a significant advance on the Soviet original SA-2 and its first-generation Chinese clones HQ-1 and HQ-2. It uses solid fuels and can be highly mobile, being mounted on a tracked TEL (Transporter Erector Launcher) vehicle. Other improvements include a better rocket motor, more G capability, better warhead, digital command link for guidance with crypto capability, a monopulse engagement radar capability for jam-resistant angle tracking, and electro-optical angle tracking. Cut off from Soviet aid for twenty years, the Chinese were trying to develop their own indigenous SAM system, but HQ-3, HQ-4, and HQ-5 were all failures. It was not until the late 1990s that the SAM force, like the other parts of the PLA, succeeded in upgrading and modernizing. The venerable HQ-2 was to be replaced with the indigenous HQ-12 medium-range SAM system, serving as a second-tier supplement to the Russian S-300PMU-1/SA-20A (NATO: Gargoyle) high-mobility long-range SAM system.

In 2007, the PLA was estimated to be operating sixteen batteries of this high-attitude long-range SAM with a range of 150 km, capable of engaging a target only 0.02 square meter in size. In theory this Russian SAM can supposedly outperform the US Patriot PAC-1 and 2 systems. So impressed with the system, the PLA has now also deployed the S-300PMU-2 in large numbers; in fact, China was the first customer of the S-300PMU-2 (known in Russia as *Favorit*), operating under the name of HQ-18. According to the US DoD, the PLA has since deployed another eight batteries with the S-300PMU-1 as well as an upgraded version, the PMU-2. The PMU-2 allows the PLA to engage reduced-signature aircraft such as the F/A-18E/F and Eurofighter Typhoon, and provides a real threat to the Joint Strike Fighter.

It is believed that the total number of SAMs deployed by the PLA is well above 1,600, distributed amongst some 300 launcher platforms. Five such SAM battalions are deployed in active duty around the Beijing region, six battalions are in the Taiwan Straits region and the rest are in other major cities like Shanghai, Chengdu and Dalian.

Beside the Russian S-300PMU system, an indigenous HQ-9 was developed to provide a long-range SAM capability. To many, the HQ-9 was seen as a Chinese version of the Russian S-300PMU that can be launched from vertical ejection tubes on 8x8 four tube TELs. While there is not a lot of open source data available, what can be gleamed from Chinese sources is that the HQ-9 is the result of almost twenty years of work developing an indigenous SAM system, but some elements of the design were borrowed or developed from various SAM systems, including the S-3000PMU. From simple observation and comparison, the 48N6 missile of the S-300PMU is larger than the Chinese HQ-9 and from the released data from the FD-2000, the export model of the HQ-9 claims to have 7–125 km range in the anti-aircraft role, 7–25 km range in the anti-missile role and 7–15 km range in anti-cruise missile role. On paper at least these performances supposedly exceed the capability of the S-300PMU-1 or even the S-300PMU-2.

A HQ-9 SAM system is a brigade-level formation that comprises six batteries with each battery consisting of one Type 305B search radar, one tracking radar, one 200 kW Diesel generator truck and eight 8x8 Taian Transporter Erector Launchers (TELs) each with four missiles, totaling thirty-two rounds ready to fire. The HQ-9 system is supported by the HT-233 phased array engagement radar carried on the Taian TAS5380 8X8 high mobility vehicle that is common to the HQ-9 TEL. It has a similar design to the S-400s BAZ-6900 series vehicle. Chinese sources claim the HT-233 is a C-band system with 300 MHz receiver/antenna bandwidth, detection range of 120 kilometers and monopulse angle tracking to resist jamming. The land-based HQ-9 system has an anti-radiation variant known as the FT-2000 for export. The export designation for air defense version is FD-2000 (*Fang Dun*, Defensive shield). In September 2013, the HQ-9 won Turkey's T-LORAMIDS program to co-produce twelve long-range air defense systems; however, multiple sources have reported that the deal has yet to be confirmed as the US Congress responded by blocking all American funds for the integration of Chinese systems into NATO defenses.

For low- to medium-range air defense, there is the HQ-61, the first-generation Chinese SARH point defense SAMs deployed during the 1980s. The series includes both land-based and shipborne versions and an anti-radiation version and air-to-air version (designated as PL-11) have also been developed. The naval and anti-radiation versions are gradually being retired from Chinese service but PL-11, the air-to-air version, and HQ-61A, the land-based mobile version, are still currently in limited service with the Chinese military. Based conceptually on the cloned Alenia Aspide missile, which itself is based on the US RIM-7E/F

Sparrow, the HQ-61 is much larger and heavier and is equipped with a semi-active radar homing seeker and midcourse command link guidance. The cumbersome HQ-61 series has been largely superseded by the HQ-7 and HQ-64 point defense SAMs.

The HQ-61 had a difficult birth. It was conceived back in August 1965 when the CMC issued the request to develop a medium-range SAM. The 25th Research Institute of the 2nd Academy was tasked to do the feasibility study, and the result was Project HQ-41. In January 1966, the plan formally became a national project and the missile was to be designated the HQ-61. To reduce risk and costs, a land-based version was to be made first, designated simply HQ-61, and then based on the expertise gained, there was to be a naval version designated as HQ-61B. Later on a land-based mobile version was added, designated as HQ-61A. However, like all things in the 1960s, military projects experienced delays brought about by the so-called Great Cultural Revolution. As a result, the HQ-61A/B was not completed until 1986, more than two decades after the project had started. Certification for mass production was not granted until 1988! The HQ-61A SAM system consists of three vehicles: launcher/transporter, radar vehicle, and C2I vehicle, all of which are based on the same 6x6 cross-country truck to simplify logistics and reduce operational costs.

For short-range air defense the PLA, Army, Navy and Air Force all use the various derivatives of the HQ-7 (its export name, FM-80) air defense missile. After the visit to China by US President Nixon, China became a strategic chess piece of the West in their grand scheme against the Soviet Union. For the first time since the 1940s, China was able to obtain Western assistance to modernize its military, albeit in a small way. From France, China imported some land and sea versions of the Thomson-CSF Crotale missile for evaluation. The Thomson-CSF R-440 Sea Crotale surface-to-air missile (SAM) and the Thomson-CSF TSR 3004 Sea Tiger E/F-band radar were installed on the destroyer *Kaifeng* and CNS *Harbin*. The army found the Crotale system to be superior to the HQ-61 SAM and instructed the 2nd Aerospace Academy (now the China Academy of Defense Technology) to reverse-engineer the Crotale, instructed the 23rd Institute to reverse-engineer the radar and fire control systems, and the 206th Institute to develop ground-based vehicle carriers for the SAM. The result was the HQ-7. It began deployment in 1986 with the PLAAF as its main airbase defense system. Expecting a huge order the French were disappointed but they soon learned their lesson and instead of focusing on just selling items to China, through technology transfer alone they were able to earn more and maintain a longer technology consultant relationship with the Chinese.

4.7 PLA Navy

4.7.1 From Brown to Blue Water—Modernization of the PLA Navy

Like the Chinese Army and Air Force, the Chinese Navy and ship-building industry were also products of Soviet aid. In the early 1950s, although the People's Republic of China had been established, many of the outlying islands on the coast of China were still in the hands of Nationalist forces. The main mission of the PLAN at that time was to liberate the outlying islands from the Chinese Nationalists and to guard the Chinese coastlines from periodic attacks and raids. Lacking in money and capacity to build a fleet, the PLAN's main strategy was to develop the "people's war concept" of guerrilla hit-and-run tactics into a naval hit-and-run "sea guerrilla warfare" strategy by using large numbers of cheap and easy-to-use torpedo and gunboats in "wolf pack" groupings. Aside from asymmetrical naval warfare tactics using MBTs and gunboats, the defense of the nation's coastlines was backed up with numerous coastal batteries, and land-based naval aviation, as well as numerous diesel submarines on the prowl off the coast of China. In the 1960s, the Chinese navy was still a force of little boats, it was only in the 1970s that a few domestically built destroyers or frigates began to come on line. By the early 1980s these vessels began to exchange their guns for guided missiles. Equipped with more capable vessels, the Chinese Navy changed its mission from Passive Offshore Defense (PSD) to Coastal Active Defense (CAD). In the 1990s, partly due to the increased possibility of war with Taiwan (Taiwan under the new People's Democratic Party threatened to declare UDI),[2] the PLAN truly embarked on the road to modernization. The trigger for rapid modernization was the

1996 show of force by US carriers. At that time the PLAN brought two modified ex-Soviet *Sovremenny*-class destroyers in 1999 and 2000 respectively, and ordered two more improved *Sovremenny* types in 2005 and 2006. Sometime in the mid-2000s, China embarked on a frenzy of shipbuilding activities and the PLAN added a host of modern missile destroyers and frigates.

The modernization did not only affect the surface fleet, the expansion of the "stealth service" was equally impressive. Twelve Russian Kilo-class diesel-electric attack submarines were purchased, and a spat of domestic building added thirteen Type 039 submarines (NATO: *Song*-class) and seven Type 041 (NATO: *Yuan*-class) diesel-electric submarines to the submarine fleet. On the nuclear side, in addition to the older *Xia*- and *Han*-class SSBNs and SSNs, China was to add five Type 094 (NATO: *Jin*-class) SSBN nuclear ballistic missile submarines.

With better ships, the PLAN is therefore reaching out more to the open seas beyond the Chinese continental shelf. Strategically PLAN regards the coastal waters up to the first island chain as "Green Waters" and as such, the first and second generations of PLAN vessels were designed for such TAOR. First Island Chain (FIC) is a set of islands that stretches from the southern tip of Kyushu, Japan, moving down to Okinawa Island, then to Taiwan and the Philippines to eastern Malaysia and Brunei and terminating in the area by the Seas of Melaka in the south. The aim is that the PLAN will be a real "Blue Water" navy by the middle of the 21st century, breeching not only the FIC but also the Second Island Chain (SIC) in the mid-Pacific (Ogasawara Islands and Saipan to Guam and Papua, New Guinea). The intention behind this is to stop the United States from intervening in disputes around the Taiwan Strait and the South China Sea region and to protect the shipping lanes in the area, as around 90% of China's trade relies on shipping routes in the South China Sea. The expansion of PLAN is not limited to the waters of the Pacific, but also across the Indian Ocean to the Middle East as a mean to safeguard stable supply routes for and to Europe. The rampant piracy off the coast of Africa and the southern Arabian Peninsula prompted the PLAN to undertake an intercontinental deployment for the first time in 400 years, as Chinese warships took part in the international anti-piracy effort in this area.

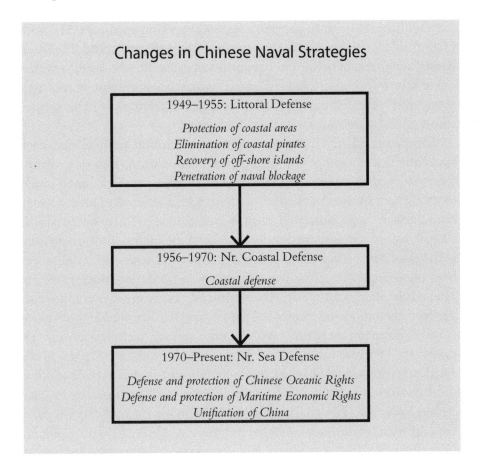

Changes in Chinese Naval Strategies

1949–1955: Littoral Defense

Protection of coastal areas
Elimination of coastal pirates
Recovery of off-shore islands
Penetration of naval blockage

1956–1970: Nr. Coastal Defense

Coastal defense

1970–Present: Nr. Sea Defense

Defense and protection of Chinese Oceanic Rights
Defense and protection of Maritime Economic Rights
Unification of China

4.7.2 Organization of PLAN

Today the PLAN is divided into five principal parts: Central Command, the three fleets (North, East, and South), naval experimental bases, academies and equipment/weaponry/ship development departments. The Naval Fleet is sub-divided into five branches: the surface fleets, the submarine force, the PLAN air force (PLANAF), coastal defense, and the PLA marines. The three fleets are subordinated to the three

Military Regions (MR) that have a coastline and each fleet is headed by a major general (vice admiral) or a brigadier (rear admiral) and each fleet has all the five branches of the PLAN as well as logistics and training facilities. Currently there are 225,000 serving in the PLAN with 26,000 in the PLANAF, 10,000 in the PLAN marines, and 27,000 in coastal defenses. Like the PLA ground force, the PLAN is still working on a selective conscription method where each recruit serves two years, and where those who then choose to continue in the service can try for NCO ranks.

Within the PLAN there are five major technical services that each applicant can choose to serve: operational, political, logistics, equipment/weaponry, and specialist/technical. As we move to a digital world so does the Chinese Navy, and the demand for educated sailors to man the increasingly sophisticated ships is ever growing. Today nearly all the PLAN sailors have attained at least a junior or high school graduation certificate. Most officers are university graduates with increasing numbers obtaining Masters or even higher qualifications. Today there are nine academies under the PLAN command. These are divided into two groups: navigation and command are grouped under the Nanjing-based Naval Command Academy, and the engineering/technical groups are under the Wuhan-based Naval Engineering Academy. Dalian Naval Academy is the most famous, and is dedicated to officer training while the Naval NCOs School is located in eastern China in Bangbu City, Anhui Province. The Marine Corps Academy is in southern China in the city of Guangzhou, and the Submarine Academy is in Qingdao City. The Naval Aeronautical and Astronautic University located in Yantai City, Shandong Province, not far from Qingdao, the Naval Engineering School is in Wuhan and the Naval Command College is in Nanjing, both inland cities but accessible by river. If Portsmouth, Plymouth and Clyde are the principal homes of the British Royal Navy and Norfolk, San Diego, and Pearl Harbor are the homes of the US Navy, then the equivalent for the PLAN are the key naval bases at Lvshun, Qingdao City and Huludao in the north, Shanghai and Zhoushan in central China, and Guangzhou, Zhanjiang, Yulin and Xisha (Paracel Islands) in the south for the Southern Fleet. While not directly part of PLAN, the state ship-building group, CSSC (China State Shipbuilding Corporation) retains close links, with major ship-building bases in Shanghai, Dalian, Wuhu and Guangzhou for surface ships, Wuhan and Shanghai for conventional submarines, and Huludao for nuclear submarines.

4.7.3 Staffing and Recruitment in PLAN

When the Navy was established in the 1950s, the plan was for an initial strength of 450,000, but this number was never really attained and almost as soon the PLAN was established the numbers began to decline. By 1995, PLAN forces numbered approximately 270,000, about 9% of the total PLA; in 2001 this fell to 225,000. Recently it has increased to 290,000. About 50% is in operational roles and the other half consists of PLANAF (26,000), PLA marines (12,000) and the remaining are with coastal defense, academies and naval bases. China's man-to-ship ratio compares well with that of other navies. China's ratio is 535, while Korea's is 525, Japan's is 470 and the US Pacific Fleet's is 430.

Finding the right recruits for PLAN and to some degree the PLANAF has been a tough task. Sophisticated warships require educated sailors, and as in many booming economies the private sector, offering higher wages and better working conditions, tempts many these clever and educated candidates away from the military. Aside from having more educated recruits, the recruiting strategy for the entire PLA is also changing. The PLAN and the PLANAF are reducing the number of conscripted personnel and are putting more emphasis on long-term career sailors. Reports say that the numbers of conscripted recruits has been reduced to 60% of all annual intakes from a previous high of 80%. To attract career sailors, service conditions have improved. Pay has been increased—some salaries have more than doubled. The annual conscription process for the PLA is identical for all three services. This usually begins in August when the GSD holds a national conference to determine the level of recruits needed by each service. For the Navy these numbers come from the fleet and then the requests are consolidated at the HQ level before passing to the GSD. The local People's Armed Forces Department (PAFD) will initiate the drafting at the local district/street committee level. Most of the conscripts will still come from the rural or township/minor cities area. Exempted are those who are physically unfit, have health problems, are in prison or charged with a crime, or those attending higher education. University draftees can be deferred until graduation. Bribery is not uncommon—some offer a bribe to avoid the military service but some bribe to have their sons or daughter accepted into the PLA, the latter is more common in poorer districts where a stable career in the PLA is seen as a way out of poverty.

The PAFD will begin the whole process by screening potential candidates, and those selected will get a number and report for health and various checks. The PAFD is staffed by serving soldiers/officers and they will choose the candidates for their unit/fleet. Conscription is now a standard two years for all the services, where previously it was three years for the PLA and four years for the SAC, PLAN, and PLAAF. Due to the technical nature of the navy, the conscription period for the PLAN is longer than the standard "Army" service of two years. For those who hold technical jobs, the service period is three years. For all PLA recruits, the basic training camp is twelve weeks in duration where recruits get "beasted" with physical exercise and general military education. Then the recruits are generally assigned to their service station or at the Fleet centralized training center for further training. However, for most, this training occurs on the boat itself. Centralized training in dedicated academies or schools is only for higher-level training such as officer candidates, petty officers, or highly technical skilled jobs.

For officers the PLAN, like the PLAAF and PLA Army, provides a five-track career: operational, logistics, political, equipment (focusing on maintenance), and technical. The PLA personnel records for officers are maintained in the offices of the GPD in Beijing as well as with GPD branches in the fleet and at the naval base where the officer is based. The political officers or commissar also double up as the unit human resource manager and manage the promotions for officers as well as their assignments. All PLA officers are graded annually as well as when they are due for promotion. PLA officers are graded on five points: their political character, physical fitness, military skills, specialty knowledge, and their achievements over the past twelve months.

Promotion is based on time served as well as merit. Officers must have the minimum time in grade and also the minimum time in rank, except for ensign to sub-lieutenant which is usually three years in rank and four years in grade. Promotion from sub-lieutenant to lieutenant takes a minimum of ten years, lieutenant to lieutenant commander fourteen years, lieutenant commander to commander eighteen years of service. From commander to captain is a minimum of twenty-two years of service and captain to senior captain (rear admiral) takes a minimum of twenty-six years. Officer candidates come from three sources: civilians attending colleges/universities, enlisted men/petty officers who have attained the qualifications and merit deemed to be good enough for officer candidates—usually found in naval academies attending courses or in high school studies entering dedicated military academies, or through the Chinese version of the Universities Officer Training Corps (UOTC)[3] program. Known as the National Defense Student Program (NDSP), this program is common to all three services and was set up with the purpose of select and sponsoring promising college/university candidates (some whilst still at secondary school or in their first year at college/university) for military service as officers. This program now covers fewer than 117 civilian colleges/universities across China.

4.7.4 Naval Paramilitaries—The Chinese Coast Guard

Supporting the PLAN are a number of maritime paramilitary organizations. Today the Chinese Coast Guard (CGC) serves as a coordinating agency for maritime search and rescue and law enforcement in the territorial waters of China. The Chinese Coast Guard was formerly the maritime branch of the Public Security Border Troops, a paramilitary police force under the Ministry of Public Security (MPS). They were divided into fleets, each under the command of the local (provincial) border defense force command; however, in March 2013, the Chinese government announced it would form a unified Chinese Coast Guard commanded by the State Oceanic Administration. The largest operational unit of the CCG is a CCG flotilla, which is a regimental-level unit in China's military administrative hierarchy. Every coastal province has one to three Coast Guard flotillas. Currently there are twenty CCG flotillas across the country and every coastal province has one to three Coast Guard squadrons. CCG ships are named *"Haijing XX,"* where XX is a number

Another paramilitary maritime service is the Chinese Marine Surveillance (CMS), a maritime law enforcement agency also under the China Oceanic Administration. The CMS's main task is coastal and ocean search and rescue. The CMS has recently been reinforced with quite a few large patrol ships (ex-PLAN destroyers with weapons removed) that will significantly enhance operational ability. In addition, these services operate their own small aviation units to assist their maritime patrol capabilities. CMS is known to operate a handful of Z-9 helicopters and a maritime patrol aircraft based on the Y-12 STOL transport. MSA ships are named *"Haixun XX,"* where XX is a number.

On the civil side, there is the Chinese Maritime Safety Administration (MSA). The MSA is a separate maritime search and rescue force, but part of the Ministry of Transport tasked with controlling marine pollution, marine safety, employment of seamen and their entry and exit, and investigation of maritime accidents and sinkings. With the changes from March 2013, the CMS and MSA are both now under the coordinating authority of the CCG. CMS ships are named *"Haijian XX."* The CMS also operates a fleet of survey ships and these have a different set of names, without the prefix *Haijian*. For example, *Xiang Yang Hong 14* (*Towards the Red Sun 14*) is a newly renovated survey vessel belonging to the CMS 8th Survey Fleet.

Finally, the Chinese Fisheries Law Enforcement Command (FLEC) is a department under the Ministry of Agriculture which is tasked with the enforcement of laws concerning fishing and maritime resources in Chinese territorial waters. It is charged with protecting Chinese fishing vessels and personnel, resolving disputes in fishing activities, preventing illegal fishing and protecting maritime resources. FLEC cutters are named *"Yuzheng XX,"* where XX is a number.

Naming of PLAN Vessels

For a long time, Western writers did not know how to properly address Chinese naval ships. Ships of the United States have the prefix USS (United States Ship) or USNS/USNV (United States Naval Ship/United States Naval Vessel), while Royal Naval ships will have prefix HMS (Her Majesty's Ship), and HMCS (Her Majesty's Canadian Ship) for Canada. In Chinese the address of naval ships is usually by attaching a suffix of *Hao* after the name of the ship. *Hao* has no meaning as such but is characterized as the "mark of a name or sign to a name." The matter of how to correctly name a Chinese naval vessel was finally laid to rest when a semi-official publication *Modern Ships* published an official announcement on the launching of the Chinese aircraft carrier as CNS *Liaoning*, where CNS stands for "Chinese Naval Ship."

The current regulation that governs the naming of PLAN ships was promulgated on the November 18, 1978 (modified July 8, 1986). Under this regulation, all PLAN vessels are divided into five classes. The naming of Class 1 vessels can only be made by the General Staff Department, while naming of Class 2 vessels can be permitted by the commander of the fleet, while the naming of smaller vessels such as Class 3 and 4 is delegated to the local flotilla commander. The classes of ship are as follows:

Class 1	Class 2	Class 3	Class 4	Class 5
Aircraft carriers	Destroyers	Large missile patrol boats	Small missile boats	Landing craft
Battleships	Escorts	Submarine hunter/chaser	Torpedo boats	Support vessels
Cruisers	Submarines	Oceangoing large minesweeper/hunters	Gun boats	Auxiliary vessels
Nuclear submarines	Large landing ships (LSD)	Medium-size landing crafts	Small minesweepers	
	Vessels over 10,000 tons	Vessels under 10,000 tons	Vessels under 1,000 tons	Vessels under 1,000 tons

For aircraft carriers, battleships and cruisers—the rules state that vessels of this type are to be named after the provinces of China, e.g.: CNS *Liaoning* is an aircraft carrier (Liaoning is a province in northeast China). As the carrier is part of the Northern Fleet it is appropriate that a province from the north of China is chosen. Destroyers and escorts take on the names of large cities, e.g.: CNS *Shenzhen 167* is a guided missile destroyer, Shenzhen is a key city in the south of China. Following the same logic, CNS *Shenzhen 167* is part of the Southern Fleet. As in all navies, submarines have their own rules. Nuclear submarines are always CNS *Changzheng* or "Long March" followed by a number, and a conventional submarine is CNS *Yuanzheng* or "Expedition" followed by a number. For example: CNS *Changzheng 1* is a Type-091 SSN Nuclear Submarine (NATO: *Han*-Class) that served from 1974 to 2000.

LSDs and large landing ships are named after mountains of China while smaller landing ships are named after rivers. The large Chinese LSD CNS *998* is officially called CNS *Kunlun Shan (Kunlun Mountain) 998*. For minesweeper/hunters the norm is to use the name of a large county which in China is known as *Zhou*, and large oceangoing fleet replenisher-oilers are named after lakes e.g.: Type-903 (Fuchi-class Replenisher-Oiler) is CNS *Weishan Lake*. Sub-chasers are named after small counties, *Xian*. Finally, other minor vessels are named by a single word/Chinese characters that depict the function they do or the port where they are based and is followed by a number when they are commissioned, e.g.: Type-81 minesweeper with pennant number 805 is CNS *Zhangjiagang-805* where Zhangjiagang is the name of a port city in central China. Another example is the Type 925 *Dajiang*-class (Great River) Submarine Rescue Ship, CNS *Nanjiu 506* (South Rescue 506) tells us that this vessel is part of the Southern Fleet, hence Nan (south) and Jiu (rescue) indicates its function.

However, there are a number of exceptions, the Dalian Naval Academy's training ship for midshipmen is CNS *Zheng He*, after a famous Chinese admiral and navigator of the 14th/15th century, and another training ship from the academy is CNS *Shichang*, named after Deng Shichang, an admiral of the 19th century. The third notable exception was a former PLAN survey ship *Li Siguang* (formerly CNS *Haiyang-81* or Ocean-81) that was named after a famous Chinese scientist, Dr. Li Siguang.[4]

The use of pennant numbers in the PLA also follows a set of rules. Destroyers are allocated with the one hundred series with 1XX as a starting point. Northern Fleet destroyers are normally 101–130, the Eastern Fleet 131–159, and the Southern Fleet 160–199. Escorts are allocated the 500 series while landing ships have the 900s and auxiliary ships have the 800 series. Nuclear submarines are 400 and conventional submarines are 200 and 300. The 700 series is for large missile boats and such, while the 600 series is kept for sub-chasers. Triple digits are combatants and this includes auxiliaries and support vessels, whereas double digits are training vessels or non-combatants. Using examples listed above, the two training vessels belonging to the Dalian Naval Academy are thus two digits and the CNS *Liaoning*, the aircraft carrier, carries a two digit-pennant number denoting that the vessel, although looking very menacing, is still a "training vessel," teaching PLAN sailors how to operate an aircraft carrier, operational procedures, and related tactics. Finally, small vessels, those under 500-ton displacement, have four-digit pennant numbers.

4.7.5 China Naval Elite—PLA Marines

The PLA Marine Corps (PLAMC) was originally established in 1953 by transferring one infantry regiment and two infantry battalions from the army to form the nucleus of the PLAMC 1st Regiment. In December 1954, the PLAMC's 1st Regiment was enlarged to divisional strength with the addition of infantry and an amphibious tank training regiment. At its height, the PLAMC consisted of eight divisions of some 110,000 soldiers. The main purpose was to conduct amphibious operations against islands held by the Nationalists as well as eventually the invasion of Taiwan. On the conclusion of these island wars and the cancelling of any CNS plan to attack Taiwan the PLAMC was disbanded in October 1957. Following the disbanding of the Marine Corps, the PLAN did continue to maintain a naval infantry force which consisted of several infantry and amphibious tank regiments. In 1979 the Central Military Commission of the People's Republic of China reestablished the PLAMC and placed it under the PLAN and on May 5, 1980, the elements of the 391th Regiment of the 131st Division, together with supporting arms, became the 1st Marine Brigade with its headquarters in Hainan Island, in view of the growing tension between China and Vietnam. Soon after the Eastern Fleet and the Northern Fleet both raised their own respective marine brigade. Each brigade consists of three infantry battalions with armor and support arms that include its own helicopter assets. In 1985 the PLA was culled by one million men. As a result, the Northern and Eastern Fleets lost their marine corps but the Southern Fleet not only was allowed to keep its marines but was strengthened, and by July 1998 the 164th Motorized Infantry Division (consisting of four regiments, 491st–494th) was transferred to the PLAN Southern Fleet and became the 164th Marine Brigade, giving the Southern Fleet a two brigade strength of PLAMC.

Today the PLAMC consists of two 6,000-man brigades with the 1st and 164th Marine Brigades—both based in Zhanjiang, Guangdong Province. PLAMC-like marines all over the world are considered elite troops and in China are now part of the rapid mobilization forces. In 1995 females were admitted to the PLAMC. Selection criteria for females are the same as for men, thus all those ladies who passed the PLAMC selection tests are indeed elite troopers as members of an all-female elite amphibious RECON commando company. Today the 1st Marine Brigade PLAMC (unit code 92510) consists of:

- Unit 91048: 1st Marine Battalion with three infantry companies supported by a HMG and a mortar company.
- Unit 92505: 2nd Marine Battalion (as above).
- Unit 92604: 2nd Antitank and AA Artillery Battalions.
- Unit 91923: Missile Battalion.
- Unit 91048: Female RECON Squadron.

- Unit 91487: Amphibious RECON Battalion and New Soldiers Training Company.
- Unit 91755: Amphibious RECON consisting of three male scuba squadrons and one female scuba squadron.
- Supporting arms that includes Chemical Defense Company, MP and Signal Company, Logistics Company, Helicopter Squadron, Medical Company.
- Training team for new recruits.

The 164th Marine Brigade PLAMC (Unit 92057) consists of the following:

- Unit 91509: 1st Marine Battalion (as per Unit 91048, with about 750 Marines).
- Unit 91376: 2nd Marine Battalion (as above).
- Unit 9xxxx (number unknown): Artillery Battalion (as Unit 92604).
- Unit 92583: Antitank and Anti-Air Missile Battalion with HJ-8 & HJ-73 ATGMs and HN-5 SAMs.
- Unit 92776—Amphibious Armor Regiment: a tank battalion, an amphibious tank battalion, and an armor battalion. All are equipped with three squadron of tanks/IFV (T-63 amphibious light tanks with T-86 IFV and T-63/89 APC all amphibious).
- Unit 92352—Reconnaissance Battalion (as per Unit 91755, three male scuba squadrons and one female scuba squadron).
- Supporting arms that include Chemical Defense Company, Military Police and Signal Company, Logistics Company, Helicopter Squadron, Medical Company.
- Training team for new recruits.

In terms of equipment, the Chinese marines receiving more than the normal allocation of modern armored fighting vehicles. The latest known example is a new light tank that features the same turret as the T-63A, but on a lighter chassis that may perform better on water than the original T-63A. This new tank comes with a new armored recovery vehicle, which features a brand new hull. In contrast to the US Marine

Corps, the Chinese Marine Corps does not have its own aviation units and relies heavily on the support of the Air Force and the Navy in direct support and airborne operations, but the amphibious capacity has been upgraded tremendously with a new series of hovercraft and the new Type-071 Landing Ship Dock (LSD), which can operate with both high-speed hovercraft and helicopters. The Type-071 (lead ship CNS: *Kunlun Mountain*, NATO: *Yuzhou*-class) is an amphibious warfare ship with a capacity of one marine battalion, and 15–20 amphibious armored vehicles that can be deployed by hovercraft such as the Type-726 (NATO: *Yuyi*-class) LCAC and helicopters. Due to the shape of the Type-726 Chinese LCAC it is often compared with the US LCAC due to their similar size and mission, but Type-726 carries less cargo because the Chinese engine on the LCAC is bulkier and offers less power than that of the US LCAC, but nonetheless it can carry up to 60 tons of cargo, enough for a T-99 tank. In contrast, US LCACs can carry more around 70 tons of cargo. In addition, China is taking delivery of up to four of the world's biggest hovercraft, the Ukrainian *"Zubr"* or *"Bison"*-type (NATO: Pomornik) air cushion assault transport with speeds exceeding 50 knots. With the PLAN's accelerating efforts to expand its capabilities beyond territorial waters, it is likely that the PLAMC will begin to play a greater role as an offshore expeditionary force similar to the United States Marine Corps and British Royal Marines.

Notes

1 The largest military AFB in Asia, it has a reputation as China's "Area 51," and is also known as Air Force Clearwater No. 14 AFB.
2 Unilateral Declaration of Independence
3 The British Royal Navy version of the UOTC program is known as Universities' Royal Naval Unit (URNU) while in the United States it is known as the Naval Reserve Officers Training Corps (NROTC).
4 Dr. Li Siguang 1887–1971. Decommissioned 2012 and transferred to fishery protection.

CHAPTER 5

CHINESE WEAPONS AND THE ARMAMENTS INDUSTRY

The modern Chinese defense industry is the direct result of aid given by Stalin in the early 1950s. Without this aid, there would be no civil industry to speak of. The modern Chinese motor transport industry, shipbuilding and civil aviation manufacturing all had their origin in armament manufacturing, whereby the excess capacity of these military factories was retooled to produce goods for the domestic market. In the early days of the republic, all that China had were workshops for repairs and the odd factory doing assembly with imported parts. There were no true indigenous manufacturing industries. The Bureau of Aviation Industry, then under the Ministry of Heavy Industry, was created for the purpose of maintaining military aircraft, not manufacturing planes. There were many ship repair facilities but no shipyard capable of building oceangoing vessels.

In the 1950s and 1960s all heavy industries were essentially geared to supporting the military, the first mass production lines for motor transport, the First Automobile Works in northeast China, began making a 4-ton Jie Fang (Liberation) CA-10 truck (based on the Russian ZIS-150) for the military. It was not until the late 1970s that China embarked on the first post-revolution "catching up" program, known as the "Four Modernizations." Because of a lack of foreign exchange, access to key military technologies was still denied to the Chinese, and the modernization of the arms industry was placed behind that of the civilian sectors (agriculture, industry, and science and technology).

To make ends meet, China's large defense sector has had to devote more and more of its resources to civilian production. For example, in the mid-1980s, approximately one-third of the ordnance industry's output was allocated to civilian production, and that proportion would rise to two-thirds by 1990. The "defense sector" produced a wide variety of products for the civil market, from furniture to telescopes, cameras to light machinery. The governmental bureaus that supervised industrial output also went through a series of transformations. For example, China's Bureau of Aviation Industry was later reorganized and renamed the Third Ministry of Mechanical Industry (1960–82) which later became the Aviation Ministry of Industry (1982–88), and the Aviation and Astronautic Ministry of Industry (1988–93). As the policy in the late 1970s was to "hold back" on the modernization of the defense industry, giving priority to the civilian sector, the true modernization of the defense sector did not really begin until 1993 when China ushered in three waves of organizational transformations in its arms industry.

The first wave of modernization of the armament industry began in 1993, and throughout the 1990s China restructured its defense industries from essentially governmental departments into large companies, albeit still state-owned. This included the China National Nuclear Corporation (CNNC), China Aerospace Corporation (CASC), China Aviation Industry Corporation (CAIC), China State Shipbuilding Corporation (CSSC), China Shipbuilding Industries Corporation (CSIC), and China Ordnance Industry Corporation (COIC). The rationale was that through transforming these entities into commercially oriented structures, the industry's manufacturing, R&D, maintenance, and sales could be better integrated so as to enhance their operation and productivity. The second wave of transformation began in 1998 when China abolished the Commission of Science, Technology and Industry for National Defense (COSTIND) originally set up by the PLA in 1982. It was confusingly replaced with an institution of the same name, the new COSTIND was to be directly under the State Council Office. In the same year, the PLA formed the General Armament Department (GAD) to assume the procurement function and integrate the various equipment-related offices that were scattered between the different ministries and bureaus. The GAD is responsible for defense procurement, the life-cycle management of weapons, and research into the maintenance of weapons, and is a testing base for the PLA.

The third wave of transformation began in the late 2000s when China established the Ministry of Industry and Information Technology (MIIT). At the same time the government reorganized the Commission of Science, Technology and Industry for National Defense (COSTIND) and renamed it as the State Administration of Science, Technology and Industry for National Defense (SASTIND), which is subordinate to the MIIT. The MIIT assumed authority to oversee the eleven major military-industrial enterprise groups originally under COSTIND, basically achieving unified management over the military and civilian industries.

To understand more about how the system worked, we can take the aviation industry as an example. Since the ending of the Korean War, the aviation industry of China has been through twelve systemic reforms. Initially in a centralized planned economy all industries were managed directly by the government bureaus; in the case of aviation this was the Aviation Industry Bureau, under the Ministry of Heavy Industry. Later, after a series of restructurings, the responsibilities of managing the aviation industries were bounced between different bureaus and departments: 4th Bureau, No. 2 Mechanical Industry Department, then 4th Bureau, No. 1 Mechanical Industry Department, 4th Bureau, and lastly the No. 3 Mechanical Industry Department. Later with the establishment of the Ministry of Aviation Industry, the habit of direct management of industries continued and this did not cease until 1993, when the Aviation Industry Corporation of China (AVIC) was formed and China began to run its defense factories like a commercial entity, albeit a state-owned enterprise (SOE). This huge company proved too big to run and in 1999 it was split into two, named—probably by an unimaginative bureaucrat—AVIC I and AVIC II. AVIC I focused on large planes, both military and commercial, while AVIC II focused on smaller planes and helicopters. In 2008, the two companies again merged into one, on the basis of increased efficiency and management of resources and to avoid redundant projects. However, a key driver was the decision to undertake the development of large aircraft by China. The Commercial Aircraft Corporation of China (COMAC) was founded with the primary duties of design, assembly, sale, maintenance, and after-sale service of large passenger aircraft with a capacity of over 150 passengers to reduce the country's dependency on Boeing and Airbus.

However, the common theme of the Chinese defense industry was the move from direct state controlled to commercial corporatization to be run on commercial terms, albeit with the state as key/major shareholders. The road to commercialization was not without hiccups. Learning from the mistakes of other industries, when the state shipbuilding industry was corporatized, two entities were created, with the aim to provide some degree of competition within the industry. The China State Shipbuilding Corporation, CSSC, was to be responsible for shipbuilding in the east and south of the country while CSIC, China Shipbuilding Industry Corporation, was to be responsible for shipbuilding in the north and west.

Today, the Army gets most of its weaponry from the CNGC (China North Industries Group Corporation). Under this group, there are two entities, NORINCO and CSGC (China South Industries Group Corporation). NORINCO itself was a result of the corporatization of the armaments industries that were previously under the Ministry of Machinery and Electronics Industry (previously known as the Fifth Ministry of Machine Industries, part of the Ministry of Armaments and in turn under the supervision of the National Machinery Industries Committee). While CSGS does deal in military equipment and parts, it was created to cater more to the commercial market for optic-electronic products, and its real strength lies in making cars and motorcycles.

5.1 Tanks and AFVs in China since 1949

The history of China's tank industry can be divided into three phases. The first period was before 1949, when China was under Nationalist administration. At that time, China relied 100% on foreign-made tanks, purchased from France: the Renault NC31; from Britain: the Vickers Mk. E Type B; from the United States: the M5A1 Stuart and

M-4 Sherman. The Chinese tank force was also well stocked with tanks seized from Japan at the end of WWII, like the Type-97 Chi-Ha. After Mao took power, and as the country was renamed the People's Republic of China, the embryonic Communist state was heavily influenced by the Soviet Union. The tank force was re-equipped with WWII cast-offs from the Soviet Red Army, and tanks like the T-34/85 and the IS-2 became the backbone of the PLA. By late 1950, China began developing its own tanks, albeit with Soviet help. The first Chinese-made tank was the T-59 MBT, which was essentially a copy of the Soviet T-54. Later the T-62 light tank (a scaled-down version of the T-59) was added to the line. These two models became the first Chinese tanks to be mass-produced in China.

5.1.1 First-Generation Chinese MBT

After the signing of Sino-Soviet Treaty of Friendship, Alliance and Mutual Assistance, the Soviets agreed to assist China in building a tank factory to manufacture the T-54A MBT in 1956. The result was the purpose-built 617 Factory (later known as the Inner Mongolia First Machine Group Co. Ltd) in Baotou City. Initially, tanks were assembled with Soviet-supplied parts, which were gradually replaced by Chinese-made components. The first Chinese-made tank, the T-59 (industrial designation WZ-120), was a direct copy of the Soviet T-54A. It first rolled off the production line in 1958 and was accepted into service by the PLA in 1959, hence the designation T-59. After the relationship between the two Communist giants soured, the Soviet experts withdrew from Baotou and for some time the Chinese had some difficulty producing anything. The Soviets destroyed key information relating to manufacturing a tank, such as how to make nickel-chromium steel, an essential item in the production of armor. Importing nickel was out of the question due to lack of foreign exchange. Forced into a corner the Chinese experimented with many types of steel, and eventually settled on rare earth treated steel (Type-601 casting steel for the turret) and rare earth thickened armored steel (Type-603 roll armor plate steel[1]) that gives similar protection as nickel chromium steel. At first the T-59 was equipped with an un-stabilized 100 mm rifled gun, incidentally also known as the Type-59 cannon, for which thirty-four rounds were carried. There was also a 7.62 mm coaxial machinegun and a 12.7 mm anti-aircraft machinegun, called the Type-54 (a Chinese copy of the Russian 12.7 mm M1938/46 DShKM) mounted on the gunner hatch. Additionally, a Type-59T 7.62 mm bow machine gun was provided for the driver with some 3,500 rounds at the ready. Very early models of the Type-59 had manual elevation; which was later replaced with a powered system allowing the gun to be aimed at between +17°and -4° (comparing poorly with Western tanks which had typical -10° depression that suited hull-down deployment). Later, vertical stabilization allowing firing on the move was made practical with an infrared searchlight which was retrofitted to the tank with an infrared periscope for the commander, gunner, and driver. The aforementioned upgrades were incorporated in the Type-59I. The T-59 was powered by a Model 12150L V-12 liquid-cooled diesel engine, which develops 520 horsepower at 2,000 rpm. A total of 815 liters of diesel can be carried, with a further 400 liters on external tanks giving a maximum road range of 600 kilometers. The Chinese T-59 is virtually indistinguishable from the Russian T-55 except for the upturned dish–air extractor that features prominently on the turret centerline, something that was not on the Type-54.

Later, as Communist China's profile improved on the international stage, China managed to get aid from the West and the T-59 received upgraded packages. The first and foremost was the 105 mm Type-81 rifled gun design provided by Austria (a copy of the Royal Ordnance L7), distinguished by the fume extractor midway on the barrel, rather than on the muzzle. Later an indigenously developed 120 mm smooth-bore gun, comparable in general performance to the Rheinmetall 120 mm gun used on the German Leopard 2 and the American M1A1/A2 Abrams (see "The Chinese 'Nashorn' Panzerjäger—T-89 120 mm Tank destroyer") was added. This upgraded tank is known as the T-59D. The T-59D is fitted with domestically produced FY explosive reactive armor (ERA). With this package, the tank's protection against the kinetic armor-piercing round and HEAT round increased by approximately 180%–260% and 200%–300% respectively. According to tests, the tank can survive a direct hit by the 105 mm

APFSDS round at a distance of 2,000 m. Additionally, the tank is fitted with an automatic fire and explosion suppression system. The Type-59D is also equipped with a 105 mm rifled gun, and when firing an APFSDS round it has an armor penetration capability of 600 mm at a distance of 2,000 m. The 105 mm gun-launched antitank guided missile (ATGM), derived from the Russian 9K116 Bastion (NATO: AT-10 Stabber) technology, with a maximum range of 5.2 km and an armor penetration capability of 700 mm, is also capable of engaging slow-flying helicopters. The T-59D is equipped with passive night vision, new fire control and a new engine. Another modification with a 125 mm gun and semi-automatic loader is reported to be in service with the PLA and the Bangladesh Army.

One unusual sidetrack of the T-59 is the T-62 light tank, which was a scaled-down Type-59 with simplified equipment for operation in southern China and more mountainous regions of the country. Development on the new Type-62 tank began in 1958 and entered batch production in 1963, and approximately 800 were produced by 1978. It weighed only 21 tons and was equipped with an 85 mm rifled gun and three machine guns. An improved T-62-I version was produced with better FCS with laser rangefinder and turret storage racks for added protection. The PLA deployed the T-62 light tank to Vietnam during the 1979 Sino-Vietnam War. They found that the thin armor of the T-62 tank could be penetrated easily by hand-held antitank weapons such as the RPG, and as result the T-62 tank suffered severe losses during the conflict, which convinced the PLA to develop new second-generation MBTs.

By the mid-1960s the Type-59 was clearly in need of replacement. Development of the successor to the T-59 began in 1967, in the depths of the Cultural Revolution. Unrealistic demands without due consideration for industrial capacity and technological limitations led the Chinese down many dead ends while searching for hte right tank design. Experimental Tanks 1224 and 1226 were two such examples. The Chinese were essentially fumbling in the dark. However, one of the unexpected bonuses from the 1969 border clash with the Soviet Army was the capture of the newest Soviet MBT, the T-62. The Chinese were able to reverse-engineer much of the technology, giving their tank designers a much-needed boost, and the new tank was eventually named the T-69 (manufacturer code: WZ-121). Improvements included a dual-axis stabilized 100 mm smoothbore gun, a new 580hp engine and an IR searchlight. Later it was found that the 100 mm smoothbore was unreliable and so the Chinese developed the T-69I, with a rifled 100 mm gun. The T-69 can carry 44 rounds, ten more than the T-59 (13 APFSDS, 13 HE-FRAG and 18 HE). The gun has a maximum range of 1,736 m. However, the PLA was not satisfied with the T-69 and only used it in limited quantities, but ironically it became one of China's best armored vehicle exports. Over 2,600 were sold worldwide in the 1980s to both armies fighting the Iran–Iraq War. Later the T-69 was upgraded with Western systems such as the British Marconi FCS and the L7-105 mm gun and the upgraded T-69 is known as the T-69III or T-79, which represented the last model in China's first-generation tank development. The T-69 is the first Chinese tank with the TSFCS fire control[2] system and later the T-69II also incorporated a Type-70 gunner sight, TCRLA laser rangefinder, BCLA ballistic computer, and Type-889 radio for which this model became the bestseller for the Chinese. It was this tank that Saddam Hussein fielded when the Western coalition force attacked Iraq in the First Gulf War. Today only a couple hundred T-69/T-79s remain in the PLA inventory, mostly deployed with training or reserve units. The T-69/T-79 is being replaced by the newer T-96 and T-99 MBTs.

The T-69, like the T-59, has a typical Soviet-style "half-egg" shaped cast turret and a conventional four-man crew layout with five large road wheels on each side, with rubber track skirt. An easy identification sign for the T-69/T-59 family of MBTs is the gap between the first and second road wheel. The early T-69 could also be identified by its large IR searchlight mounted on the right side of the main gun and a laser rangefinder mounted above the main gun. The T-69 can be distinguished from the T-59 by the position of the headlight: the T-59 has only one headlight located on the hull front (to the right); while the T-69 has two headlights mounted on the track wings.

5.1.2 Second-Generation Chinese MBT

At the end of 1970, the T-122 Experimental Medium Tank[3] project was abandoned following just three years of development. By February 1977, work on another second-generation MBT named T-1226 began but the delay caused by infighting between different factions led to the project being so delayed that the group was told that they should be working on a third-generation tank and not a second (see "T-98 MBT").

While the "second-generation" MBT design team was locked in bitter disputes about the finer philosophies of tank design, another design group was working fastidiously on an upgrade of the T-69. Instead of starting from zero, this group was merely working on an upgraded version of an earlier design and very quickly reached the prototype stage. After settling on the design work, the group was asked to meet with the Minister of Defense, Zhang Aiping. After looking at the remodeled T-69 design proposal, he suggested that this new type should be known as the T-80, as this was seen as the replacement for the aging T-59 as a second-generation MBT. Although initiated in 1980, the tank was not operational until 1988, meaning that it is also referred to as the T-88, as it is a habit of the Chinese to name weapons for the date they were brought into service. The 1980s was an era when China opened up to the West, and as a result Western companies began to see China as a vast untapped market.

The T-80 was the first Chinese tank to incorporate Western technologies, a hybrid of a Russian tank body with Western add-ons. Mr. Fang Wei was appointed chief designer. The T-80 is essentially a T-69 with a NATO standard 105 mm rifled gun, a British fire-control system, GM-09, that incorporates passive night sights and a ballistic computer, and a German diesel engine. The T-80 can be equipped with ERA armor and additional external storage racks which give the tank a new silhouette. The tank only saw limited service with the PLA, but its technology was used in the development of the later T-85 and T-96 series MBTs.

As result of rapprochement with the United States in the early 1980s, and US assistance on the new Chinese tank, T-80 was redesigned with an M-60-style wheel arrangement. The original five large road wheels of the T-59 and T-69 were replaced by an arrangement of six smaller road wheels with three track rollers. The wheel spacing is key for recognition purposes—the gap between the first and second road wheel is easily visible as is that between the second and the third wheel, and on the turret center there is a narrow tube-snorkel placed between the commander and gunner's hatch cover. With better equipment and thicker armor, the T-80's weight was increased to 38.5 tons, and as a result a new more powerful engine was required. The result was a German-designed 730hp diesel engine, but despite the improvement the T-80 did not win any overseas orders—the type of clients who buy arms from China are usually poorer nations wanting something "cheap and cheerful," all the Western add-ons were beginning to be too expensive. However, the T-88B or T-88II (built-in ISFCS-212 laser range-finder integrated with FCS, image intensifier, built-in test system to identify malfunctions) can be reinforced with Type-683 composite armor on the glacis plate. In addition, it is painted with anti-IR detection paint, VRC-8000 voice encryption, frequency-hopping radio and a 105 mm gun capable of APFSDS, HEAT and HESH. On top of that there is a built-in NBC protection with overpressure (so that the crew need not to wear individual NBC protection gear inside the tank). The T-88B did eventually find service in the PLA. Production of T-88-series MBTs was halted in 1995 after a production run of some five to six years. Over 400 T-88-series tanks are currently in service with the PLA.

Sometime during 1985, with an eye for the export market, China's North Industries Group Corporation (NORINCO) in association with 201 Institute (now China North Vehicle Research Institute), unveiled their own version of an upgraded T-80. The final result was the T-85 MBT. The T-85 has a new all-welded turret but in all other respects it is essentially a T-88B and was marketed by NORINCO as the "Stormer" in the international arms market. The PLA did not initially accept the T-85 but the tank eventually found favor with the Pakistanis, renamed as T-85-IIAP[4] or the T-85-III. After Pakistan bought the T-85-IIAP, the PLA changed its mind and had a rethink on adopting the T-85-IIAP.

This change of mind occurred after tests conducted on the Soviet T-72 in the late 1980s (reportedly from Iran with captured Iraqi samples) and the Chinese discovered to their satisfaction that the Chinese T-80 105 mm guns could defeat the armor of a T-72. That was the good news, but the bad news was that the main gun of the T-72 could also easily defeat the armor of not only the T-80 MBT but all the armor of all China's current tanks!

In the early 1990s, the world's attention was suddenly all focused on the Middle East. The 1991 Gulf War soon became a showcase for Chinese vs. Western weapons. The Iraqi Army was equipped with all sorts of Chinese MBTs and AFVs and the Chinese-made T-69 MBT was the key tank in Saddam's "elite," the Republican Guard. *Desert Storm* proved that these Chinese tanks in the hands of the Iraqi elite were no match against Western MBTs. Hundreds were destroyed with hardly any loss to the Western Coalition Army. As a result of this awesome display of Western superiority, China rapidly upgraded the T-85 and renamed it the T-85-IIM, or known in the PLA as the T-88C. The T-88C, boosted with a 125 mm gun and autoloader, was rapidly accepted into service with the PLA. Today it is estimated that the PLA has some 600 T-88Cs still in service.

NORINCO entered the Pakistan tank tender with a T-85IIA (an upgraded T-85II), but after extensive testing the Type-85A proved to be under-armored against the T-72M1, the main MBT of India. In 1987, under a technology transfer agreement, Pakistan began to locally manufacture the T-85 under the new name T-85IIAP, and they soon began to upgrade the tank with a 48 caliber 125 mm gun with automatic loader, thus reducing the crew from four to three. According to the Chinese, the Chinese-supplied APFSDS can penetrate 500 mm rolled homogenous armor (RHA) at 2,000 m, which on paper at least is equal to the 125 mm on the Indian T-72M1. After the Pakistani military introduced the upgraded T-85 into its fleet, the Indians soon upgraded their tank force with the Russian T-90. Fearing that they were losing the arms race, Islamabad took the Ukrainian T-84 (essentially an upgraded T-80UD) as a stopgap measure. However, after buying the T-84, to the shock of the Pakistan

Army, the 125 mm on the T-84 was no match for the Chinese 125 mm on the T-85IIAP. Some "know-it-all smart Alec" decided that as both tanks use 125 mm guns, if they transferred the Chinese ammunition into the Ukrainian tank it would compensate for the low penetration power of the T-84. However, the longer Chinese tank round did not fit the autoloader on the T-84. Another "smart Alec" decided that they could cut part of the penetrator with the Chinese APFSDS. Now shorter, the Chinese round would fit the Ukrainian autoloader. Of course with the round shortened, the aerodynamics of the Chinese round changed, and also reduced the penetration power. The "new" shortened Chinese round failed to defeat the Indian T-90, and the Pakistani government was left with lots of expensive tanks that were inferior to the Indians' MBT. Whether this had to do with the eventual move by the Pakistan Army to adopt the MBT-2000 is difficult to say, but after this fiasco the Pakistani government stuck firmly with Chinese arms!

The T-90 was a new experimental Chinese tank for the 1990s. It was essentially an upgraded T-85, but besides manufacturing a few test vehicles for evaluation, this tank was not adopted by the PLA. Instead, the PLA decided to adopt the subsequent upgraded model, the T-90II. With the fiasco of the Ukrainian tank behind them the Pakistani government began to look for a replacement and they also chose the T-90II. After making some modifications to it for local desert conditions, it was eventually renamed the MBT-2000 (Al-Khalid). This tank was jointly developed by the Beijing 201 Institute (China North Vehicle Research Institute) and the 617 Factory (Inner Mongolia First Machine Group Corporation), and the chief designer for the MBT-2000 was Mr. Ma Chengmeng. The T-90 is unique as it was the first Chinese tank to incorporate modular attachable armor that gives a pointed arc outlook instead of the old flat turret silhouette of the T-88.

The MBT-2000, or as it's better known, the *Al-Khalid* tank (Urdu for The Immortal), is today Pakistan's main MBT, and since 2001 about 500 have been in service. In 2011 the Bangladesh Army ordered forty-four MBT-2000s and it is reported to be in service with the Royal Moroccan

Army, while an unknown number have been reported to be in service with the Myanmar (Burmese) Army.

The MBT-2000 is equipped with an automatic loading 125 mm 48-caliber smoothbore main gun that is capable of firing the usual set of ammunition (APFSDS, HEAT-FS, and HE-FS) as well as the Ukrainian *Kombat* or the Russian 9M119 Refleks (NATO: AT-11 Sniper) ATGMs. Since it is automatically loaded, the tank is served by a crew of only three men. As the T-88 was a hybrid Soviet tank with Western technology, the T-90II/Al-Khalid is no different. The Al-Khalid is unusual in that it was designed to be adaptable for manufacture, so that it can be easily integrated with a variety of foreign engines and transmissions. It is the first Chinese tank that incorporates a wheel-type steering column instead of the old twin sticks method, and is equipped with an LSG-3000 automatic power shift transmission from Zahnraederfabrik Friedrichshafen AG that gives four forward and two reverse gears and increases cross-country mobility. However, in the mid-1990s the German government, for security reasons, forbade exports of the LSG-3000 to China and this forced the Pakistani government to choose a new power and transmission pack. Initially they settled on a British Perkins Shrewsbury CV12-1200 TCA diesel engine (as used in the Challenger 2), and a French SESM ESM 500 automatic transmission (used in the Leclerc MBT), however, the project was abandoned due to the arms embargo following the 1998 Pakistani nuclear tests.

A Chinese engine was chosen as a replacement but it failed to live up to its capability in the desert of Pakistan. Denied Western technology, the Al-Khalid eventually settled on a diesel engine and transmission supplied by the KMDB design bureau of Ukraine, and the tank was re-designated as T-90IIM or MBT-2000—a name used by NORINCO for marketing the T-90IIM at the 2001 Abu Dhabi arms show. Initially the Al-Khalid had an ammunition capacity of thirty-nine 125 mm rounds, 500 12.7 mm rounds and 3,000 7.62 mm rounds, but the improved version Al-Khalid I had its ammunition capacity increased to forty-nine 125 mm rounds, 1,500 12.7 mm rounds and 7,100 7.62 mm rounds, with improvements on the fire-control system, Sagem third-generation thermal imagers, sensors,

IBMS, side-skirts, track pads and autoloader (rate of fire increased to 9 rounds per minute). The Al-Khalid also had a Ukrainian Varta electro-optical jammer (disrupts laser rangefinders, laser designators and antitank guided missile tracking systems) and an improved air conditioning system. Later an upgrade on the Al-Khalid I yielded the Al-Khalid II, incorporating a redesigned turret and an upgraded armor package which has been tested to withstand all known 120 mm and 125 mm rounds. The new engine produces 1,500 hp, a 300 hp increase over the older Ukrainian engine. With more horsepower, the top road speed has been increased to 72 km/h. The MBT-2000 is also one of the best value-for-money tanks on the market. At US$2 million per tank it is one of the cheapest—Germany's Leopard 2, the British Challenger tank and Indian Arjun are all approximately US$4 million per tank and America's M1A2 is US$6 million, with the Japanese MBT-90 being the most expensive at US$8 million. For many developing countries, the Chinese MBT looks extremely good value.

Besides the Al-Khalid, the versatile T-85 also yielded another new tank, the T-96. This is a hybrid of new developments as seen on the T-85III, such as the 1,000-bhp diesel engine and explosive reactive armor (ERA) and modular armor concept as seen on the T-90. The result is the T-96, which entered service with the PLA in 1997, replacing the T-88; in fact, the production of the T-88 ceased altogether. The T-96 features a new integrated thermal imaging/day sight for all three members of the crew, a Chinese infrared/laser jamming system, improved electronics and a Western-style all-welded turret. Currently an estimated 2,000 to 2,500 are in service with the PLA, becoming the standardized MBT in service with the PLA throughout the decade. The modified variant T-96, the T-96G, was first revealed in 2006. This variant features arrow-shaped spaced add-on armor modules, which replaced the original vertically faced front armor on the basic variant T-96.

5.1.3 Third-Generation Chinese MBT

In 1984, after a series of meetings the PLA eventually settled on the Soviet T-72-based design as the basis for the third-generation Chinese main battle tank. The third-generation Chinese MBT (T-99, manufacturer designation WZ123) had its nucleus with the T-98 tank hunter. Design work began in 1984 and by the first quarter of 1989 NORINCO signed a contract with the Chinese government to manufacture the prototype of this third-generation tank. The 617 Institute was subcontracted to produce the first T-99 prototype. In August 1994, two prototypes underwent climate durability tests in southern China. During the tests, the prototypes were driven 3,800 kilometers and 200 rounds were fired. In September 1994, reliability and fording tests were carried out in the Huiahuling regions outside of Beijing. Additionally, from 1995 to 1996, three prototypes underwent Arctic climate tests in Tahe County, Heilongjiang province.

In March 1996, the T-99 project reached the final stage of its development process and by December the two prototypes (albeit incorporating many modifications based on the results of earlier tests) were again transported to Tahe for further cold-weather testing. Finally, at the end of 1999, after over five years of extensive research, the design of the T-99 prototype was finalized and was renamed the T-98. This new tank met all, and at sometimes exceeded some, of the Army's expectations and passed the final examination with flying colors. The T-98 was then accepted into the PLA. The T-98 is unique in some ways because the Chinese abandoned the autoloader system and reverted back to a four-man crew setup, loading Western-style single unit ammunition rounds, whereas the traditional Soviet-style autoloaders were designed to separately load the propellant and warhead components. Another major difference is in the transmission system, as the tank uses a manual instead of automatic like those on the T-90. Small-scale production of the T-98 began in time for it to be featured as one of the new "stars" in the 1999 National Day parade.

As soon as the T-98 went into service with the PLA, gremlins were found, and research was immediately carried out by China's 201 Institute to arrive at an "improved versions" of the tank known as T-98G (G of Gai, the Chinese for "change"). The most obvious feature of the T-98G is that the autoloader (albeit a modified and improved version of the Soviet model) was re-installed so that the crew for the T-98G was reduced to three from the original four. To boost the cross-country performance, it also incorporated a new domestically made 1,200-bhp diesel engine. At the end of 2001, the first batch of 40 T-98G tanks entered service with the regular Army, which eventually gave rise to what is now known as the T-99, which was officially revealed in 2001. The final version of the T-99 included a 1,500 hp engine, as opposed to its immediate predecessor's 1,200 hp power train, and although it matched the power output of the US Abrams, the Chinese engine still could not match the reliability of Western-made engines. Also added were a Leopard 2A5-style sloped-arrow armor plate on the front of the turret and additional composite armor layers on the sides. The T-99 is manufactured by China's Northern Industries Group Corporation (CNGC and) is the most advanced MBT fielded by the PLA. The T-99 was only built in a small number (~200) due to high unit price (16 million Chinese RMB, approximately US$1.9 million in 1999 at an exchange rate of 8.4). These tanks are currently deployed by only two elite armor regiments, in Beijing and Shenyang Military Region respectively. Some of the T-99's technologies have been used to upgrade the less expensive T-96.

5.1.4 Chinese made MBT/tanks since 1949

Type	Manufacturer designation	Main gun (mm)	Export	Comments
T-59	WZ-120	100 rifled (Type-59)	Yes	34 rounds
T-59I		100 rifled (Type-59)	May be	Incorporated laser range finder, Simplified fire control system, hydraulic steering control, a larger round escape hatch, automatic fire extinguish system and many improvements as a result from lessons learnt from 1979 Vietnam War. 34 rounds
T-59II	WZ-120B or ZTZ-59C	105 rifled (Type-79)	No	38 rounds, including APFSDS, AP, and HESH. New radio, automatic extinguisher system
T-59IIA		105 rifled (Type-81A)	No	37 rounds. Can mount ERA

(Continued)

Type	Manufacturer designation	Main gun (mm)	Export	Comments
T-59D	WZ-120C	105 rifled (Type-83A)	Possibly	Equipped with 580 hp 12150L7 engine
T-59D1		105 rifled (Type-79)	Possibly	ISFCS-212 fire control system, second-generation passive night sight, FY1/FY2 ERA. 37 rounds
T-69I	WZ121	100 smooth	No	
T-69II		105 rifled	Yes	
T-69III	WZ-121D	105 rifled	Yes	Also known as T-79
T-80	WZ-122	105 rifled (Type-83)— fume extractor and thermal sleeve	Yes	4-man crew
T-80II	BW-122	105 rifled (Type-83)— fume extractor and thermal sleeve	Yes	Export only
T-88A	ZTZ-88	105 rifled (Type-83A, copy of L5 British gun obtained from Israel) −5°−+18°	No	Autoloader, crew of three, optical sight gunner—7x or 3.5x 2,000–8,000 m ± 10 m. FY series double explosive ERA— which can resist APFSDS and HEAT-FRAG rounds
T-88B		105 rifled	May Be	Auto-loader, Crew 3, improved loading assembly for main gun. FC is image-stabilized system.
T-85	WZ-1227	105 rifled	Prototype	
T-85II		105 rifled	Yes	
T-85IIM	WZ-1228	125 (48 caliber)	Yes	Export only
T-85III		125	Prototype	
T-96	ZTZ-96	125	No	Also known as T-88C
T-98	ZTZ-98/ WZ123	125 (50 caliber)	No	"9910 Project"—to fast-track T-98 ready for 1999 National Day parade
T-99	ZTZ-99/ WZ133	125	No	

(Continued)

Type	Manufacturer designation	Main gun (mm)	Export	Comments
T-99A2		125	No	1500 hp domestically made engine with the latest FY4/FY5 ERA
MBT-2000		125 (48 caliber) smooth	Yes	Export only—eventually developed into the Al-Khalid, 1200 hp 6TD-2 engine—same as Russian T-80UD
MBT-3000		125	Yes	Export—Al-Khalid II

The Chinese "Nashorn" Panzerjäger—T-89 120 mm Tank Destroyer

After the border clash with the Soviet Union in 1969, the Chinese realized that they were totally outgunned with the emergence of the latest Soviet MBT, the T-62. Marshal Ye Jianying immediately set up a national emergency meeting with the PLA and the weapons development institutes to see how China could meet this challenge. At first China placed her hopes on obtaining the latest L44 120 mm smoothbore tank gun technology from West Germany, but under pressure from the United States, West Germany turned down China's request and the PLA was forced to develop its own 120 mm gun. After some research the best military minds in China proposed the development of a high-pressure smoothbore 120 mm antitank gun mounted on a self-propelled antitank artillery weapon system and this task was given to the Fifth Machinery Department and the PLA Armor Corps. By 1984 the initial development of said gun and its munitions, Armor Piercing Fin Stabilized Discarding Sabot (APFSDS) rounds, was completed and trials showed that the gun matched international standards closely . The main aim of the gun was to defeat the two principal Soviet tanks of the day—the T-72 and T-80. The defining characteristics of the Chinese 120 mm smoothbore gun are:

Caliber, barrel length	120/52 caliber, 6250 mm long
Ammunition	Armor Piercing Fin Stabilized Discarding Sabot (APFSDS), High Explosive Antitank (HEAT, Tracer shell and High Explosive (HE) using two-piece ammunition system— projectiles and combustible bag charges.
Penetration ability	Design targets: 1500 m or above using abovementioned ammunition, can penetrate 204 mm 68° inclination composite armor (face: 20 mm, rear: 80 mm, center 104 mm glass reinforced plastic (GRP)), Actual penetration test at 3100 m on 150 mm at 68% inclination armor
Accuracy	Result at test: 0.18 x 0.24 m at 1000 m using APFSDS
Rounds per minute	Barrel can sustain no less than 6 rounds/minute, actual using semi-autoloading can sustain 14 rounds per minute
Inclination and depression, operating temperature	−8°–+18°, −40°C to +50°C
Muzzle velocity	1740 m/s at normal temperature
Easy to maintain	No need to dismount the turret to dissemble the gun

	First prototype 120 mm	Second prototype 120 mm	Third prototype 120 mm
Recoil (mm)/ (KN)	450/490	670/390	620/450
Chassis	Model-321 prototype	Model-321 production model	Modified Model-321 with Dozer-blade
Fire Control	As Type-69 tank	TSFCS (see feature)	TSFCS
Night Vision	None	None	Yes (1100 m)
Smoke Discharger	None	None	Two sets of 4
Fire Extinguisher	Handheld	Handheld	Automatic
Radio/Intercoms	Type-889*/ Type-803	Type-889*/ Type-803	Type-889D/Type-86B (common to all SP guns)

*Vehicle-mounted FM VHF voice communication with maximum range 25–30 km VHF set, 200.00 to 499.75 MHz, Capable of 16 kbits/s data transmission in wideband mode and connected to a digital terminal set at 3 or 20 W output.

After six years of extensive testing the 120 mm smoothbore gun was finished, three prototypes were made, and the third gun was selected as the final finished product.

In a rare initiative, without obtaining any directions from the powers that be, Factory 447, a military design and production house that specialized in SP guns, continued the developmental work on the chassis and turret design. In order to keep the development work as simple as possible, the designers decided to place the gun on a model 321 chassis. The 321 chassis is the same as the 152 mm SP gun and the T-89 122 mm MBRL, two major supporting armor vehicles of its day which had the obvious advantage in simplified logistics, however the shortfall on choosing the 321 chassis was that the 321 was NOT a MBT chassis and as such the mobility and protection characters of the T-89 tank destroyer fell short of requirements for a MBT. The T-89 SP tank destroyer design philosophy followed the WWII German Nashorn Panzerjäger, light on armor but with a heavy punch and it was cheap to produce. The turret only had 50 mm armor which can at best only survive against artillery splinters and small arms fire to 12.7 mm caliber, but the relatively light body meant that the T-89 when powered by the 12150L Model 520 bhp engine, same as the T-59 MBT, could reach a relatively high road speed at 56.6 km/h.

The T-89 is equipped with the China North Industrial Group-made Tank Simplified Fire Control System (TSFCS) with night vision and laser rangefinder input, essentially the same as the T-69 MBT, that can acquire a target at 5,000 m and complete ballistic calculation and loading at 3,000 m. According to the Chinese, the T-89 could complete its first round cycle time on a stationary target within 7 seconds and 10 seconds for moving targets and the first round hit rate on a 2.3 x 2.3 m stationary target at 2,000 m was as high as 90.7% and 75.1% for similar-sized moving targets.

After completing all the tests in 1987, the T-89 Tank Destroyer went into small-scale production and between 1988 and 1989 and soon began to be deployed in selected units within the 38th and 39th Group Army for trials. Total deployment did not exceed 300 vehicles. The original plan was to showcase the T-89 Tank Destroyer to the public during the 1989 National Day parade, however because of the Tiananmen Square incident, the plan was shelved and it debuted in a 1991 movie, and it was only then that its official name was revealed as the PTZ-89 Model 120 mm SP Antitank Weapon System.

Despite the T-89's success, the necessity for such a weapon system became questionable soon after it entered service, as by 1991 the principal reasons for its existence, China's arch-enemy the Soviet Union, had ceased to exist. Following the end of the Cold War and the restoration of Sino-Russia relations in the early 1990s, the possibility of a large-scale over-land invasion was becoming more remote. As a result, the T-89 total production run was limited to just 300. As newer tank destroyers such as the 120 mm and 100 mm wheeled tank destroyer and ZTZ-99 MBT came on line, the days for the T-89 were numbered and it will soon be withdrawn from active service. However, the legacy of the T-89 should be seen as a stepping stone for the development and the total upgrading of the military industrial complex value chain, better metallurgy, better production, and better design that enabled the development of today's 125 mm high-pressure guns.

Chinese Tank Simplified Fire Control System (TSFCS)

The Chinese TSFCS is a relatively simple tank fire control system, consisting of an optical sight for the gunner, laser range finder, ballistic computer and a control panel, power source for the aiming dot, light dot driver, target azimuth velocity and speed detector, barrel-distortion sensor and a dual-axis stabilizer. The commander has his own general observation scope and his dedicated night-viewing devices plus four or more vision-block periscopes. The gunner and loader have their own fixed vision-block periscopes.

The operation procedure for the TSFCS is as follows: After the gunner has acquired the target he will illuminate the inverted arrow in the center of his scope which he has already aligned with the target. The gunner will track the target for two seconds after which he will engage the laser range finder and a number will then appear in the gunner's scope as well as the aiming off mark if the target is a moving target. At the same time the gun aligns to the target and after the gun is stabilized using the control panel it is then moved to the aiming point to be aligned with the target. Once it is aligned the gun can fire.

The gunner's sight is a single eye scope with 3.5x and 7x magnification points. Angle of view is 9° and 18° respectively for 200–800 m. Data from the range finder, azimuth velocity sensor, and barrel distortion are all automatically entered into the ballistic computer, but the temperature, cross wind, characteristic of the rounds such as muzzle velocity, charge temperature etc. have to be entered into the computer by hand, which makes this obsolete equipment. The computer operational scope is from 200 m to 3,000 m and accuracy is ±0.1 mils.

T-98 MBT

The Chinese Type-98 was the first of the new third-generation MBTs to enter service with the PLA. The plan for a third-generation MBT started in April 1978 at a fateful meeting held in Datong, Shanxi province. The National Defense Technological and Industrial Committee and the Fifth Machinery Division, under the direction of the National Armament Department, initiated a meeting that was known as the 784 meeting where the design standard for the second-generation (later to be the third-generation) MBT were set. At the end of the meeting the committee decided that the new

Chinese MBT would use the Leopard 2 as a comparison and the tank was to be designed with the Soviet T-72 as the main adversary.

In 1979, with 617 Factory as the manufacturer and 201 Institute as the design office successfully revealed the basic test model, named Model-1224. This test model was equipped with a 120 mm smoothbore gun and hydraulic automatic transmissions, friction shock absorbers and the German-made MB8V331TC41 engine. Later two more prototypes, Model 1226 and 1226F2 were made, with the purpose of testing the 8V165 diesel engine developed by 636 Factory and the rival 12V150 engine by 616 Factory. The design of these prototypes were heavily influenced by the Leopard 2, as for a time the PLA was considering importing the Leopard 2 as the Chinese MBT. During this heyday, Chinese tank designers and the PLA's armor corps specialists were frequent visitors to Germany. However due to cost and political reasons the Chinese decided to drop the Leopard 2 option and continued to design an all-Chinese tank, albeit with much German influence. In 1981, after T-80 was named as a second-generation MBT, the yet to be developed Model-1224 and 1226 and 1226F2 were later renamed as third-generation MBT projects.

In the years between 1981 and 1984, the Chinese tank designers were engaged in a big debate as to how the third-generation MBT would take shape. The conservative school of thought argued that the new MBT would be best based on the T-72 design; as the Chinese military industrial value chain was set up based on the Soviet model and Soviet tank designs are familiar to generations of Chinese tankers and designers. This would formulate an easy, cheap, low-risky option for the new Chinese MBT. However, a group of progressive designers lobbied for the Israel Merkava MBT design. In fact, the two camps could not see eye to eye on anything: among the issues debated were whether the main gun should be the 120 mm Western gun or the Soviet 125 mm gun; a crew of four or a crew of three with autoloader; front-mounted versus rear-mounted engine; petrol versus diesel fuel etc. The dispute was settled only in 1984 with the conservative camp coming out on top. As a result, the conservatives pushed for a new start by getting rid of the designers "tainted" by the progressive camp; 201 Institute, a new tank design house was appointed to lead the project and with this came a new tank designer, the infamous one-armed Professor Zhu Yusheng.

In the spring of 1989, the General Staff Office signed a contract with NORINCO for three third-generation MBT prototypes, with 617 Factory given the job to manufacture these test vehicles. In 1992, four more prototypes appeared and more stringent technical standards were incorporated into the design. For example, one of the key changes was a more substantial survivability rate, and as a result the frontal armor on the turret was increased from 600 mm to 700 mm. In August 1994 two of the four prototypes were put through their paces in the tropical heat of south China, and later in September carried out reliability and water fording tests in Beijing. Testing continued from 1995 to 1998, including cold weather trials in Tahe of Heilongjiang in northeast China. The trials were completed only in 1998 and the success of the new MBT was such good news to the politicians that the tank was chosen to be a highlight in the 1999 National Day parade, the 50th year of the founding of the republic. All in all, the T-98 project lasted almost ten years and cost hundreds of millions RMB, making it the costliest tank in the history of China.

No sooner had the development of the T-98 been completed than work on the improved T-98 began, not only to iron out gremlins and to improve overall reliability, but because designers soon found out that the T-98 was inferior to the MBT-2000. Both tanks were equipped with the same engine but the MBT-2000 had the engine mounted sideways, not only reducing the overall length to 6.5 m from the 7.6 m of the T-98, but also the weight, the MBT-2000 weighed only 46 tons and thus had a much better power-to-weight ratio. After some consideration, the designer decided to mount the T-98 turret on the MBT-2000 chassis, giving improved performance. This feature was then incorporated as "standard" in the improved T-98 MBT. Delay caused by production and technological glitches meant that the improved T-98 only began to be deployed in numbers as late as 2001.

The general outlook of the T-98 has an unmistakably Soviet feel. The body looks almost exactly like an enlarged version of a T-72; in fact, the T-98 is almost one meter longer than the T-72. The glacis plate of the tank bears the unmistaken "V" of the T-72. The driver sits centrally in the front of the tank and is equipped with a night viewing as well as a day view vision block. In addition to that the driver has access to passive night goggles for night driving that can add 200 m of viewing ability. Driving is conventional with two levers, left and right, the accelerator is the right pedal as in a car and also, unique to a tank, there is a fuel tank selector. The driver must first engage which tank to pump fuel from before starting ignition. In the turret the commander sits on the starboard side and gunner on the port. The commander has five 360° vision blocks and one forward-mounted gyro-stabilized day and night observation scope and a radar range finder that is integrated with the gunner and the digitized fire control system. The commander and gunner have dual control of the gun and can share information from each other's data screens. The system is connected with a host of external sensors such as cross-wind sensor, barrel alignment sensor and turret gyroscope. This system differs from the older TSFCS that was essentially an optical system, not an image-stabilized sight system. The older TSFCS had no means by which the gunner and commander could exchange information, a feature that is coming in the modern new fire control system. According to the Chinese the first shot time for a stationary-to-stationary target is less than 5 seconds and a moving-to-moving shot is less than 9 seconds with an 85% hit rate at 2,000 m range. In the improved T-98, there is a built-in error detection and correction system that tracks the shot as it leaves the barrel, and shots that miss the target will automatically adjust the data for the second shot, thus increasing the hit possibility to 100% (as claimed by the data released). Like all modern tanks the Type-98 is equipped with a SPRITE (Signal Processing in the Element) thermal imager with two magnifications, 11.4x and 5x, with a detection range of 2,750 m in the dark. The improved Type-98 has an upgraded second-generation thermal imaging system that employs an infrared thermograph instrument technology that does not need to be super cooled with liquid nitrogen, thus easing the logistics burden, and on top of that it gives a much improved performance at 4,000 m observation range.

During the design phase, the designer, Professor Zhu, did consider seriously using the 120 mm gun. It was eventually dropped in favor of the smoothbore 125 mm (derived from the Soviet 2A46m-1 125 mm gun) with autoloader. This was due to a number of factors: first the 125 mm system is well-known to the Chinese, and using this option would not only be cheaper but also reduce design lead time. Second, the 120 mm autoloader is not only much larger than the Soviet model but mechanically also very complicated. After looking into the French Leclerc and the Japanese MBT-90 tank, which both have adopted the autoloading 120 mm gun, the Chinese still prefer the 125 mm gun using two-piece ammunition, first as a matter of safety, second the Chinese simply love the Soviet-style APFSDS tungsten/uranium penetrator. It is reported that this round, with its extreme high muzzle velocity of 1,780 m/s, can penetrate 850 mm HRA at 2,000 m. In recent years, news from the Chinese press refers to an even more powerful AT round. This is a depleted uranium kinetic energy penetrator AFPSDS that is reported to have penetration capacity up to 960 mm. In addition to the AFFSDS round, the Type-98 also carries some special ammunition that includes four Chinese copies of the Soviet 9K119 Svir laser beam riding, guided antitank missiles (NATO: Sniper). The Type-98 normally carries a coaxial Type-86 7.62 mm machine gun, and a QJC88 12.7 mm turret-mounted HMG for the driver, but in special circumstances three additional HMG AA gun mounts can be mounted on specially prepared mounts on the turret. The crew carry their normal sidearms, which is normally the Model-56C or Model-95 carbine.

The low profile of the T-98 is one of its best defenses—from top to bottom it is just 2.3 m in height compared with 3.03 m for the German Leopard 2A6, 2.53 m for the French AMX Leclerc, 2.49 m for the British Challenger, and 2.44 m for the M1 Abrams. For protection on the glacis plate and the turret mantel there is upgradable composite armor comprised of a complex mix of steel and glass-fiber. It has an actual thickness of 220 mm, but the actual protection level is equal to 600 mm RHA steel. The turret is protected by a still-classified armor composite that has the equivalent of 800 mm RHA of protection. During the trials, one T-98 prototype survived fourteen rounds of APFSDA from a 105 mm gun and six rounds from a Soviet T-72C 125 mm gun. On the side is a belt of 8 mm thick rubber that gives some protection against HEAT antitank rounds like the RPG.

To reduce chances against top penetration attack, the T-98 is the first Chinese tank to be equipped with a protection system against top-attack guided missiles that comprises an IR disrupter, smoke generators and laser warning sensors which are especially designed against mainstream Western weapons such as the TOW, Hellfire, Dragon, Milan, Maverick and HOT antitank missile systems. Although not sold as a foolproof system, the protection available to the T-98 can reduce the hit rate by 60%. In addition to passive protection, the improved T-98 also carries active defense such as the Doppler radar system and Russian AREAN Active Protection System (APS).

As far back as 1960 the Chinese were already working on an AFV automatic fire suppression system. However, due to the disruption caused by the Cultural Revolution, progress was slow. The lessons learnt from the 1979 Sino-Vietnam War put a renewed urgency into the project, but as the country opened up in the 1980s, Western technology became available. Instead of making its own the Chinese just bought a Western Automatic Fire Extinguish System (AFES) off the shelf. It was soon made mandatory in all Chinese AFVs and from which over the years the Chinese made improvements to the system to include explosion suppression. The Automatic Explosion Suppression System (AESS) that the T-98 had installed is the Type-92 AESS using Halon 1301 as its fire suppression agent.

Communication-wise, the T-98 is equipped with a VHF-2000 FM AFV radio system that incorporates an IFF (Identification Friend Foe) system and optical laser communication system that can carry data as well as voice transmissions. On top of the turret toward the rear is a Model 9602 GPS system that is accurate only to 100 m. On the improved T-98 the GPS system is upgraded to the GLONSS/GPS system that gives accuracy to 20 m.

The T-98 is the first Chinese tank to be equipped with the laser suppressed observation and sighting system. Mounted towards the rear of the gunner hatch it is operated by both the gunner and the commander. It uses lasers to suppress the enemy's sighting system, with also the capacity to incapacitate the enemy's observation and sighting system and even to blind enemy personnel. After depressing the engaged button for one second, the system will emit 1,000 joules of pulse repetition frequency at 10 cycles per second up to 4,000 m range.

Originally the T-98 was to be powered by a MTU's MB871ka501 engine from Germany, but the international embargo that was imposed on China after 1989 led to the Chinese making its own version of the German engine. Named 150HB, it is a turbocharged diesel engine that develops 1,200 bhp giving the 51 tons T-98 23.54 bhp/ton power to weight ratio with a top speed of 70 km/h on the road and can accelerate 0–32 km/h in 12 seconds. The improved Type-98 has an uprated 150BH that gives 1,500bhp, increasing the top road speed to 80 km/h and cross-country speed to 60 km/h. The T-98 is equipped with automatic transmission with two epicyclical gearboxes (or planetary gearing) with seven forward gears and one rear gear.

5.2 Chinese AFVs

The limitation of this book forbids me to go into every type of Chinese AFV; however, if I were forced to make a choice from the list of many, the obvious choice is to focus on probably the best known of all the Chinese AFVs, the T-63 APC. If the US-made M113 APC holds the honor of the most ubiquitous tracked AFV in the world, second on the list is the Soviet Union's BMP IVF. Coming in third on this list is the Chinese-made T-63 family[5] of APCs. While the first two on the list have ceased production, the Chinese are still making the venerable T-63, and reports claim that some 8,000 have been made so far.

The story of the T-63 begins in July 1958, when the central government of the People's Republic of China proclaimed a national scientific development strategic plan that called for a tracked armored personnel carrier that could be ready for mass production in 1960—in less than two years, a tall order by any measure! Yong Ding Machinery Factory—later incorporated into the NORINCO Vehicle Group—was to be responsible for the manufacturing of the new APC and the design work was left to the No. 1 Institute of the First Machinery Works, assisted by the Fourth Faculty of the Harbin Engineering Academy, all under the supervision of the Scientific Department of the PLA Armor Corps, Fifth Department of First Machinery Works, and Soviet experts. In the beginning, much hope was placed on the Soviet experts, but the Chinese were soon to discover that most of them had no clue how to build a tracked AFV, probably as the Soviets themselves did not have a good tracked APC. Located in the southwest of Beijing, Ying Dong Machinery Works was at that time nothing more than an armored vehicle repair workshop—it was as though a high street car repair workshop was asked to mass-produce a car! To make matters worse, while there was external help from the Soviets to make a new tank, the agreement did not cover APCs and the Soviets would not provide any technical drawings nor equipment to aid manufacturing.

Soon thereafter, a name needed to be assigned to the project, a name which—like all previous Chinese armament projects—would disguise the project's real purpose. With this intention in mind it became known as "Project 58-72." The initial design was based on the US M-59 APC, and after much debate it was decided to go for a 12-ton amphibious tracked fully enclosed armored personnel vehicle. By September 1958, a draft design was ready and handed to the Soviet experts for comments. The experts threw the paper back saying that it would never run, let alone float. Furthermore, the Soviet military thinking at that time still preferred an open-top design where infantry debark from the carrier by leaping over the top, despite the experience of the 1956 Hungarian revolt where countless APCs were destroyed in narrow streets with homemade Molotov cocktails. The Chinese decided that the Soviets were wrong, and soon after the Chinese decided to go it alone with no further consultations with the Soviet experts. The first prototype was ready on March 28, 1959, and on the next day it was taken for flotation tests during which it promptly sank because the vehicle was unbalanced and too front heavy. Such was the level of engineering competency in China at that time that centers of gravity and buoyancy were not part of the calculations! The generals were eager to have their new "tanks" on parade, however, and "requested" the new APC participate in the October 1959 National Day. Thirty sample vehicles were rushed off the production line but were taken off the march-pass at the last minute as they were still deemed mechanically unstable. By September 1959, the vehicle received a new name, albeit from the design bureau code: Vehicle 531.

The system used by the Chinese in naming their tanks and armored vehicles has always been a mystery to many in the West. According to a document issued by the Fifth Machinery Works, all Chinese tracked AFVs were to be codified in a three-digit code. The first number, in this case 5, means the AFV is a transporter, the second digit, in this case 3, is the code for amphibious capability, and the third and last digit is the code from the factory, in this case 1, as it was the first vehicle that Yong Ding Works designed. Models made for exports have two alphabet letters preceding the three numbers. For example, export model YW-531 APC (a T-63), where Y stands for Yong Ding, the manufacturer, and W stands for Wai Mao, which means external trade. In models that are destined for domestic service, the prefix is WZ followed by a three-digit code. WZ stands for the Armored Fighting Vehicles from the Fifth Machinery Works, with W short for Wu (number 5) and Z is *Zhuang Jia*, or armored. Sometimes a suffix would appear, such as WZ-531G where G is the manufacturer design order code.

In 1961, WZ-531 went into troop trials and feedback soon pointed out a number of modifications required. The result was an improved APC that was to be known as the A531 and it was this version that eventually became the mass production model known as the T-63 (a PLA name) in March 1963. Externally there is little difference between the 531 and A531, the only notable difference being that WZ-531 was armed with a 7.62 mm MG while the A531 was upgraded with a 12.7 mm HMG. By 1965 all older 531 models were upgraded to the A531 standard.

In the 1970s, as demanded by the army, NORINCO was tasked with mounting a 122 mm field gun on the T-63 to create a SP gun for the PLA, which later saw service as the T-70-1 122 mm SP gun. However, the designers at NORINCO soon found out that the chassis needed to be strengthened and the characteristic four road wheels needed to upgrade to five with three idlers; as a result the chassis was also extended by 226 mm. The result was the B531, which later evolved into the T-85, or exported under the name of YW-531H. Domestically the B531 found service with the PLA as the T-63-1 or WZ-302 according to NORINCO's standard. Mechanically it is a big improvement on the previous T-63 model—more firing ports and vision blocks, larger exit hatches, and an armored shield were installed for the commander around the 12.7 mm HMG, all as a result from lessons learnt from the 1979 Vietnam War. By the mid-1970s the Western attitude toward China began to soften. This allowed the Chinese to access Western technology, particularly a diesel engine from Klöckner Humboldt Deutz AG of Cologne, West Germany. This engine proved to be superior to the Chinese 6150L water-cooled diesel power plant, and soon became the standard driver for the T-63, and by 1979 the Chinese loved it so much that NORINCO became the licensed manufacturer of the Khd 413F engine in China.

In the 1980s, the "new" China was recovering from years of seclusion, and hungry for foreign exchange, the Chinese government started looking at the overseas market for its weapons. The T-63 was a candidate for export and it was marketed as the YW-531C and later expanded to the YW-531D model as well (equals to the T-63C, and the YW-531E was in fact the T-63CA). To upgrade the technology, the Chinese soon began to cooperate with foreign arms manufacturers. NORINCO founded a partnership with Britain's Vickers and this union yielded the YW-531L, or according to the British, the NVH1. The NVH1 was essentially a T-85 mounted with a Vickers design turret that mounts a 30 mm British Rarden cannon or can also mount an American M242 25 mm Bushmaster auto-cannon.

Another attempt in Sino-Western cooperation created the YW-531M, which was essentially a T-85 with a LSG-1000 transmission unit from Zahnraederfabrik Friedrichshafen AG of Germany. However, neither of these "marriages" lasted, as all died a premature death due to the fallout from the 1989 Tiananmen Square incident. As one door closed, another opened however. The Iran-Iraq war of the 1980s created an unprecedented opportunity for the Chinese. In July 1981, to the astonishment of the Chinese, on their first export drive they netted an order for 450 T-63s from Iraq. The Iraqis asked for six points of modifications that included, understandably, an improved cooling system for a hot desert environment. True to their promise, the Iraqis made a down payment of US$25 million and the first batch of forty modified T-63s, renamed the YW-531C, was delivered on January 31, 1982. Striking while the iron was still hot, NORINCO tried out a new modification of the T-63 on their new deep-pocketed customer, Iraq, the all-new YW-750 armored ambulance and its sister the YW-701A armored command post. To their astonishment, Saddam made an order for 600 more on the spot! Other lovers of the T-63 include Thailand. In 1988 the Royal Thai Army purchased 450 YW-531H APCs, later named the T-85. This order included a small number of YW-304s with 81 mm and YW-381s with 120 mm mortar carriers as well as the YW-306, a MBRL with thirty 130 mm rockets. Although the T-85 of Thailand never saw combat, it played an active role in the coup d'état of 2006 and "Red and Yellow Shirt" civil disturbance of 2010. Sri Lanka bought twenty YW-531s in 1991–92 and later added a host of YW-309s, which were essentially T-85s with a BMP-style turret, a model that is unique to Sri Lanka.

While a great number of T-63s saw action around the world, the only time that the T-63 went to war in the hands of the PLA was in the 1979 Sino-Vietnam War in which only limited numbers were involved. The original intention was to use the T-63 to carry infantry to accompany and protect the tank columns. Each infantry division would contain a battalion's worth of T-63s, while it was designed as personnel carriers, but in essence many of the T-63s ended up as command and communication vehicles, rendering what was already limited in quantity truly scarce, forcing many of the infantryman to ride on the tanks. The lack of APCs was a major source of PLA casualties. According to PLA sources, the largest infantry unit that was truly armor protected was only a company-sized formation. The troops loved the T-63 as it not only offered much-needed protection but had excellent cross-country capability. However, the T-63 was also prone to breaking down, especially its running gear, and to throwing its tracks. Other variants of the T-63 that saw service in Vietnam included WZ-751 armored ambulances, where often they doubled up as MASH, and T-81 armored command centers which were only seen at divisional level.

The T-63 also saw service in civilian applications. The YD-801 is an adapted 531 APC used for fighting forest fires, while the BFC-802 is a newer version that is based on the T-85 chassis. Characteristically they are painted bright red and serve as fireproof carriers for firefighters, able to take them safely to the heart of a burning forest.

While China was making the T-63 tracked APC, it also embarked on making a wheeled 8x8 APC, with the manufacture designation WZ-552-1, which was first trialed in 1971. Despite passing all tests, however, it was not accepted into service.

NORINCO's Northern Industries Vehicle Group

NORINCO or China North Industries Group Corporation (or "Northern Industries") is also known in China as the China Armaments Industries Group Corporation (CNGC). NORINCO is a Chinese company that manufactures vehicles (trucks, cars and motorcycles), machinery, and many other items.[6] In addition, NORINCO is also involved in domestic civil construction projects. Northern Industries Vehicle Group is a subsidiary of NORINCO that specializes in tracked vehicle manufacturing.

Northern Industries Vehicle Group was founded in 1980; it traces its roots to an armored train repair workshop during the Japanese occupation of China. After WWII, the Chinese Republican Government incorporated this workshop into the No. 27 Vehicle Factory, which essentially was still responsible for the repair of rail carriages and engines. After the founding of the People's Republic of China, the factory became a military establishment and was renamed the PLA Railway Corps' Third Corps Repair Workshop and later it was renamed The First Factory of the PLA Motorized Armored Corps. In 1951 it was named the Northern Vehicle Manufacturing Factory. During the Korean War, the factory was responsible for repairing Soviet-made tanks such as the T-34/85, the IS-2, and the Su-76. The T-63 is the Northern Industries Vehicle Group's most famous military product, but it also manufactured a range of buses and coaches for the civilian market. During the 1980s, when China was in the grip of nationwide commercial fever, the PLA also wanted to get into some form of money making venture. The result was the establishment of the Poly Group Trading Corporation. The main aim was to deals in arms and weapons. The establishment of the Poly Group coincided with the Iran-Iraq War, and both sides purchased arms from China in great numbers, making the Poly Group one of the most profitable companies in China, though it diverted many of the PLA's soldiers away from their true profession.

5.3 Modernizing the PLAAF—"Project 906," Bringing the SU-27 to China

Having been starved of modern technology for almost thirty years, the PLA's Air Force realized that it needed to modernize pretty rapidly. One of the key operational issues that plagued the PLAAF in the late 1980s was the combat radius of its planes, particularly its fighters. Even the upgraded J-8II was unable to operate at the distance China demanded. The clash with the Vietnamese on March 11, 1988 was just such an example. Although the PLA Navy was able to retake the Johnson South Reef, due to lack of air cover the PLAN had to retire as soon as the battle was over. The Chinese had at that time nothing to counter the Soviet threat that was based in Cam Ranh Bay with a formidable force of sixteen TU-16 (NATO: Badger) long-distance bombers and fourteen MiG-23 (NATO: Fencer) fighter bombers. Furthermore, Vietnam was equipped with the SU-22M4; all were capable of threatening the Chinese warships should they remain at Johnson Reef.

The urgency was clear, and within a week of the battle the PLAAF initiated "Project 883," with the single purpose of extending the operational radius of the J-8II fighter by enlarging its fuel-carrying capacity. Gone were the two 760-liter wing tanks and the fuselage 850-liter tank to be replaced by a single FYX1400 fuel tank that added 610 liters to the fuel-carrying capacity. In September that year, the PLAAF initiated another project to tackle the issue of limited operational range, by attempting to test the possibility of mid-air refueling using a modified H-6 bomber with the J-8II. The project was named "Project 8911" and such was the urgency that all tests were completed by the end of October and the J-8II that was modified with a fixed air-to-air refueling probe became known as the J-8D.

Besides the issue of limited operational radius, another handicap that plagued the PLAAF was the fleet of second-generation fighters that it depended on. Fully realizing that it was at least a generation behind in fighter technology, the Chinese were increasingly worried. By the mid-1980s, the Soviets were beginning to renew its fighters with the MiG-29 and SU-27; furthermore, in 1987 a visit to Beijing by the USAF display team, the "Thunderbirds," with their F-16s, truly stunned the Chinese. The military and economic embargo brought on by the 1989 Tiananmen Square incident limited the PLAAF's options, while at the same time the Nationalist Chinese in Taiwan managed to add F-16s and Mirage 2000s to their ORBAT. The strategic balance over the Taiwan Straits suddenly tipped towards Taiwan's favor. Things were looking pretty grim for the generals in Beijing.

With the Western option closed, the Chinese turned to their old enemy, the Soviets. In May 1990, the Deputy Chairman of the CCC, General Liu Qinhua, made a visit to Moscow and signed a MOU to initiate discussions for purchasing Soviet warplanes. The technical team soon followed in June to kick-start serious discussion. For the Russians, the deal with the Chinese was providential. The financial difficulties they were facing at the end of the Soviet era were crippling, but at the same time the Russian government was also fearful of the Chinese. Chinese SU-27s with their longer ranges might have security implications for Russia; with these issues in mind the Russians decided to push the short-range air superiority fighter, the MiG-29.

The Chinese, however, were after a long-range fighter and the MiG-29 was not what they wanted. Furthermore, its ability to take on F-16s and Mirage 2000s was not convincing. The negotiation soon fell into a deadlock. But then General Yevgeny Shaposhnikov, the last C-in-C of the Soviet Union, personally intervened and made a push for the SU-27, much to the annoyance of the Soviet government and its Minister of Defense.

The Chinese were overjoyed at the change in the Soviets' stance and the Chinese CCC confirmed that the SU-27 was the plane they wanted. Negotiations followed till the end of December 1990, at which point both sides were able to confirm the purchase of twenty-four SU-27s (twenty SU-27SKs and four twin-seat trainer SU-27UBKs) with an option for another twenty-four. The Chinese SU-27 was to be designated as SK, "S" being production model and "K" being modifications made as per client request, in this case the Chinese, which in Russian is spelled with an initial "K." The Soviets drove a hard bargain, requiring the Chinese to pay 70% up front with the rest on delivery, with the deal carried out through a counter trade rather than hard cash as China in the early 1990s was still pretty poor.

The Chinese SU-27 raised the maximum lift-off weight from 28,000 kg to 33,000 kg and increased the weapon-carrying ability with a total of ten external hardpoints that could carry a host of bombs (250 and 500 kg dumb bombs and incendiaries) and FFR rockets (100 with 80, 122 and 266 mm). With the extra weight the undercarriage and parts of the airframe needed to be strengthened as well, but the increased weight meant a slight loss of performance, especially on the two-seat training model. As with all exported military hardware, Russia retained some technological secrets. The SU-27SK model was equipped with the L203/L204 active jammer and not the regular Russian L005 model. The early batch of twenty-four MiGs was equipped with the SUV-27 fire control system with flight instrumentation incorporating two CRT multifunction displays (MFD) of similar size, one on top of the other with the upper MFD fitted to the right of the HUD. The Su-27SK was equipped with RLPK-27 radar couple with a N001E antenna that was capable of 80 –100 km search range and 60–70 km tracking range with up to ten targets at the same time. However, due to the limited computing power of the TS101M processor, it could only attack one of the ten targets at any given time. The latter deliveries were upgraded with a N001P antenna with the Baguet series BCVM-486-6 processor that increased TWS accuracy and allowed for two simultaneous target attacks. Furthermore, only the latter batch of Sukhois had the A737 GPS navigation system.

If the Chinese Sukhoi were to be deployed as an air superiority fighter, it could carry up to six R-27 long- to medium-range air-to-air missiles (NATO: AA-10 Alamo) and four R-73 (NATO: AA-11 Archer) IR heat-seeking short-range missiles. However, the twin-seated SU-27UBK could not carry the R-77 AAM medium-range active radar homing air-to-air missiles (NATO: AA-12 Adder).

Despite the collapse of the Soviet Union, the new Russian Federation kept to the deal and the first of the twelve "modern" fighters duly arrived on June 27, 1992 and the second batch on November 25, 1992; however, the arrival of the twenty-four modern Russian fighters was not the end of the story. In any plan the Chinese always look at the long term. The strategic aim of the Chinese was always to make their own weapons: as soon as the Sukhoi landed, in early 1993, the Chinese took the opportunity to learn as much they could from the Sukhoi experts, pilots, and engineering teams coming to China. The Russian experts were there not only to train the Chinese in using and maintaining the Sukhoi but also to inspect the Shenyang aviation factory, a site which would do the local maintenance and upgrades of the plane. Much to their surprise, the Chinese experts soon discovered some "unknown" limitations to the SU-27SK, such as the maximum fuel load under normal circumstances was 6 tons; the vertical fin was so flimsy that if the plane was travelling at over 600 km/h, the speed reduction spoilers could be deployed, etc.

China began to ask certain questions; such as could Russia transfer a SU-27SK production line to China. Initially Russia was not keen, however China indicated that if that was so, the Chinese would limit the SU-27SK purchase to just the forty-eight planes and that would be the end of future deals. After much banging of heads, eventually a deal was reached; Russia agreed to supply China with a SU-27 production line. First Russia would supply China with knockdown kits and parts to facilitate the eventual production of the entire SU-27SK in China.

Fast forward to May 1993, when the Chinese Vice-Minister of Aviation Industry, Wang Ang, led a team of aviation experts to Russia. The delegation made a number of visits to the factories that produced the Sukhoi and its components. In addition to the main site at Komsomolsk-on-Amur in the far east of Russia, the team also went to see the production of the SU-30 in Irkutsk. The Irkutsk team was facing financial difficulties and was hoping to rope the Chinese into helping them develop an upgraded version of the SU-30 fighter. They decided to hijack the project to persuade the Chinese to produce this upgraded SU-30 in China instead of the SU-27SK. Stunned by this backstabbing the Komsomolsk-on-Amur factory team, the principal production base of the SU-27, was fuming, but the SU-30 proposal fell flat as soon as the Chinese saw the price tag. The instruction from the CCC was simple, stick to the SU-27.

By the end of August 1993, the Chinese reached an internal understanding that the SU-27SK production line would only consist of airframe and power system production as well as the capacity to conduct a major overhaul of the Sukhoi engine. The project officially received the name "Project 11," and after six rounds of negotiations the final contract was signed on December 6, 1995 in Moscow. To Russia's delight the Chinese also confirmed the follow-up order of twenty-four SU-27SKs, and this time paid for the order in hard cash: US dollars.

Project 11 was not without its hiccups. The data and CNS received by the Chinese were often incomplete and at times also quite confusing. CNS from the Sukhoi design office and the Komsomolsk-on-Amur factory were at times conflicting. Furthermore, the abbreviations, symbols and terms used by Sukhoi office were different to those used by the Mikoyan-and-Gurevich team, which the Chinese were familiar with. A lack of Russian speakers amongst the new generation of aircraft designers was also a problem. Many of the old retired experts who had been schooled in Moscow were invited in to help. These and other problems delayed the project somewhat and it was not until the end of November 1997 that the production drawings, all translated to Chinese standard, were delivered to the Shenyang Aircraft Corporation. The first two SU-27SKs, No. 0001 and 0002 rolled off the line in the first half of 1998. After extensive testing, the two SU-27s were handed over to the PLAAF on Christmas Eve 1998 as training aids. These two planes would be eventually deployed to an operational squadron in Tibet.

The first sixteen SU-27SKs were essentially test planes, while the initial batch was largely made from Russian-supplied parts, the later batches were increasingly made with local components. For example, No. 0004 was a test bed for the Chinese Tai Hang WS-10 power-plant[7] and No. 0013 became the test plane for locally made fire control system and weaponry. Like all things new, there were glitches to be fixed. The compatibility of Russian-supplied systems with Chinese weaponry and current PLAAF in-use ground support/logistics systems were key problems. The translation and modification of Russian-made navigation and fire control systems was especially difficult. Fully localized with Chinese components, the SU-27SK was to be named the J-11, after "Project 11." Soon after deployment the PLAAF came back with series of comments and suggestions for improvements; these included the use of the Chinese Tai Hang power plant, full EFIS electronic cockpit with new locally made avionics with AESA radar and power systems, domestic Chinese helmet-mounted sight (HMS), use of composite materials (reducing the weight by 700 kg) and reduced RCS, MAWS, IRST, and standardization of parts and components to be compatible with Chinese logistics and support systems were just some of the items on the wish list.

Incorporating these upgrades resulted in a new designation for the J-11. The J-IIB, as it was to be known, made its first flight on December 6, 2003. By mid-2006 the J-11B became fully operational with the PLAAF.

As the PLAN launched its first aircraft carrier in 2012, the need for a suitable carrier fighter became apparent. The SU-33 was the obvious choice as it was designed for Soviet carriers. However, the SU-33 was a 1975 design armed with 1980s weaponry and avionics, and was no match for the US F-18 Hornets or the French Rafaels. With this in mind the Chinese were hoping to "navalize" the SU-27SK and wanted to obtain a few SU-33 as test-beds. The Chinese soon made a request to buy the SU-33 for its carrier but were rejected on the count of insufficient order size. The Chinese then turned to Ukraine for help and managed to buy the early production model of the SU-33, the T-10K-3 prototype. The SU-33 airframe was essentially the same as the SU-27, so using the Ukrainian sample and their experience in developing the J-11B the Chinese soon came up with a naval version of the J-11B, named J-15 (*Flying Shark*). The J-15 differs from the J-11B mainly on account of the additional canards or foreplanes, foldable main wings, an air-to-air refueling probe, strengthened undercarriage with twin wheel supports, night refueling lamps, the IR probe positioning on the starboard, and finally an arrester hook. The J-15 prototype made its first flight on August 31, 2009 and its first carrier launch on May 5, 2010 with a Russian-supplied AL-31 turbofan engine, later changed to a Chinese-made FWS-10H turbofan engine with an increase of thrust to 12,800 kg, compared to the J-10s FWS-10 turbofan's 12,500 kg. There is still plenty of testing to be done before full deployment of the J-15; but as the PLAN's indigenous carrier is now launched the Chinese will still have time to iron out a few bugs before full operational deployment.

5.3.1 In Search of Even Greater Range—the SU-30MKK

The US military interventions into Afghanistan and Iraq clearly show what war in the 21st century will look like. The USAF precision strike capability has clearly demonstrated the differences between them and the Chinese, and with this in mind the PLAAF began to change its mission focus from air defense to air attack. The demand for even greater range continued, such that during the visit of Premier Li Peng to Moscow at the end of 1996 he signed an MOU for a massive arms sale worth US$180 million that included forty multirole fighters. In 1988 the Sukhoi design team was tasked with meeting this challenge. Because of their prior cooperation with the Komsomolsk-on-Amur factory on the SU-27SK project, the Chinese specifically required the same team to partner with them on this project and to deal directly with the factory in Komsomolsk-on-Amur.

The Sukhoi team used the SU-30 as a base and made modifications to it to squeeze more fuel-carrying capacity into the jet. The final solution was a SU-30 but incorporating SU-27M technology to develop this new plane for the Chinese. New materials were used, especially for the tail fin that could incorporate fuel tanks for the first time. In addition to the added fuel tanks on the tail fin, the fuel-carrying capacity of fuselage and wings was also increased. The forward No. 1 tank was increased to 3,150 kg; the rear No. 3 fuel tank to 1,053 kg; and the mid-section No. 2 fuel tank capacity was expanded to 4,150 kg. The No. 4 wing tank now holds 1,552 kg. The total lift-off weight now is a massive 38 tons, making the SU-30MKK one of the heaviest fighters of the Sukhoi family.

After two years of negotiation the contract was finally sealed at the 1988 Zhuhai air show, and during the visit of Premier Zhu Rongji to Moscow in March 1999, a contract for thirty-eight SU-30MKKs was confirmed. As Premier Zhu was signing the deal, the first unarmed SU-30MKK prototype (named T10PU-5, "Blue 05") made its maiden flight on March 9, 1999. The second prototype, "Blue 502," flew in the summer of 1999 and even made it to the 2000 Zhuhai air show to stun the crowds. Two more prototypes, "Blue 503" and "Blue 504," followed, and after extensive testing all were handed to the PLAAF. Deliveries were made in three batches: the first ten were delivered on December 20, 2000, the second ten in August 2001 and the last eighteen before the end of 2001. Happy with the SU-30MKK, the Chinese placed another order for thirty-eight, for delivery by December 2002.

With two more additional hardpoints, the SU-30MKK is capable of carrying even the heaviest 2,000 kg air-to-ground missile. The weapons load has increased from the 6 ton of the SU-27SK to 8 tons.

In the air superiority role, the SU-30MKK can be equipped with all missiles, including the R-77 AAM medium-range and R-73 short-range missiles, while in its air-to-ground role the SU-30MKK can carry precision-guided air-to-ground weapons such as the Kh-59, 29 and three guided missiles as well as the KAB laser-guided missile.

The Chinese SU-30MKK is a unique one-of-a-kind airplane. The fire control system is comprised of two parts: the SUV-VEP air-to-air system and SUV-P air-to-ground system, to better meet different targeting conditions, and the two separate systems are each equipped with their own detection systems. As with the SU-27SK the Russians kept back their own secrets and only equipped the SU-30MKK with RLPK-27 radar, but lined to a simplified version of the N001V antenna, named N001VE that limits search range to 80–100 km and simultaneous strikes by R-77 AAM on two targets at the same time.

Satisfied with the SU-30MKK, the Chinese placed another order for twenty-four aircraft in January 2003, this time for PLA naval aviation, to be named the SU-30MK2. Delivered in two batches, the final twelve arrived in China in August 2004. The Navy's Sukhoi differs from the PLAAF's, with a better antenna system, the N001VEP, with a greater detection range that reaches 110 km, and with a weapons system that incorporates the Kh-59MK and Kh-31A anti-ship missiles.

5.3.2 The Future of Sukhoi in China

The SU-27/J-11 has been serving the PLAAF and PLAN for twenty years together with the locally designed J-10 "*Vigorous Dragon*," now the principal fighter for the PLA. As the development of the fourth-generation fighters, the J-20 and J-31 stealth, is still ongoing, China is looking for a stopgap fighter that will breach the gap between the SU-27 and the new J-20. The Chinese love affair with Sukhoi may not end with SU-30MKK. As of the end of 2012 the Chinese have already signed an MOU for buying the SU-35S. If the SU-35S is brought to China, it will incorporate the Chinese-designed Type "E" fire control system that is already deployed on the "*Snow Leopard*" JH-7 fighter (NATO: Flounder). Capable of detection ranges of 350–400 km, it can commit up to eight active missiles simultaneously and is a far cry from the current installed Russian fire control system. Another interest the Chinese have in the SU-35S is the Saturn (Al-41F-1S) 117S Turbofan engine with trust vector technology, something that the Chinese lack, and if the SU-35S can indeed be introduced to China, it will massively support the development of jet power technology, an area where the Chinese still lag behind.

The latest reports in China talk of a new strike plane by Shenyang Aircraft Corporation, known as the J-16 fighter/bomber. It is based on the Shenyang J-11 airframe but incorporates design elements of the Russian Sukhoi Su-30MKK.

5.3.3 China's F-16—Development of the J-10

The J-10, known in the West as the "*Vigorous Dragon*," is a multirole all-weather fighter aircraft designed and produced by the Chengdu Aircraft Industry Corporation (CAC) for the PLAAF. The development of the J-10 can be traced back to the 1960s and China's attempt to develop its own fighter, the J-9. In 1961, soon after the Soviets agreed to transfer the MiG-21 manufacturing rights to China, Sino-Soviet détente broke down and the Soviet Union withdrew all their advisors from China. Plodding along on its own, China had no choice but to complete the final prototype without Soviet assistance. Soon the Chinese found out that the MiG-21 F13 had two major limitations: short combat range and limited payload, which meant it could only serve as an area interceptor, quite unsuitable for a vast country like China. Even before the first J-7 (locally manufactured MiG-21) left the factory in 1964, Institute 601, as Shenyang aircraft design and research center was then called, began working on improving the model. Soon an ambitious plan emerged that called for an uprated version of a MiG-21 with twin engines that matched the F-4 Phantom's ability in every respect, and which eventually was named the J-8. However, a rival plan by another institute, the 611, to develop a second option—a single-engine air superiority fighter and interceptor, the J-9—was also approved. To ensure success China was betting on two options: the J-8 was seen as the safe option while the J-9 was more ambitious and adventurous. The development of the J-9 faced many challenges: the "too many cooks" syndrome was one, and the chaos caused by the Cultural Revolution also did not help. However, the less glamorous J-8 was proceeding ahead on its own with little interference, and by July 5, 1969 it made its maiden flight.

By 1978 when China decided on a new path by opening up the country, many of the unproven projects still requiring work were terminated—including the J-9, and the PLAAF's hope for a new fighter rested on the J-8II and the improved J-7III.

However, during the height of the Cultural Revolution another fighter development project was initiated. The J-12 was a single-seat lightweight, supersonic, inexpensive, STOL (short take-off and landing) fighter design with low-set swept wings, swept control surfaces, tubular fuselage, and nose intake with small or absent shock cone. The aim was to have the J-12 replace the J-6, which was a local copy of the

Changes in Specifications for the J-9				
Time	Speed (Mach)	Ceiling (m)	Range (km)	Combat radius (km)
October 1964	2.2	20,000	1,600	–
	2.3 (fighter)	20,000	–	450
April 1965	2.4–2.5 (interceptor)	21,000–22,000	–	350
April 1966	2.4–2.5	21,000–20,000	–	600
June 1970	2.2–2.5	20,000–21,000	3,000	800–1,000
November 1970	2.6	26,000	–	–
January 1975	2.3–2.5	23,000	2,000	600

Key events of the development of the Chinese fighter prior to J-10			
Year	J-9	J-13	Others
1964	601 Institute made two proposals for new Chinese fighters, J-8 and J-9		
1965	601 Institute came up with four options for the J-9		Approval given for J-8 design to start work

(Continued)

Key events of the development of the Chinese fighter prior to J-10			
Year	J-9	J-13	Others
1966	Proposed specification for J-9 approved		J-7 entered into mass production
1967	601 Institute proposed a delta wing design for J-9		
1968	Delta wing concept entered into detail design stage		Approval given for J-12 design to start work
1969	Design work move to 611 Institute		J-8 and J-12 made its maiden flight
1970	PLAAF changed specification twice in one year!		
1971	J-9 became a research project for advance aerodynamics research	J-13 design work started by 601 Institute	
1972-1974			
1975	Restart development work on J-9 and funding for five prototypes were approved.	PLAAF affirm the need for J-6, production is to continue	Brought Spey Mk202 engines from the UK
1976	Final design accepted— settled on canard configuration	Initial design and avionics needs on J-13 completed. J-13 to be powered by the WS-6 engine	Commence development work on J-8I
1977			Approval on new design of bomber H7
1978	Major design work finished		J-12 project terminated, J-7II made its maiden flight
1979		Re-equipped using WP-15, a copy of the Soviet MiG-23's R-29	
1980	Project terminated	WP-15 engine is approved for production	Design work for J-8II given the green light
1981		Project terminated	Design work on J-7III and J-7M to start. J-8II made first flight

MiG-19 (NATO: Farmer). The lead designer was the Nanchang Aircraft Manufacturing Company (NAMC), and just one year after the start of the project the prototype flew, but the performance was disappointing, so additional prototypes were built with improvements such as simplified control surfaces, a lighter area ruled fuselage and revised intake. In 1978, development of the J-12 was abandoned. The reasons cited were insufficient firepower and engine thrust, and at the same time the mature J-7 design, based on the Soviet MiG-21F, was considered superior. Another rival fighter project that died while still at embryonic stage was the Shenyang J-13, also a lightweight, single-engine fighter design by the 601 Institute with a similar intention as the J-12, i.e., a replacement for the J-6.

Problems with producing suitable airframes continued to be a constant problem in many Chinese aircraft projects. The lack of viable, high-performance engines was another key problem area, which incidentally is an area in which the Chinese aircraft industry is still weak. The initial plan was to use the WS-9 (turbofan) engine (a copy of the British Rolls-Royce Spey Mk. 202 engine), but setbacks in its development led to initial testing with the WS-6 turbofan engine (which was capable of providing 12,200 kg of thrust). In August 1978, the Chinese purchased two MiG-23MS (NATO: Flogger-E, export variant of MiG-23M), two MiG-23BN (NATO: Flogger-H; ground attack version), two MiG-23U (NATO: Flogger-C, twin seat trainer), ten MiG-21MF (NATO: Fishbed-J), and ten KSR-2 (NATO: AS-5 Kelt) ASM cruise missiles in exchange for spare parts and technical support for the Egyptian air force's large fleet of MiG-17 (NATO: Fresco) and MiG-21s that was left stranded after the break in Soviet-Egyptian relations. One of the Egyptian MiG-23MS was sent to the 601 Institute and by March 1979 an order to reverse-engineer the MiG-23's Tumansky R-29 turbojet engine was placed by the project, which by the late 1970s had finalised its design and officially been allocated the designation J-13. The Chinese R-29 copy, called the "WP-15" (WP—Turbojet, capable of 12,500 kg of wet thrust), like the earlier WS-6 engine, proved to be disappointing. Delays caused by engine problems and the success of Shenyang with its redesigned J-8II caused funding to be severely cut by 1981. No prototypes of the J-13 were ever built, but one airframe was later incorporated into the further development of Chengdu's J-10 project. Although an entirely Chinese design, the J-13 bore a passing resemblance to the French Dassault Mirage F1 fighter aircraft. The tailless delta-canard is aerodynamically unstable, and to control it requires a sophisticated computerized control system, or "fly-by-wire" (FBW) on a digital quadruplex (four-channel FBW system), which was developed by the 611 Institute. The J-10 incorporates many of China's latest technologies, including indigenous fire control radar, the KLJ-10, developed by the Nanjing Research Institute of Electronic Technology (NRIET). For the J-10B, the up-rated J-10, the nose cone is modified to accommodate an active phased array airborne radar (AESA) developed by the 607 Research Institute that, according to the Chinese press, took eight years to develop and is capable of tracking ten targets and engaging two or four of them simultaneously, depending on whether it was equipped with a semi or active homing missile system.

The J-10B was made with increased radar absorbent material composites, a new EW suite and avionics with a diverter-less supersonic inlet (DSI), an infrared search and track (IRST) sensor, and is powered by an upgraded WS-10B engine developed by the Shenyang-based AVIC Aviation Engine Institute (also known as 606 Institute). The Shenyang Liming Aero-Engine Group carried on the development of the indigenous WS-10. The revised design was known as the WS-10A, or "Taihang," its commercial name.

The controls take the form of a conventional center stick and a throttle stick located to the left of the pilot. These also incorporate "hands on throttle and stick" (HOTAS) controls and a zero-zero ejection seat was provided for the pilot, permitting safe ejection in an emergency even at zero altitude and zero speed. The cockpit had three liquid crystal (LCD) multi-function displays (MFD) along with a Chinese-developed holographic head-up display (HUD), all of which are fully compatible with a domestic Chinese advanced helmet-mounted sight (HMS).

The weapons internally stored by the J-10 consisted of a Type-23/3 twin-barrel 23 mm cannon and it was equipped with eleven external store stations for weapons carriage, three under each wing and five under the fuselage. For interception missions, the J-10 could carry a mix of medium-range air-to-air missiles (MRAAM), short-range air-to-air missiles (SRAAM) such as the PL-11/PL-12, or the short-ranged PL-8/PL-9. Another first for the J-10 was that it was the first Chinese-made fighter to have surface attack capabilities in mind right from the design stage and was also capable of all-weather offensive strikes.

5.4 China's Rotary Wing—the rise of vertical aviation in China

As with fixed wing aircraft, China's attempt in producing helicopters was at first totally dependent on Soviet assistance. The Harbin ZHI-5 (Vertical-5) is a Chinese copy of the Soviet Mi-4 (NATO: Hound) piston engine helicopter built using Soviet-supplied blueprints, and the first flight was made on December 14, 1958. That year China was in the depth of the "Great Leap Forward," a political campaign that called for rapid industrialization and collectivization and placed undue priorities on quantity over quality. As a result of these unrealistic demands, the first ten ZHI-5s were all written off. After the Sino-Soviet split, the Chinese were initially lost on how to proceed, and it was only after many years of trial and error that serial production became possible in the mid-1960s. The ZHI-5 saw service with the PLA, PLAAF, and PLANAF and was exported to a number of Communist states, but the PLA was unhappy with the ZHI-5, as improvements in power and metallurgy allowed for greater range and flying ceiling.

China's first attempt in rotary wing aviation was a total failure. It was launched in 1958 by leading aviation academies throughout the nation. Up to nineteen separate projects were initiated, but despite some early promises all failed to develop beyond the prototype stage.

In 1966 China was propelled into further chaos by the Cultural Revolution. During this period there were numerous attempts to bring a Chinese helicopter to reality. Of the many projects, four notable attempts were made and cloning the Bell 47 was one. In 1963 an unusual exhibit became a crowd pleaser in the Beijing Military Museum—it was an Indian Army Bell 47-G3, captured in the 1962 Sino-India border war. The Harbin Aircraft Factory was tasked to clone the helicopter and by 1968 a Chinese Bell-47, renamed as "helicopter 701," became reality.

However, the PLA did not take a liking to this helicopter, calling it "out of date," and despite early promises it never made it to mass production. Another helicopter that suffered the same fate was the 1978 "Yanan No. 2," a light observation helicopter that resembled the Mi-4 (NATO: Hound) and which lifted off from Nanjing Dongshan aerodrome on September 4, 1975. Despite exceeding many of the parameters demanded by the PLA, it too failed to move to mass production and the project was terminated. The third attempt was a larger troop- and freight-carrying helicopter that resembled the Soviet Mi-6 (NATO: HIP). This helicopter was named ZHI-6 and never made it to the production line due to many insurmountable technological problems. Flight tests revealed excessive vibration and insufficient tail rotor thrust, as well as the engine and main rotor gearbox overheating; a fatal crash of a prototype in 1972 killed all six occupants including the pilot. Political turmoil took a great toll on the economic and industrial development. Armament manufacture was also affected such that by 1979 the Chinese themselves had given up on the ZHI-6 because the single engine design was deemed unsafe and under-powered. While the 701, ZHI-6 and Yanan No. 2 were all light utility helicopters (LUH), the ZHI-7 was an equally ambitious attempt to develop a Medium Support Helicopter (MSH) with a load-carrying capacity of 4,500 kg. By 1979 the ZHI-7 had passed all wind-tunnel tests, but the opening up of China in 1978 meant that foreign assistance was again on the agenda and all Chinese attempts at developing a home-grown helicopter were suspended.

5.4.1 The ZHI family of Chinese helicopters

By 1978 the Chinese were painfully aware that the ZHI-5, the only helicopter in service in China was totally out of date; a design built in the 1950s was serving twenty years beyond its intended service life. After making the rounds, the Chinese chose two potential targets for cooperation, the Bell-212 and Bell-412, the Huey family of twin blade utility helicopters from the United States, and the Dauphine range of helicopters from Aérospatiale in France. Initially Bell had the upper hand because during the two preceding years, the Ministry of Forestry and Petroleum had purchased eight Bell-212s and since this was the first time the Chinese had operated Western helicopters, they had nothing even close to compare. At the end, however, the French won the Chinese over, mainly because they were more open and willing to share more of the technology with the Chinese. On July 2, 1980, China signed an agreement to purchase fifty SA-365N/N1 Dauphine helicopters from France and there was also a technology transfer to enable local production of SA-365N1 Dauphine II and the Arriel turbo shaft engines. The first fifty Dauphine and 100 Arriel engines were assembled from French-supplied parts (of the fifty locally assembled Dauphine, twenty-eight were ZHI-9, twenty were ZHI-9A, which was equivalent SA-365N2 standard, and two were of the ZHI-9A-100 model—domestic market versions with locally manufactured Arriel engines known as WZ8A engines) then moving to gradual substitution by local manufactured parts. Later on the ZHI-9 was upgraded to the SA-365N2 standard and a further twenty-two ZHI-9s were made under license as well as eight ZHI-9 civilian models.

An armed variant has been in service with the PLA since the early 1990s, known as the Z-9W; it was essentially a Dauphine SA-365 with pylons fitted for antitank missiles. However, the Chinese were not content with the Z-9W and measures were made to develop a true attack helicopter, later known as the Z-10W. While the Z-10 was being developed, upgrading of the Z-9W continued. The Z-9WA and later the ZHI-9G were essentially Z-9Ws with night-attack capabilities achieved by mounting a FLIR on the nose. They also incorporated a Chinese-designed helmet-mounted sight that was compatible with anti-tank missiles such as HJ-8/9/10, as well as light anti-ship missiles such as the C-701/703 and TL-1/10 when they were used as air-to-surface missiles. It is also compatible with air-to-air missiles such as TY-90 and other MANPAD missiles used for helicopter self-defense. The Z-9C is a naval variant first introduced in 1987 and was actually a locally manufactured Eurocopter AS-565 Panther. As well as SAR and ASW duties, the Z-9C can carry two YU-7 torpedoes (reverse-engineered US Mk-46 torpedoes) and other ASW depth charges. In addition, the Z-9C was fitted with an X-band KLC-1 surface search radar to detect surface targets beyond the range of shipborne radar systems.

In addition to the ZHI-9, China also received from the French CNS for the Aérospatiale SA-321 Super Frelon (Super Hornet) and a locally produced version is known as the ZHI-8. China's first experience with the Super Frelon was back in 1977–78 when it purchased thirteen SA-321 helicopters for the navy. These helicopters came in two forms: anti-submarine warfare (ASW) and search and rescue (SAR). These versions were the first helicopters of the PLA to be capable of operating from the flight deck of surface vessels. China's quest for a large helicopter went back to 1973 when Changhe Aviation Manufacturing Company initiated a development project for a large helicopter. The Ministry of Aviation invested 45 million RMB to build a new factory with new machines and tools for this project. At least one of the Super Frelon helicopters was disassembled for survey and reverse engineering. By 1980, 70% of the design work was completed for the Chinese copy of the SA-321, designated ZHI-8, but the opening of China in 1978 saw the reprioritizing of resources and the project was nearly halted until the intervention of CMC Deputy Chairman Yang Shangkun. The first flight was made on December 11, 1985 but the design finalization was not completed until 1994.

For ASW missions, the ZHI-8 was equipped with a surface search radar and a French HS-12 dipping sonar while carrying a Whitehead A244S torpedo under the starboard side of the fuselage. The SAR version, the ZHI-8S, had upgraded avionics and a searchlight, FLIR turret and a hoist. Another rescue variant with dedicated medevac equipment onboard is known as the ZHI-8JH.

The ZHI-8A version was developed as an army transport variant but only one batch of about six ZHI-8As were delivered to the PLA. Starting in 2007, the PLAAF also acquired dozens of upgraded ZHI-8Ks and ZHI-8KAs for SAR missions; they were equipped with a FLIR turret and a searchlight underneath the cabin, plus a hoist and a flare dispenser.

A third Chinese helicopter, named the ZHI-11, was a Chinese development based on the French AS 350B Squirrel helicopter, which first flew in 1974. However, the ZHI-11 was not simply a reverse-engineered copy of the AS 350B. The major changes were in nose shape and internal structure. China's Helicopter Design Institute and Changhe Aircraft Industry Group

(CAIG), both located in Jingdezhen, Jiangxi Province, were appointed as main contractors for the project. The maiden flight was in December 1994 and production began in 1997. The PLA Army Aviation Corps Training Regiment has received a total of thirty-seven ZHI-11s in the ZHI-11J (military) model for training since September 1998.

An armed variant of the ZHI-11, known as ZHI-11W, was made for battlefield surveillance and reconnaissance, ground attack, and medical evacuation roles. It is comparable to the US OH-58D Kiowa. The ZHI-11W employs an optical TV/IR sighted mount on the roof of the cockpit and has external weapon pylons for four HJ-8 antitank missiles or four unguided rocket pods. It also has an improved cockpit featuring a color LCD multi-functional display.

The ZHI-10W is China's first true attack helicopter. Known to the Chinese as Fierce Thunderbolt, it was designed and built by Changhe Aircraft Industries Corporation (CAIC) primarily for antitank missions but it has secondary air-to-air capability as well. The ZHI-10 is thought to have some influence from the South African Rooivalk, via the secretive cooperation between South Africa and China which was often mentioned but never officially publicized. The development of a dedicated attack helicopter began in the mid-1990s and by April 29, 2003 the first prototype made its maiden flight.

In the 1970s, after the border clash with the Soviet Union, the Chinese military found that they had a major problem countering large armor formations. The ground forces went for a tank killer, a long-range cannon solution, as a missile solution was still beyond the reach of the PLA then. In the 1980s, as technology improved, the idea of missile defense resurfaced. It concluded that the best conventional solution was attack helicopters. The PLA decided that a dedicated attack helicopter was required. At the time, the only available helicopters were civilian helicopters converted for the military, but they were not adequate in the true attack role and were only suitable as scouts.

Following this, China evaluated the Agusta A129 Mangusta, and eight Aérospatiale Gazelles armed with Euromissile HOT were procured for evaluation. In 1988 they secured an agreement with the United States to purchase AH-1 Cobras and a license to produce BGM-71 TOW missiles;

the latter was cancelled following the Tiananmen Square incident of 1989 and the resulting arms embargo. The fall of Eastern Bloc nations prevented the purchase of attack helicopters from Eastern Europe, and both Bulgaria and Russia rejected Chinese offers to purchase the Mi-24.

Despite the setbacks the PLA went ahead with developing helicopter tactics. This led to the formation of the People's Liberation Army Ground Force Aircraft (PLAGFAF), with an initial strength of nine ZHI-9s. Research by the PLA also decided that the new Chinese attack helicopter needed to be a missile-centered design with antitank missiles, but the BGM-71 TOW was deemed inadequate and the PLA favored something more like the AGM-114 Hellfire.

To bypass the Western technology embargo, the 602nd and 608th Research Institutes started development of the 6-ton class China Medium Helicopter which was promoted as a civilian project. Support was gained from Eurocopter (rotor installation design consultancy), Pratt & Whitney Canada (PT6C turboshaft engine) and Agusta Westland (transmission); the medium helicopter could continue to develop technology used by both military and civilian aircraft.

In 2000, the Chinese again attempted to obtain a Russian attack helicopter, but the deal for the Kamov Ka-50 and the Mil Mi-28 deal both fell apart. With no choices left to them the Chinese decided to ignore foreign options and develop its own aircraft, and work on the ZHI-10W was accelerated.

The ZHI-10W was revolutionary in many respects. First, instead of using French standard DIGIBUS, the ZHI-10W is built to the Chinese GJV289A standard, the Chinese equivalent of MIL-STD-1553B. The adaptation of Western military standards means that Western weaponry could be readily deployed on the ZHI-10W and this would also help to expand the export potential in the future. ZHI-10W was also the very first indigenous Chinese helicopter to adopt HOTAS, but a traditional conventional control system had been developed in parallel as a backup, just as in the case of cockpit MFDs and for exactly the same reason that two configurations of flight instrumentation were developed in parallel. Unlike previous Chinese helicopters which had different independent navigational systems on board, the navigational systems of ZHI-10Ws are fully integrated and a modified Blue Sky navigation pod can also be carried, thus allowing information to be shared via secured datalink that provide real-time and near real-time information. The ZHI-10W also has the capacity to incorporate helmet-mounted sight (HMS) designed by the 613th Research Institute that is fully integrated into the overall FCS.

Whereas the initial production of the ZHI-10W was all powered by foreign engines, in the future, long-term, they will be the domestic WZ-9 (*Wo Zhou* turboshaft), designed by the 602nd Research Institute with Ukrainian and Russian assistance. Although the WZ-9 is not as powerful as the P&W engine, it enjoys the advantage of lower operational cost because there are no foreign components. Furthermore, since it is 100% built in China, there are no political issues that would affect the purchase of vital parts.

Another new engine is under development, by China and Turbomeca. It is called the WZ-16 turboshaft engine. After the installation of the new engines, power for ZHI-10W will be capable of carrying sixteen missiles instead of the current ten on the four hardpoints.

The heart of the ZHI-10W is the antitank missile system, and the HJ-10 (*Hong Jian*, Red Arrow) is the key. The HJ-10 thought to be similar to the AGM-114 Hellfire. The main air-to-air missile deployed is the TY-90, a missile specifically designed for use by helicopters in aerial combat, although more traditional PL-9s can also be carried.

The latest model of the Chinese ZHI family of helicopters is the ZHI-19, which is a tandem twin seat version of the ZHI-9W. The ZHI-19 is a new Chinese light scout and observation helicopter locally developed in China by Harbin. The whole development program was kept highly secret and the ZHI-19 was only publicly revealed in 2012. First to be equipped by the ZHI-19 were the 8th and 9th Regiments based in Beijing, then later Chengdu's 2nd Brigade and Lanzhou's 3rd Brigade. It will operate alongside the dedicated ZHI-10W attack helicopter.

The cooperation between France and China in helicopter development is not likely to end in the near future, and a new ZHI-15 helicopter will be another model created by the two nations. The ZHI-15 is a 7-ton class medium utility helicopter being developed by Eurocopter and AVIC. Two production lines were set up, one in Europe and one in China; each is responsible for production and marketing in its respective area. In Europe, it is known as the Eurocopter EC175. The PLA is reported to have taken delivery of the ZHI-15 as a replacement for much of its existing fleet (older Mil Mi-8, Sikorsky S-70, ZHI-8 and ZHI-9).

Other works in progress include the trinational (China, Singapore, and France) EC-120 light helicopter. The Eurocopter EC-120 Colibri (English: Hummingbird) is a five-seat, single-engine, single main rotor light helicopter that is produced in China as the HC-120. The PLA Army and local police forces have purchased a small number of HC-120 helicopters.

Naming of Chinese Aircraft

The original system used by the manufacturers consisted of fancy-sounding and sometimes Communist-flavored names that were appropriate for the times—East Wind (*Dongfeng*) for fighters, Flying Dragon (*FeiLong*) for bombers, Mighty Eagle (*XionYing*) for attack aircraft, Red Craftsman (*Hong Jiang*) for trainers—and a three-digit numbering system. The first digit was a code for the aircraft class (1 = fighter, 2 = bomber, 3 = attack aircraft, 4 = transport aircraft, 5 = trainer) and the other two ran consecutively (for example, Dongfeng-101 through Dongfeng-l13). The military, however, used two-digit service designations matching the last two numbers of the year when the type was accepted for service, in 1959, for example, became the Type 59, Type 59A and Type 59B respectively.

In 1964, China switched to a new system used by both the manufacturers and the PLAAF/PLANAF, which designated the aircraft by role. The Chinese word(s) denoting this role were usually abbreviated to a one- or two-letter prefix followed by a sequential number within each class of aircraft: BA (*Baji—*target plane), CJ (*Chuji Jiaolianji—*primary trainer plane), H (*Hongzhaji–* bomber plane), J (*Jianjiji—*destroyer plane or fighter), JH (*Jianji Hongzhaji*—fighter-bomber), JL (*Jiaolianji*—[advanced] training plane), Q (*Qiangjiji*—strong attack aircraft), SH (*Shuishang Hongzhaji* maritime bomber, i.e.: flying boat), WZ (*WurenZhenchaji*—unmanned reconnaissance plane), X (*Xiangji*—glider), Y (*Yunshuji*—transport), Z (*Zhishengji*—"vertically rising plane," i.e.: helicopter). A curious aspect of this system was that the numeric designator was not lower than 5; this was reportedly due to superstitious reasons, as the Chinese numeral "four" sounds very similar to the Chinese word for "death"—in some buildings in China and especially in Hong Kong there is no fourth or fourteenth floor.

Consecutive versions were identified by Roman numerals; thus, the J-7 fighter was followed by the J-7 I, J-7 II, J-7 III and J-7 IV. After 1987, the Roman numerals were replaced by Roman letters; thus, the H-6 IV became the H-6D, though this is not a hard and fast rule—in some cases, the letters did not match the former numerals, denoting a different version. Export aircraft wore further "Westernized" designations—for instance, the Q-5 III became the A-5C, where A is for Attack. In the case of specialized planes, an extra letter is used: for example, D for electric/electronic (*Dian*), U for Oil (*You*, tanker) and Z for *Zhenchaji* (reconnaissance plane).

5.5 Building Warships for the PLAN

This chapter does not serve to be an encyclopedic listing of the entire history of warship building in China but by highlighting a particular example, and building around anecdotal tales that surround the design, construction and service of this vessel, I hope to give the reader an insight into what the PLAN was then and how these experiences fostered the building of the modern Chinese Navy. The vessel in question is the Type 65 frigate. I choose this because it is the first "large" vessel entirely designed and built by the Chinese.

In the early days of the Republic, the Communist Chinese received massive aid from the Soviet Union. For the PLAN, they received four ex-Soviet *Gremyashchiy*-class destroyers (the official Soviet designation was Project 7). Better known as *Gnevny*-class destroyers, these WWII leftovers were to become principal warships in the early 1950s. In Chinese literature these four ex-Soviet destroyers, then renamed as Type 6607 Destroyers, or later just Type 07 (NATO: *Anshan*-class) were collectively known as the "Four Heavenly Guardians" after the mythical Four Heavenly Guardians that are commonly seen in Chinese temples. These were purchased in the 1950s after the plan to buy former British Royal Navy vessels fell through due to the onset of the Korean War. Instead, the Chinese turned to the USSR to buy four worn-out destroyers with 17 tons of gold—a hefty price by any calculation. With the four ex-Soviet *Gnevny*-class destroyers also came materials and instructions to build a further four Soviet Project 50 *Gornostay*-class (NATO: *Riga*) frigates, assembled in China as Type 6601 (NATO: *Chengdu*-class), but before the 6601 was finished Sino-Soviet relations turned sour and the Chinese were left with CNS ownership of the boat but without weapons, radar key, and other essential items. Therefore, no further 6601s were built. As China moved into the era of turmoil of the "Great Leap Forward," which morphed into the Cultural Revolution, mad concepts were dreamt up by political hotheads. One such program was the Project 022 frigate that demanded specifications beyond China's ability. In the 1960s, raids and harassment by the Nationalist Chinese and the United States intensified, especially in southern China. With only one old escort, CNS *Nanning*, pennant number 230 (ex-IJN Type 1C coastal defense escort) in the Southern Fleet and reinforcement from the Eastern and Northern fleet out of the question on the account of the naval blockage by the US Pacific Fleet, the only option was to build a modern frigate using what material was available to the Southern Fleet. The result was later known as the Type 065 (NATO: *Jiangnan*-class), and the lead boat was completed in 1965.

As with many weapons systems that were built by China in the 1960s, the break from the Soviets left the Chinese in a lurch. The first issue was finding an appropriate power source for the Type 065. The *Riga*-class frigate was powered by a TV9 steam turbine that China was incapable of copying; furthermore it was also too big and the heavy demand on fuel made it unsuitable for the new Type 065. Although China was, at that time, trying to clone the TB-8 and TB-9 steam turbine, the success was uncertain and it was deemed too risky to choose this power source for the new frigate. The designer soon turned to the diesel 37D and 9EDZ43/76 models as they were available at the time. Both these engines were being manufactured in China. However, whereas the 37D model was available, as it was the power source for the *Whiskey*-class submarine, a vessel that was being manufactured in China, the 37D was incapable of going into reverse. Not a good choice for a frigate! There was, however, a possible option in the 37DR engine that did have a reverse mode. Nevertheless, the Soviets never gave the CNS instructions to do so and reverse engineering it was not guaranteed to succeed. Although the model 9EDZ43/76 was not hampered by its ability to go into reverse gear, the engine was huge and its power was poor, so that if it was to power the Type 065 this new frigate would have a poorer performance than the Type 6601 *Riga* clone. The Chinese were left with no choice. 9EDZ43/76 was to be the engine for the Type 065. Initially the designers came up with three options:

Option 1: Power plant of three 37DR diesel engines giving 26 knots top speed. Main armaments are three single-barrel 100 mm guns.

Option 2: Power plant of two 9EDZ43/76 diesel engines, giving top speed of only 20 knots. Armaments same as Option 1.

Option 3: A smaller version of Option 2 that, by reducing the total displacement, gave the boat a top speed of 24 knots. The main armament was reduced to two 100 mm guns and anti-submarine weapons were discarded.

By June 1962, as the effort to clone the 37DR engine was deemed totally impossible, Option 1 was therefore scrapped. Option 3 was deemed too weak in the eyes of the PLAN, so at the end Option 2 became the final approved design. However, as one problem was solved, another appeared. The gigantic size of the 9EDZ43/76 diesel engine became an issue. It has a height of 4.5 m, which meant if it were to fit in the vessel the overall keel to deck depth had to be expanded to 6.8 m. In a vessel that displaced only 1,000 tons this would affect stability as the boat would have a higher than normal center of gravity.

To solve the problem, the naval architects chose to have a split-level deck with a long raised deck stretching from the bow to about three quarters down the hull and a shorter freeboard at the stern of the ship. Further efforts in improving the efficiency of the engine and a better propeller to create less cavitation would further enhance the speed of the vessel. The designed speed was pushed up to 20.5 knots, but at the end during testing, a top speed of 21.5 knots was achieved. It was beyond the capacity of the Chinese to clone the 100 mm B-31 gun that was supplied on the Type 6601 Chinese *Riga*. However, the Soviet Union did supply a number of 100 mm V-34 56 caliber shore battery guns that were found to be similar to the naval gun of the *Riga*. The Chinese took these shore guns and mounted them on the Type 065. With a range of 22.4 km, these guns were entirely manually loaded and fired and had only a semi-enclosed turret which left some of the gun crew exposed. The question of gun positioning was also a problem for the naval architects. After it was decided that the vessel would mount three 100 mm guns, it was a question of 2 front/1 back or 2 back/1 front mounting. If it was to be the former, in a staggered design, the bridge needed to be raised in order to have an unobstructed view of the bow, but a heightened bridge meant a higher center of gravity and poorer stability which, since the South China Sea is prone to typhoons, would definitely cause problems. In the end, a compromise was reached and the designers settled for a 1 front/2 rear design. Auxiliary weapons-wise, the Type 065 had four Type 61 twin barrel 37 mm (copy of the Soviet Bu-11 37 mm) manually operated open gun mounts. These are the most commonly carried gun systems on Chinese ships. These guns are highly limited—they can be operated only in clear weather conditions and are effective only in daylight conditions since they lack radar coordination or any form of automatic or autonomous targeting. They are, however, economical and highly reliable. Their firepower has been effectively utilized not only against aircraft but also against surface and land targets.

In addition to the anti-aircraft role there was one 14.5 HMG on each side of the bridge. Due to its low speed, the boat did not have any torpedoes but was mounted with two Type 65 five-barrel ASROC launchers (copy of the Soviet RBU-1200) and four Type 64 432 mm depth charge dischargers. The Chinese ASROC suffered from an inherent design flaw from being on a fixed mount and unable to swivel to aim; to fire the ASROC the whole boat had to be maneuvered to aim the weapon. In terms of search capacity, it was very limited. There was a Soviet Zarnitsa (NATO: Skinhead) search 80kW S-band radar with only 20 km range, and a Soviet Tamir HF sonar (NATO: Stag Hoof) that could only provide 800–1,300 m range. Another first for this unique vessel was that it was the first surface warship in China to be equipped with an air-conditioning system, an ultimate luxury at a time when most Chinese had never seen or heard what an air-conditioner was, and even the mayor's office in Guangzhou did not have any air-conditioning. Getting a posting to a Type 065 was like a ticket to the ultimate dream job for sailors in the Southern Fleet.

The building of the Type 065 started in 1964 with the laying of the keel in Shanghai. The lead vessel CNS *Haikou* (pennant number 529) had an overall length of 90 m, beam of 10.2 m and a depth of 6.8 m. The average draft reached 2.9 m displacing 1,250 ton when fully loaded and was capable of 21.5 knots top speed and a cruising speed of 16 knots with a range of 50,000 kilometers. The subsequent vessels CNS *Dongchun* (504), *Xiaguan* (501), *Nanchong* (502), and *Kaiyuan* (503) were all built in Guangzhou and saw service with the Southern Fleet.

The most famous of all the Type 065s launched was no doubt the CNS *Nanchong* (502). At launch the vessel bore the pennant number of 232 but did not have a name—during the 1960s, the Chinese had very different ship naming rules, 232 was just a number on the list of vessels and it happens this vessel was the 232nd vessel in the PLA Navy.

Prior to the arrival of the Type 065 frigate, the PLAN was reactive to events. Due to the limitations of the vessels at hand, the Nationalist Chinese had a relatively easy time conducting raids and nuisance attacks on Communist China. China at that time was only able to conduct littoral defense, much of it supported by militias in coastal cities and villages. However, with the arrival of these new frigates, with their greater range and bigger guns, the Communist Chinese were able to assert greater rights to the nation's maritime territories. It was under these conditions that the two naval clashes with Vietnam, first in 1974 (see "Battle of the Paracel Islands") and then in 1988 over the Johnson South Reef or Chiguajiao materialized.

On both occasions, CNS *Nanchong* played a role. In 1974, when the vessel was just known as CNS *232*, it was part of the reinforcement/amphibious force that came to the rescue. In the 1988 battle CNS *Nanchong* was front and center of the event. *Nanchong* continued to serve the PLAN until 1994 when it was transferred to the Qingdao National Naval Museum. For many years it became a key attraction of the museum until September 2012 when the rusted hull proved too expensive to repair and sadly it was scrapped. This unlikely decision caused a ferocious protest, which may force the PLA to relook into its whole policy of how to protect military heritage.

Another very important warship in the history of the PLA was the Type 051 (NATO: *Lvda*) missile destroyer. It was the first Chinese ocean-going warship to be fitted with an integrated combat direction system. Based on the Soviet *Kotlin*-class destroyer design, which was partially transferred to the Chinese before the break in Sino-Soviet relations, the Chinese had to overcome many technical problems to build the new destroyer. Research began in the late 1950s at the Seventh Academy. By the mid-1960s, the No. 701 Institute, under the auspices of the Seventh Academy, began developing a first-generation guided missile destroyer under the leadership of Mr. Li Fuli and Mr. Pan Jingfu as chief and deputy designers. The destroyer's standards were to have 3,000 tons of displacement or more and to be powered by steam power. Construction began in 1968 in the Dalian Shipyard. The *Lvda* is significant because it was the first vessel that was not obsolete as soon it was constructed but was able to hold its own against vessels from the USSR or USA. The killer app was its six HY-1 guided missiles. With a range of 50 km, it could outshoot and outgun the Soviet *Kashin*-class destroyers which had only four first-generation P-15 Termit (NATO: Styx or SSN-2) anti-ship missiles that had a range of only 40 km and also the standard missiles of the US Navy of the 1960s—the RIM-2 Terrier system had only a range of 32 km and could only be matched by the later RIM-8 Talos SSM. Although some sixteen of the class were completed, each with new upgraded variants with better electronics and weapons, the vessel was ultimately still a boat designed in the 1950s. Whilst the Type 051 had fearsome AShM, it lacked SAM and was largely still a gun-dependent vessel. The integrated combat center was not incorporated until the late 1980s, so for most part the *Lvda* was still a WWII-style design with controls spread over the boat and with no integration of the data and control of these systems. Furthermore, the PLA recruits of that era often had only a limited education, and the constant turnover of experienced sailors meant that those with some degree of competence needed to dash between these different control rooms to supervise and relay messages. Although this constant turnover of men was not unique to the PLA, the poor educational level of the average PLA recruit in China during the 1960s and 1970s created extra challenges to the PLAN and also to the PLAAF, which was increasingly moving to technology-based warfare.

The Type 052, which the West called *Lvhu*-class, a second-generation guided missile destroyer marked a step up in terms of technology and design from the Type 051 *Lvda*-class. Only two were ever made: the CNS *Harbin* and CNS *Qingdao*, both of which served in the Northern Fleet. The lead vessel CNS *Harbin* was designed in the early 1980s when China entered into what "The Honeymoon Decade" with the West, where China was able to have access to Western technology after a hiatus of decades. Therefore, CNS *Harbin* was the first CNS to be designed with Western armaments in mind. This proved to be a steep learning curve and a double-edged sword. For example, the Type 052 was designed with General Electric's LM2500 marine gas turbine in mind after the Americans promised to conduct a technology transfer deal; however, after the Tiananmen Square incident the deal was called off and the Chinese were left with five LM2500s, one for training, and the embargo on parts and technical service was also a problem. Therefore, the naval architects were left with a dilemma: should the Type 052 still use the LM2500 or switch to an alternative power source? Various options were considered, including buying Russian marine gas turbines, but in the end the both the lead vessel *Harbin* and the second boat CNS *Qingdao* adopted a CODAG (combined diesel and gas) power plant configuration that used two LM2500 and two MTU 12V-1163/T83 marine diesels. The impetus for this decision was that the initial worries about spare parts were partly solved through the successful cloning of some of the parts which most commonly suffered from wear and tear, and later the United States also relaxed the embargo, and many suppliers began setting up factories in China, thus further easing the problem of parts supply. The final nail in the coffin of the US embargo was that the Chinese started to discuss with the Ukraine their AM-50 marine gas turbine. Fearful of losing a lucrative market to Ukraine, America soon relaxed its tough commercial stance.

5.6 Building Chinese Submarines

Like many things in China, the first Chinese submarine was only possible through Soviet aid. The first stage was the purchase and assembly through knockdown kits. In June 1954 China imported from the Soviet Union two submarines of the early *M*-class (*Malyutka*-class; baby or little one), along with two Soviet *S*-class submarines, (S-52 and S-53) and two *Shchuka*-class submarines (under lease, S-121 and S-123). Both the *M*- and *S*-class submarines were sold to China and subsequently two more M–XV series of the *M*-class sub, M-278 and M-279, were also sold to China a few years later. Those purchased by China received Chinese names and the two leased *S*-class submarines did not. The four *M*-class submarines bought by China were named as National Defense #21, 22, 23 (ex M-278) and 24 (ex M-279) respectively, and after some preparation on June 19, 1954, the PLAN's submarine force was born. As part of what was then called the 6.4 agreement with the Soviet Union, which agreed to transfer the building knowledge on what the Soviets called the Type-613 SSB (NATO: *Whiskey*-class), known in China as 6603-class or later abbreviated to "03" diesel electric submarines. With the package came with it a number of Soviet naval architects and ship-building experts.

The first 03-class submarine was started in April 1955 and was launched on March 1956 in Jiangnan Shipyard in Shanghai. Subsequently Wuchang Shipyard participated in the mass production of the 03-class. In what is known as the second stage, in the late 1950s and early 1960s, the Chinese attempted to design and build their own submarines, but both attempts ended without any boats being built. In the third stage, an agreement signed on February 4, 1959, known by the Chinese as the 2.4 agreement, was intended to lead to the transfer of six submarines. This was known as Project 633 in the Soviet Union and the 6631-class in China, later abbreviated to just 31-class (NATO: *Romeo*) conventional submarines. However, the break in Sino-Soviet relations in the late 1950s forced the Soviet Union to unilaterally terminate all agreements and withdraw all experts almost overnight. Despite initial difficulties, the lead boat of the Type 033 was completed in 1965, taking a total of almost five years. A total of eighty-four Type 033 submarines were built in China between 1962 and 1984, plus several exported to other countries. The Chinese Type 033 incorporated some improvements over the original *Romeo*, including noise reduction and better sonar. Today most of the Type 033 subs have been retired or preserved, with a few remaining for training purposes.

A total of six Chinese *Romeo*-class submarines were developed. Type 6633, which was the original Chinese-built "*Romeo*," using Soviet-supplied kits. By 1967 all the "*Romeos*" were produced in China and were renamed as Type 033 with improvements in refrigeration and the air-conditioning systems for the boats stationed in tropical regions. In September 1969, Huangpu Shipyard in Guangzhou was responsible for building these hot-weather Type 033s. ES5As were upgraded Type 033s with improved sonar. Type 033G was a development of ES5A, with the added ability to launch acoustic homing torpedoes with analog computers added to achieve automation in order to speed up the calculation of torpedo fire control calculations that had previously been done manually. All Chinese *Romeos* have been converted to this standard. One experimental missile-carrying Type 033 known as Type 033G1 was modified to carry six YJ-1 SSMs, which could be launched while the boat was surfaced. Finally, there was ES5B, a Type 033G primarily intended for export. This was an upgraded package for the *Romeo* submarine users. Egypt was reported to be the only customer when China won a contract to upgrade its *Romeo*-class submarine fleet, including both the Soviet-built and Chinese-built units.

With the success of the Type 033, the CMC ordered the building of the *Ming*-class submarines in 1967, known as Project 035.

In the 1970s, the 701 Institute built an improved submarine based on the Type 033 hull, named Type 035 *Ming*. The construction of the first began during October 1969 at Wuhan Shipyard with Mr. Wei Xumin the chief designer. The last boat was built in 2002. A total of twenty boats were built, of which seventeen are left, and most served in the North Sea Fleet. The Type 035 *Ming* had an improved diesel-electric engine, improved hull design with less hydrodynamic resistance, better underwater speed, and a more capable sonar. The most significant difference between the Type 035 *Ming*-class and Type 033 is that the former is driven by a single shaft instead of the twin shafts of the latter.

As far as the Type 6631 (later abbreviated to Type 031, NATO: *Golf*) is concerned, which was also part of the initial Soviet aid, the Chinese only built one boat—partly due to the fact that China did not purchase SLBMs, and thus Type 6631 was an empty SSB. In the end it was retrofitted with simulation systems and was mainly used for training. Originally with pennant number 1101, it was subsequently changed to 200 in 1967. The Type 6631 went through a second major refit, completed in November 1978. The most important improvement was its ability to launch SLBMs underwater. In addition to changing from the original Type 6631 to Type 031, the unit also received the name *Great Wall*, when China begun to restore the practice of naming its warships in the 1980s. The unit is hence usually referred to as *Great Wall* pennant number 200.

A little known fact, perhaps revealed to the Western world for the first time, is that in 1964, about the time that the Type 6631 was launched, there was an attempt by the Chinese to develop a mini-submarine capable of 11 knots underwater and carrying eight torpedoes in four tubes. The task was given to 701 Institute's 14th Department and was named as Type 030. The design was finalized in August 1966. The chief designer was Li Jianqiu and they were to be built in Shanghai by the Jiangnan Shipyard. A full-size wooden replica was made for construction which was to begin in 1968. In 1973 the project was cancelled. No explanation was given but technical difficulties and the Cultural Revolution may have been contributing factors. After a hiatus of almost twenty years the Chinese at last managed to develop an indigenous submarine entirely different from the Romeo concept. The result was the Type 039 submarine (NATO: *Song*-class) diesel-electric SS, the first Chinese submarine to adopt a teardrop hull shape.

Like all self-developed weapon systems by the PRC, development of the Type 093 was not without problems, as a lengthy testing period for the first vessel attests. Problems with noise levels and underwater performance led to revisions in the design, and only a single boat was ever built to the original specifications. Essentially it was a work in progress. Improvements led to the specification for the Type 039G, which became the bulk of production and with seven of the type entering service. The elimination of the stepped design for the conning tower—an effort to shrink the submarine's acoustic signature—is the main visual identifier of the G variant.

The primary weapon for the Type 039 is the 533 mm Yu-4 (Fish) torpedo; a locally produced passive-homing 40-knot (74 km/h) torpedo which is roughly comparable to a Russian SAET-50 ASuW passive acoustic homing torpedo which has a range of 15 km. There is also the Yu-6, a Chinese counterpart of the US Mark 48 torpedo. Guidance can be by wire, active and passive-homing or wake-homing that can be used for targeting submarines. The Type 039 is capable of carrying the YJ-8 anti-ship cruise missile, which can be launched from the same tube as the boat's torpedoes, and can target surface vessels from a range of up to 80 km. The missile is subsonic and carries a 165 kg warhead. For deployment of mine operations, the submarine can carry up to thirty-six naval mines, deliverable through the torpedo tubes. The general designer of the torpedo and missile launching system was Mr. Sin Zhuguo and the launching system was compatible with AShM, ASW, and torpedoes of both China and Russian/Soviet origin. Although it is not an indication of the capacity of the *Song* SSK, on October 26, 2006, a Chinese *Song*-class submarine did "pop up" within 9 km of the carrier USS *Kitty Hawk* well within firing range of its torpedoes and missiles before being detected.

CNS *Liaoning*—The Chinese Aircraft Carrier

Since the 1970s, the PLAN has expressed interest in operating an aircraft carrier as part of its blue water aspirations. Since 1985, China has acquired several retired aircraft carriers for study: the Australian HMAS *Melbourne* and the ex-Soviet carriers *Minsk* and *Kiev*. The HMAS *Melbourne* was acquired in 1985 but was not dismantled for many years. *Minsk* and *Kiev* ended up as floating amusement parks for tourists. There was an attempt to purchase the old French carrier *Clemenceau* but talks fell through. In addition to buying secondhand carriers, China also tried to get plans and blueprints. One such example was its effort to purchase the blueprints for proposed conventional take-off/landing ships from Empresa Nacional Bazan of Spain; the 23,000-ton SAC-200 and the 25,000-ton SAC-220 designs, but it did not result in any purchase. China also approached the Russian warship firm Nevskoye Design Bureau, who completed an aircraft carrier design for China in the late 1990s. However, China did get a complete set of the decommissioned Soviet aircraft carrier *Kiev* as part of the purchase of the old carrier.

The first Chinese aircraft carrier, CNS *Liaoning*, was a rebuilt and refitted old Soviet warship, the *Admiral Kuznetsov*-class multirole aircraft carrier *Riga*, but later renamed *Varyag*. Bankrupt and in severe financial difficulties, the stripped hulk was purchased from Ukraine in 1998 for US$25 million by Chong Lot Travel Agency Ltd., a small company in Hong Kong. The initial proposal (or cover story, depends how one see this) was to tow *Varyag* out of the Black Sea, through the Suez Canal and around southern Asia to Macau, where they would moor the ship and convert it into a floating hotel and gambling parlor, as had been done with other ex-Soviet carriers (*Kiev* in Tianjin and *Minsk* in Shenzhen) which had proven to be popular theme park and tourist attractions.

Before the auction was closed, officials in Macau had warned Chong Lot that they would not be permitted to berth in Macau, but Chong Lot bought it anyway. Chong Lot was owned by Chin Luck (Holdings) Company, another Hong Kong-registered company.

However four of Chin Luck's six board members were listed as having their domicile in the seaside city of Yantai in Northern China, where a major Chinese Navy shipyard is located, and incidentally Chin Luck's chairman is a former career military officer with the PLAN. After a long journey around the Cape of Good Hope, the *Varyag* eventually landed in Dalian on March 3, 2002. However, when the Macau government announced the awards for new casino licenses in February 2002, Chong Lot was not among the successful bidders. The hulk was tied up at Dalian. The total cost of acquiring the hulk was over US$30 million: US$25 million to the Ukrainian government for the hull, nearly US$500,000 in transit fees, and some US$5 million for the towing.

After fourteen years of refitting, the ex-*Varyag* was commissioned into the PLAN on September 25, 2012 carrying the pennant number 16, and was classified as a training ship, intended to allow the Navy to practice with carrier usage. As it is a training ship, CNS *Liaoning* was not assigned to any of China's operational fleets.

Prior to being commissioned, the vessel undertook ten sea trials and on post-commissioning the carrier took six more trips in the Bohai area, with the last one from December 3, 2013 to January 3, 2014 in the South China Sea. CNS *Liaoning* will continue to play a role primarily as a training ship, but if needed can also double up for operations. However, the first true all-Chinese built aircraft carrier will be a larger version of CNS *Liaoning*, supposedly based on plans obtained of a Soviet-era 80,000-ton vessel capable of carrying sixty aircraft. In comments on Chinese news websites, the Communist Party boss of the northeastern province of Liaoning, where the first carrier is based, said the second carrier was being built in the port city of Dalian, construction would be completed by 2018, and in the future China would have a fleet of at least four carriers.

5.7 Chinese Nuclear Submarines

The story of Chinese nuclear submarines began back in 1958 when Marshal Nie Rongzhen tabled a secret memo to the CCP for the development of a missile-capable nuclear submarine. Initially the idea was to start with a SSBN; this line of thought was partly influenced by the Soviets and the world situation at that time, including the need for a strategic nuclear response capability. The program was terminated in the early 1960s but in 1965 it was resurrected and the CCP decided to take a less ambitious two-step approach; first developing a simpler SSN and then the SSBN. The logic to this was that to build the SSN, the Chinese only needed to master the nuclear reactor technology, while when building a SSBN there are three essential technologies: the nuclear reactor, the missile, and the underwater launching system. By June 1967, the PLAN submitted a white paper on the use of nuclear submarines and the plan called for a relatively simple SSN design during the first stage before moving to a SSBN design, allowing time and space to master the operation and upkeep of such complicated technology.

The first nuclear submarine was the 5,500-ton Type 091 *Han*-class, pennant number 401,[8] (Chinese designation 09-I) SSN. The chief designer of the SSN was Mr. Peng Shilu, who was later succeeded by Mr. Huang Xuhua. The first Chinese SSN T-091 submarine was commissioned into the PLAN in 1974. This was followed by a number of launches with the fifth and final boat of the class commissioned into the PLAN as late as 1990. The *Han*-class SSN was essentially a learning tool for the Chinese. They wanted a simple and easy to operate vessel, such that when compared with the West's SSNs it is often regarded as poor and backwards. The *Han*-class is well known for having a noisy reactor and poor radiation shielding, which meant higher health hazards for her crew. The subsequent boats had upgrades and are essentially used for training. The boats have six 533 mm torpedo tubes and carry twenty torpedoes. Alternatively, they can carry thirty-six mines in their tubes. The *Han*-class is capable of firing sub-launched variants of the C-801 anti-ship missile as well as a range of indigenous and Russian torpedoes or mines. The first of the *Han*-class, hull 401, had been retired from active service by 2005.

Next on the line was the 6,500-ton *Type 092 Xia*-class (Chinese designation 09-II) submarine, which was the first ballistic missile-carrying, nuclear-powered submarine class (SSBN) deployed by the Chinese

Navy and the first SSBN designed and built in Asia. It shared 85% common parts with the *Han* but stretched the hull to accommodate twelve missiles. It had the same nuclear reactor as the *Han* SSN but, due to its larger size and displacement, the *Xia*-class was reported by the Western press as only capable of 22 knots compared to the 26 knots for the *Han*-class. The *Xia* SSBN was also designed by Peng Shilu and Huang Xuhua. The preparation for construction began in September 1970 and it was projected that the first hull would go down the slipway in 1973; however, due to various reasons, the first *Xia*-class SSBN, *Changzheng* (pennant number 406) was not launched until April 30, 1981 at Huludao, 190 km northeast of Beijing, and became operational on October 19, 1983. *Changzheng* 6 was fitted out with twelve JL-1 (*Ju Lang*: Huge Wave) missiles. Designed by Huang Weilu (1916–2011) and Chen Deren (1922–2007) it was begun initially for the Type 31 or Project 629A (NATO: *Golf*) SSBN. However, the *Golf*-class of SSBN submarine with its three silos fitted in the rear of the large sail behind the bridge could only be fired with the submarine on surface, and by the mid-1960s all the world's nuclear powers were equipping their navies with SSBNs that could fire missiles while submerged, so the Chinese Navy also demanded this capability for their SSBN.

Mastering the underwater launching of ballistic missiles was no easy matter; and a dedicated testing facility was built in southern Liaoning province with full-size testing of underwater launching of the full-size mock-up JL-1 model in October 1972. Although the development work on the warhead was essentially completed by 1974, the solid fuel system and the fuel itself were more problematic and it was not finished until March 1979. First- and second-stage rocket motors were completed by 1980 and full-scale land launch with a mock nuclear head was successfully carried out in April 1984 in a modified Type 031 *Golf*. However, the subsequent trial with real missiles in 1985 was a complete failure and the program was set back until 1988 when, under Operation 9188, two JL-1s were successfully launched and both achieved bull's-eye hits on the target zone in the Pacific. Aside from its twelve ballistic missiles the *Xia* SSBN can also carry twelve 533 mm torpedoes in six tubes, and by 2006 wire-guided torpedoes were in operation in all submarines. Despite the success of the *Xia* and *Han*, one of the reasons that China did not mass produce both of these classes was that the PLAN fully realized that by the time the two submarines became operational they would already be obsolete. By the late 1980s/early 1990s, the USSR and the United States were moving to third-generation SSBNs. Compared with the Western and Soviet technology at the time, the *Xia* SSBN and the JL-1 were clearly not in the same league. First, the *Xia* could carry only twelve missiles while American *Ohio*-class SSBNs had twenty-four tubes. The second key limitation was that the range of the JL-1 SLBM was only 2,200 km and it was a single warhead SLBM, whereas the UGM-73A Poseidon C3, a similar SLBM of that time, could travel 4,600 km and was equipped with MIRV multiple warheads. Limitations in metallurgical science meant that the boat was noisy and thus its survival in a modern battlefield was very doubtful. Despite these constraints, the experience of going it alone allowed the Chinese to master the essential strategic technology to develop a truly independent strategic nuclear deterrent.

With the improvement of the economic and political environment with the West in the 1980s, the positive atmosphere allowed China access to essential Western technology that allowed them to begin developing their second-generation SSBN in around 1996/97. The new SSBN design was completed in 2000 and the boat was built in Huludao Shipyard and launched in just one year. According to the Chinese press, the new SSBN, Type 094, was hurried through the development and building stages due to "international pressure" and "international uncertainties." As to what these "pressures" and "uncertainties" were the Chinese sources (books and TV) never made clear. The nuclear submarine has always been the secret of any nation and China is not an exception. The first sign of a new SSBN was only revealed through the accidental release of a picture onto a Chinese website in 2006. However, the subsequent release of information clarified that first Type 094 was delivered to the PLAN in 2004.

The Type 094 (NATO: *Jin*-class) is a 12,000-ton SSBN capable of carrying twelve of the more modern JL-2 SLBMs with a range of approximately 8,000–14,000 km, capable of reaching targets in the Western Hemisphere from Chinese coastal waters. As the JL-2 is much larger than the JL-1, the *Jin*-class is bigger than the older *Xia*-class. In comparison with the older Type 092-class submarine, it has been elongated from 122 m to 133 m and the breadth is at least 10 m wider. In addition to the twelve missiles, the Jin SSBN submarines have six 533 mm torpedoes tubes armed with twelve torpedoes.

The design of the JL-2 began back in 1986 and the development work was completed by 1990. During this stage there were many ideas what the JL-2 should be, but the end conclusion was that, in order to save time and avoid uncertainty with new technologies, the designer Huang Weilu would develop the JL-2 by "navalizing" the proven land-based ballistic missile DF-31. As such, it shares many features of the DF-31 missile, such as its operational characteristics. During this design debate, the original criteria was set at 6,000 km, but this distance was too small to reach the continental USA, and in order to do so the sub needed to reach the mid-Pacific for launching, thus exposing the SSBN to unnecessary risk. So the range of the JL-2 was increased beyond 6,000 km.

The JL-2 SLBM has three subtypes: the JL-2, the upgraded JL-2A (Jia, A class) and the latest version JL-2B (Yi, B class). JL-2B is the current operational version and some reports claim that the JL2B has an operational range of 14,000 km. The first land launch of the JL-2 was carried out in June 2003. The first sea, albeit surface, launch of the JL-2 was reported to have taken place in June 2005 from a modified *Golf*-class submarine—*Vessel 200,* as it was called in the Chinese media. The underwater launch of the JL-2 was carried out in 2006 but news reports tell of "problems," and it was not until 2008 that the redesigned JL-2 completed the underwater launch tests. News on the Chinese SLBM program was never disclosed to the public, until on February 25, 2013 during a regular primetime radio broadcast, the announcer suddenly and unexpectedly mentioned China's nuclear program: "If we calculate from the beginning, today is the 24th birthday of the JL-1 SLBM, and looking back at the life of the JL-1 program the baton of protecting the nation has already been passed on to a new generation of ballistic missiles on a new generation of submarines."

Some interpreted this to mean that the JL-2 or JL-2B and the Type 094 *Jin*-class SSBN were already fully operational, but some more cautious observers say that it only meant that the JL-2 and Jin-class submarine have completed the last of their testing programs. No matter what, the Type 094 with the JL-2 is sure to be the next generation of SSBN for the PLAN.

However, even before the Type 094 SSBN is fully deployed, the PLAN is already working on its replacement, the design of the Type 096 (NATO: *Tang*-class) SSBN was reported to have begun as early as 1995. The vessel is to have similar capacity to the USS *Seawolf* SSN. From the model shown at a recent arms show, the Type 096 is equipped with twenty-four SLBMs, and according to some unnamed US officials, the Type-096 entered service with the PLAN in 2014. The reason for developing the Type 096 was that the PLAN was unhappy with the Type 094. The enlarged missile silos for the JL-2 that protruded through almost three quarters of the submarine hull were causing severe hydrodynamic problems and creating unnecessary turbulence and hence noise. A second major defect of the Type 094 *Jin*-class SSBN is its nuclear reactor. The nuclear reactor installed on the *Jin*-class is essentially the same as the Type 094, albeit with minor upgrades. The *Tang*-class SSBN is a much larger boat than the *Jin*, reportedly carrying twenty-four JL-2Bs, such that the power requirement for such a heavier boat, reportedly at 20,000 tons, is beyond the capacity of the older reactor. As a result, the Type 096 is a totally new design with a new reactor and a radically different shape hull. Finally, aside from the JL-2 ballistic missiles, the Type 096 is equipped with six 533 mm torpedoes tubes with twelve torpedoes and six cruise missiles, most probably the YJ-83 anti-ship type.

The importation of advanced Type 636 SSK (NATO: *Kilo*) from Russia allows the Chinese to examine the anechoic tiles fitted on the hull to absorb the sound waves of active sonar, which results in a reduction and distortion of the return signal. These tiles also help attenuate sounds emitted from the submarine, thus reducing the possibility of detection by passive sonar, making the Type 636 SSK one of the quietest submarines in the world.

The T-093 (NATO: *Shang*-class) SSN is a new type of SSN that has been in development since the 1980s as a replacement for the *Han*-class. Type 093 was officially approved by the PLA leadership in July 1983.

However, the development program only made very limited progress in its early stages due to enormous technical difficulties, especially with the nuclear reactor and onboard weapon systems.

The Type 093 design is comparable to the Russian Project 671 (NATO: *Victor*) III class SSN, signifying a significant step forward for Chinese nuclear attack submarines. The first hull was launched in 2002 by the Bohai Shipyard in Huludao with six to eight boats planned. As soon as the first boat was launched, defects found were immediately rectified in the second boat, resulting in an improved Type 093G variant. The Type 093 is estimated to have roughly 7,000 tons' displacement when submerged and is armed with six 533 mm torpedo tubes that launch wire, acoustic and wake-homing torpedoes as well as anti-ship and land attack cruise missiles, most probably the anti-ship YJ-83. A radical offshoot of the Type 093, first known in China as Type 093A, later referred to as a Type 041 submarine (NATO: *Yuan*-class), is a class of diesel-electric SS. This class was first launched at Wuhan Shipyard and is the successor of the Type 039. The *Yuan* incorporates some of the best features of the *Song* and the *Kilo*. The *Yuan* is fitted with two AIP systems developed by the 711 Institute and integrated with advanced noise reduction techniques including anechoic tiles, passive/active noise reduction, and asymmetrical seven-blade skewed propellers as well as an indigenous active/passive torpedo and the YJ-8 (C-801) submarine-launched anti-ship missile.

Notes

1 In 1966, Type 601 steel was replaced with Type-623 rare earth treated steel that contains 50% less molybdenum displaying greater strength at low temperature. Later 601A and 622 castling steel replaced Type-603 Steel.

2 Such an FC unit means the T-69 cannot fire on the move.

3 A US/German MBT-70 lookalike with 120 mm smoothbore gun weighing 45 tons.

4 The "P" depicts Pakistan.

5 T-63, T-63-1, T-63C, T-85, T-89, T-90.

6 Optical-electronic products, oil field equipment, chemicals, light industrial products, explosives and blast materials, civil and military firearms, and ammunition

7 Tai Hang power plant was designed for the J-10, but at the time the J-10 was not ready for testing.

8 Initially it was 1701, this SSN is now decommissioned.

CHAPTER 6

CHINA'S STRATEGIC VIEW

The history of the PLA, in the eyes of the Chinese, is of a glorious and heroic struggle, and ultimate triumph over insurmountable obstacles. A fundamental lesson learned by the PLA is that the weak can triumph over the strong, no matter how daunting the difficulties or how asymmetrical the fight, and victories are always possible if selfless PLA soldiers doggedly pursue their tasks. After all, despite being abandoned by the Soviets, and the humble beginnings of all three PLA services, the Chinese nevertheless built the A-bomb, nuclear submarines, and ICBMs. This mentality of persistent struggle, overcoming obstacles no matter how formidable, is the eternal hallmark of the PLA and of China.

The trademark of the PLA, if it has one, is: surprise, mass, maneuver, and strategic employment of terrain. In the Chinese Civil War, Korean War and the Sino-Indian War this was the battle-winning formula. The PLA also learned the hard way that positional warfare is not their forte; trained to fight and retreat, the army was not skilled in immobile defense. Furthermore, the PLA realized that to take advantage of their numerical strength, the army must use the element of surprise. In the Sino-Vietnam War the PLA learned another set of lessons—misdirected policies left the army in tatters, and poor logistics, poor combat engineering and lack of artillery/fighter support weakened the 1979 campaign. Case studies from this campaign are required lessons in the PLA academies. The Gulf War taught the PLA that they need to modernize quickly, while the 1996 Taiwan Straits missile crisis taught the PLA that unification with Taiwan and other still outstanding territorial disputes cannot be carried out without US intervention, and so keeping America out is the key to any successful operation. The Cultural Revolution and Tiananmen Square incident taught the leaders of China that PLA intervention in domestic disturbances should be avoided if all possible. The Tiananmen Square incident also clearly illustrated that the PLA is the armed wing of the CCP; and the interest of the CCP is paramount.

The history of the Chinese People's Liberation Army is the history of modern China. The PLA played a paramount role in the rise to power of the Chinese Communist Party, and has been a key political kingmaker and powerbroker in Chinese politics. For all of the 20th century the fundamental purpose of the CCP and its military wing, the PLA, was the struggle to regain control of China from foreign powers, rid the nation of its protected enclaves, and recover its lost territories and colonies with the ultimate aim to establish a strong and sovereign China within firm borders. As the name suggests, the Chinese People's Liberation Army is all about the pursuit of liberty and self-determination for the Chinese people.

With the above fundamentals in mind, it is not hard to understand the core values of the Chinese National Defense Mission Statement. The Chinese national security concept is divided into two parts: internal security and external security. On internal matters, there are four key points. Top of the bill is safeguarding the national integrity and cohesiveness of the nation, and defending the nation's land and sea borders; the second concerns nation building; third is developing national security in line with development needs; and the fourth and last point is a focus on developing social order, for a cohesive society. From this simple statement it is possible to discern the priorities of Chinese leaders, and on what issues the nation's leaders will resort to arms if pushed.

The long-term goal for modern China is the recovery of "lost" territories and defense of the nation's boundaries. These "lost" territories were areas of land and sea sovereignty lost during the 19th and 20th centuries, and means a redress of the humiliations that were levied on China during the period of Western colonial expansion. Whereas some in the Western world may not agree, areas like Tibet, Diaoyu Islands (Senkaku Islands to the Japanese), Xinjiang, Taiwan, and the South Sea Islands are areas which the Chinese regard as part of modern China. Hong Kong and

Macau were lost to colonial powers (Britain and Portugal) when China was weak, now they are back (1997 for Hong Kong and 1999 for Macau) and the great mission is to continue to regain Taiwan, the South Sea Islands, Diaoyu Islands, etc., which are still regarded as "lost" territories. Ideally, they will be recovered without the use of arms, as in the cases of Hong Kong and Macau, but if needed, such as in resistance to secession/separatist movements, or foreign intervention that treads on the issue of national territorial rights, the use of arms cannot be excluded, at a time and place of the Chinese leadership's choosing.

Second is striving for an orderly society and the support of national development. Through most of the 20th century, China was in a mess. Wars, civil commotions, famine and natural disasters, not to mention ill-conceived policies such as the Cultural Revolution, brought nothing good to the nation and its people. To the Chinese leadership, the era of "trouble and chaos" had to end in order for the society to advance. Events such as the Cultural Revolution must not be repeated, and sustaining a peaceful and orderly society is at the forefront of every Chinese leader's mind. To the Chinese, without order nothing could be done, no advancement of the society and nation was possible. By the end of the 1980s China was at last free from wars, but was a poor and underdeveloped nation, and the Chinese leadership knew that China badly needed to "catch up." Thanks to the "opening up" policy established by the late Deng Xiaoping, China has made tremendous progress in the last thirty years or so, though it has not crossed the finish line to be regarded as a "developed nation," and so more effort on national development is needed. If anything gets in the way of national progress and development, the PLA or PAP will act!

The second part of the PLA mission statement focuses on external matters; the main aim here is for the PLA to support a peaceful, independent non-aligned diplomatic and security framework. The second part of the "external security" mission statement is to promote Chinese values of peaceful coexistence, and peaceful resolutions of difference without the use of force, if possible. China has stated repeatedly that she will never become a hegemonic state and adopt a militaristic expansionist policy. However, many may doubt this claim, as in recent years the Chinese as well as the PLA are beginning to show their strength further afield.

The increased prominence of the Chinese on the international scene was a result of the rise of China in the last thirty years; much of it was fueled by the intense industrialization of the nation. As such the demand for natural resources has risen tremendously. Much of this has to be supplied from aboard. As of 2013, 59% of China's oil comes from overseas and 30% of its natural gas. China is now the largest buyer of iron ore in the world, projected to reach 6.8 million tons compared to 2.7 million last year. This places a massive demand on overseas transportation, and these trading links mean that China, like any nation, has to protect its national interests, its overseas investments and its long logistics supply chain. It is inevitable that the PLA will have to play a role in protecting the nation's lifeline and assume greater exposure on the world stage. The active participation in UN peacekeeping missions and international anti-piracy patrols off the coast of Somalia and Gulf of Aden are just two examples. More will come for sure.

As the Chinese are becoming more visible around the world, there are some elements in the West that are beginning to play up the "threat" of Chinese expansion and the need for "containment." To the West there is the "String of Pearls" theory that is supposed to be evidence of a newly expansionist China.

According to some military strategists and commentators, this "String of Pearls" was supposed to be an attempt by China to secure a maritime sphere of influence, using the energy shipping route as its baseline. The key locations for this strategy are the ports of Gwadar in Pakistan, Hambantota in Sri Lanka and Chittagong in Bangladesh, as well as the Coco Islands and Hainggyi Island in Burma, Songkhla in Thailand, and Phu Quoc Island in Cambodia. China has been pushing to use these ports, and in some cases providing huge amounts of economic support to build new ports at these locations.

Whereas in the West we see the "Strings of Pearls," in the East across the Pacific it is seen as the "Two Island Chain" theory. The first island chain (Okinawa–Taiwan–Philippines–Malaysia) and ultimately the second island chain (Ogasawara Islands–Saipan–Guam–Papua New Guinea) are containment lines of a series of nations, all friendly to the United States, which can be used to restrict China's eastward expansion, especially blocking key passages in order to limit the movements of the PLAN deep into the Pacific Ocean. Around 90% of China's trade to the east relies on shipping routes in the South China Seas, therefore protection of these key logistics routes is also vital to the continuation of the development of the nation. True or false, it's up to the observer to decide.

Between 1978 and 2009, China's GDP grew by almost 2,000%. In 1980, China's share of world GDP was only 1.72%, but by 2010 it had grown to 9.32%. With money from thirty years of trade stashed up, the PLA could afford to spend. To protect this trade, China is expanding its armed forces, especially the Navy.

Wealth from trade inevitably brings in more to spend, and this includes the PLA. Neglected in the initial stages of the country's modernization, the real expansion of the PLA budget occurred after the First Gulf War. During the twelve years following 1996, China's (officially published) defense budget grew at an average annual rate of 12.9%. The latest announcement by Premier Li Keqiang revealed that national defense spending for 2014 was 12.2% higher than that of 2013, reaching 808.2 billion RMB, or US$ 132 billion.

On the question of China's arms spending, it is often claimed that the rise in its defense budget is posing a threat to the world. Whereas it is true that China defense spending is rising rapidly, it is still low compared to that of other countries, especially the United States. Furthermore, the defense budget also relates to the size of the nation: China is big, and spends US$ 13,598 per square km while the United States spends US$ 53,589 per square km. In 2012 the US military spending was not only the highest in the world at US$ 682 billion but was more than the defense budgets of the next eight highest spenders put together (in order: China, Russia, UK, Japan, France, Saudi Arabia, India, Brazil, totaling US$ 652 billion at the 2012 US$ rate). In 2014, 17.4% of the US federal expenditure was on defense-related matters, while China's defense budget for the same period was only 11.6% of the national budget. Therefore, militarily, the United States is still far ahead of the game with its superior technology, and while the Chinese may want to be eventually become as strong as the United States, this will take many decades.

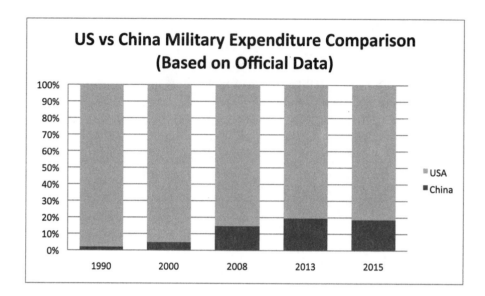

The PLA is currently applying resources to its Navy and Air Force at the expense of the ground forces. However, by expanding its naval power it is directly challenging the United States' dominance in the Indian and Pacific Oceans. The South and East China Seas are both of strategic importance to the United States and countries of Southeast Asia as well as to Japan and South Korea. Some 80% of Japanese and South Korean trade relies on using the South China Sea route, and 80%–90% of the crude oil and natural gas heading for Northeast Asia comes that way. The United States cannot ignore the threat to its maritime hegemony, and if the United States were to be pushed much further east into the Pacific Ocean it would be difficult for it to provide support to its allies in the region, obviously an area for potential conflict.

In 2012 the highlight for the PLAN was when it successfully commissioned its first aircraft carrier, the CNS *Liaoning*, making it the tenth country in the world to possess an aircraft carrier. It is currently building a further four carriers. It is also known to have procured ten nuclear submarines with ballistic missile capabilities. In 2013 a number of other major ships entered PLAN service.

Meantime, the Chinese Air Force is busy developing fourth- and fifth-generation stealth fighters, called the J-20 and J-31 respectively,

2013 PLAN—New Ships Commissioned				
Ship Type	Name (CNS)	Pennant Number	Date in service	Fleet
052C Destroyer	Changchun	150	31.1.2013	East
	Zhengzhou	151	26.12.2013	East
054A Escorts	Yueyang	575	3.5.2013	South
	Weifang	550	22.6.2013	North
	Sanya	574	13.12.2013	South
056 Light Escorts	Bengbu	582	25.1.2013	East
	Datong	580	18.5.2013	North
	Shangrao	583	10.6.2013	East
	Huizhou	596	1.7.2013	Hong Kong
	Qinzhou	597	1.7.2013	Hong Kong
	Meizhou	584	29.7.2013	South
	Yingkou	581	1.8.2013	North
	Baise	585	12.10.2013	South
093 Replenishment	Caohu	890	12.9.2013	North
	Taihu	889	18.6.2013	East

and both have already carried out successful test flights. The Chinese strategic transporter Y-20 made its debut and the J-16 (the improved J-11B/S) is now approved for mass production. The Zhi-20 (the 10-ton general purpose helicopter) made its maiden flight. The photos reveal that it is heavily inspired (or cloned) from the S-70 Blackhawk series of helicopters. Two major UAV projects also took a step forward: the X-47B stealthy UCAV and the "second generation" of Soaring Dragon.

The PLA is also testing more sophisticated high-tech weapons. On January 9, 2014, a Chinese hypersonic glide vehicle (HGV), referred to as the WU-14, was allegedly spotted flying at high speed over the country. The flight was confirmed by the Pentagon as a hypersonic missile delivery vehicle capable of penetrating the US missile defense system and delivering nuclear warheads. The WU-14 is reportedly designed to be launched as the final stage of a Chinese ICBM traveling at Mach 10, or 12,360 km/h. China is the third country to enter the "hypersonic arms race," after Russia and the United States. Russia is meantime jointly developing with India the Mach 6 (7,300 km/h) scramjet-powered Brahmos-II.

Once President Xi Jining came to power and consolidated his position, he began reforming the PLA. His defense modernization/reforms are probably an attempt to achieve improved combat effectiveness through organizational, doctrinal, training, educational, and personnel reforms (including recruitment, promotion, and demobilization). On March 15, 2014, the Chinese press announced that Xi was to head a working group described as a "deep and comprehensive reform group" of the CMC. What this reform entails it is too early to say, but in a recent report from the Hong Kong press, 200 PLAAF airmen were "sacked" and dismissed from flying duties, so something momentous is going on, or at least deadwood is being cleared. Corruption in the PLA is a problem that President Xi has not been afraid to tackle. As recently as November 2014, nine generals were taken away for questioning, not to mention the arrest of the former deputy head of the CMC, General Xu Caihou. Looking more broadly, President Xi's "reform" plan is not limited to the military but is being applied in the Party as well as in society.

The military modernization also involves the transformation of the defense industrial establishment into a system capable of independently sustaining modern military forces without reliance on foreign technology, or most importantly, dependence on foreign supplies in technology and weaponry. Since the founding of the People's Republic in 1949, the desire for local control of vital military technology has been uppermost in the minds of Chinese leaders. From Mao to Xi, whenever the Chinese acquire new military technology, the package is always to include local production. If licensing is given all is well, but if licensing is not given the Chinese will still find a way to achieve local manufacturing, including cloning and reverse engineering. The desire for control of vital military technology stems from the need not to have the defense of the nation dependent or held ransom by foreign supplied weapons and vital parts. Twice in the republic's history, foreign suppliers withdrew help at critical points: the Soviet Union in the late 1950s and the West in 1989. The lesson learned from bitter experience is that there are no true friends in global politics; while friends are there, acquire as much from them as possible, but if China has to go it alone so be it. Often China is described as a copycat nation; while this is true, in fact reverse engineering, copying, even stealing vital technology through espionage is practiced by all nations. Take, for example, the Japanese automobile industry. Isuzu's first attempt in automobile manufacturing was in a venture with British automaker Wolseley Motors in 1918, but by 1927, having learned all its secrets, Isuzu terminated the relationship and booted out Wolseley altogether. In fact, everybody was at it: Toyota's AA was a copy of the Chrysler Airflow; Mitsubishi's Model A was a copy of the Fiat A3-3; Ohta cars of the 1930s were based entirely on Fords; while Chiyoda built a car resembling a 1935 Pontiac and Sumida copied from LaSalle. Having learned all they could, the Japanese innovated and since then they have not looked back. China is doing the same, following the path that every industrial nation has trod.

Finally, I have mentioned various likely areas of contention, which may see China deploying its forces in a "hot" battle/skirmish. One area is the South China Sea where there are claims and counter-claims of territories. However much trading relations with China continue to grow, the countries of East and Southeast Asia have a big concern about the economic and military rise of China. These countries have historical enmities and territorial disputes with China, and these disputes can be exacerbated in an economic crisis. The United States has been attempting to use these very concerns and position itself as a "regional balancer" in order to "contain" China through its new "Pivot to Asia" strategy. On the carrot side of the strategy is a focus on boosting US economic and diplomatic influence while checking China's expanding influence using the Trans-Pacific Partnership (TPP) free trade agreement against China's East Asian Free Trade Agreement (EAFTA). On the stick side, the United States is attempting to boost military influence in the region with the intention to neutralize China's naval strategy—or what the United States calls its "Anti-Access/Area Denial Strategy." This involves an increased naval presence and the construction of regional missile defense systems with its Asian allies as well as increased arms sales. To Taiwan, America sold AH-64 Apache attack helicopters, F-16 C/D fighters, and P-3A Orion anti-submarine warfare planes. To the

Japanese, the United States both sold and deployed more Global Hawk UAVs and its revolutionary Osprey VTOL aircraft, which are based at Fatima, despite fierce opposition from the locals of Okinawa.

To complement the increased US presence, the Japanese have increased military spending under the banner of increased regional/international status. This partly reflects Washington's need to cut its military spending due to the financial pressure that the United States is experiencing. Despite the fact that the United States wanted its two North Asian allies to increase cooperation and form a US–Korea–Japan trilateral alliance, issues involving Japan's colonial past have been an obstacle. For the containment strategy to work the United States needs to have cooperative allies that grant access to overseas bases as well as cooperative allies' forces. For these reasons, the United States is strengthening its existing alliances with Japan, South Korea, Australia, and others while reinforcing security cooperation with other states such as Vietnam, Singapore, the Philippines, and Indonesia.

Is it the United States' intention to oppose head-on China's attempts to push the US military out of its neighboring seas, beyond the First Island Chain and possibly even the Second Island Chain? If this is true, to the Chinese, the United States is sending a message that it will continue to dominate the Asia-Pacific region and as a quid pro quo, oppose the rise of China in the region. If this is indeed the "Grand Strategy" which the United States is acting upon, then it may explain the recent rise in tension over the South China Seas as well as the tussle between China and Japan over the Diaoyu (Senkaku) Islands. In the eyes of the Chinese, all these developments were the work of the United States.

In the unlikely event that China and Japan actually "trade bullets," it will inevitably draw the United States into this tussle through Article 5 of the US–Japan Security Treaty. In her speech of July 2010, Secretary of State Hillary Clinton emphasized, "The United States supports a collaborative diplomatic process by all claimants for resolving the various territorial disputes without coercion." This puts pressure on China's claims to possession over the South China Sea and offers a protective shield to those countries that are in conflict with China over these issues.

In a concerted diplomatic intervention by the United States to delink Myanmar (Burma) from China, Secretary Clinton and President Obama made a number of visits to Myanmar, Laos, and Cambodia, previously viewed as Asian bogeymen by the United States. In view of the fact that Myanmar has been supported economically and diplomatically by China throughout the last twenty years of economic sanctions imposed by the West, the "loss" of Myanmar to the United States came as a shock to China, as China had heavily invested in Burma including a strategic oil pipeline project that granted access to Indian Ocean. The series of actions by the United States in infringing, or getting very close to the core interests of China is a very big concern in Beijing.

In face of the advances made by the United States, China has not sat idly by and has been making continuous efforts to expand its influence, not only economically but also geopolitically and to protect its "core interests" from the United States and its allies. On his visit with President Obama in February 2012, President Xi Jinping argued that China and the United States should work out a "new type of relationship between major powers," which can be simply translated as "mutual trust and respect each other's core interests and concerns: I am not trying to replace you, but respect my interests and we will do the same for you." The "core interests" of China include "sovereign and territorial integrity"—as stated in the core mission statement of the PLA, which means maintaining its rule over Tibet and Xinjiang and adhering to the "One China Principle" regarding Taiwan. Since 2010, China also counts the South China Sea among its core interests. Beijing will not back down easily in disputes regarding these issues, considering China's characterization of its "core interests" as national imperatives that must be defended at all costs and under any circumstances, using force if necessary.

In recent times many Western commentators see the current disputes in the south (with the Philippines) and eastern seas (Japan) as Chinese "aggression" given the fact of a "rising China." However, in the eyes of the Chinese (and I am talking about "now" and "before 1949") the loss of territories to Western powers when China was weak was a national humiliation, and the recovery of these lost territories is at the core of modern Chinese nationalism. This "recovery" process was put on hold in the early years of the People's Republic as China was then a poor and weak country, and "lost" territory was not a top priority. A stronger and richer China is now less willing to eat "humble pie" in any future disputes. A resurgent China is not going to allow its sea or land boundaries to be decided by third parties. As Lee Kuanyew, former Prime Minister of Singapore, wrote in Forbes magazine (April 2014): "A rising China is asserting its position by claiming historical rights, and many of these disputes which arise from claims based on different principles are unlikely to be resolved [easily]. If historical claims can define jurisdiction over waters and oceans, the Chinese can point to the fact that 600 years ago they sailed the South and East China Seas unchallenged." However, China's leaders also know that war will disrupt the "peaceful rise" which China has embarked on so successfully.

While a military clash between the United States and China is not inevitable, nevertheless, an amber warning light is flashing in regard to a proxy battle involving China and one of the United States' allies. Unless pushed over the edge, China will prefer to settle any disputes without firing a shot; after all China settled border disputes with Russia and Kazakhstan, and reclaimed Hong Kong as well as Macau without armed conflicts. Therefore, it's not all doom and gloom. Although China and the United States are now economically interdependent of each other, history has told us that economic interdependence and increased trade and investment do not necessarily bring peace. Both Germany and Britain and the United States and Japan just prior to WWI and WWII had close economic ties with each other. Above all, Asia is rife with destabilizing factors such as territorial disputes and a divided Korean peninsula, any one of which could trigger a rapid escalation of military tension in the region. China knows that at this moment it would be foolish to trigger a war or battle that would involve the United States. Any clash that drags in the United States could easily spiral out of hand to involve the United States' allies such as Australia and even the ever China-skeptic India. War on multiple fronts is simply not winnable. However, China is also very wary that the current actions by Japan and the Philippines, both junior allies to the United States on the Pacific Rim, suddenly appear very aggressive on the issues of disputed territory. For years these disputes were kept out of the limelight and China was focused on building better trade and national relationships; but China is increasingly concerned with developments and sees the United States as the chief instigator of these "troubles." In a recent program shown on the national Chinese state television channel, CCTV, a commentator offered an "explanation" of these developments, which does provide insight into how the Chinese think. The commentator explained that the "actions" were a grand strategy; while the United States is mired in economic problems it is looking for a way to break out by increasing trade with an economically vibrant Asia through the EAFTA trade pact. To strengthen the United States' influence on Asia and lessen China's, especially those countries who were once stout US allies, forgotten disputes are being stirred up to make China react to "infringement" on its core values, and these nations, instilled with fear of China's "hostile" nature, would embrace the US security umbrella. The danger is that if this is the real intention, then one misstep could lead to calamity. The year 2014 was the centenary of the beginning of the Great War and miscalculations amongst the European powers allowed a sideshow in the Balkans to lead to a global war in just thirty-seven days.

In terms of military technology, although China is catching up fast there is still a big gap between the United States and China. The Chinese themselves know well that they are not yet a match for the United States. The Russian weapons, although formidable, are not on a par with the latest US/Western arms. To win any battle China would still have to rely on numbers; providing that losses can be sustained and replenished, a David versus Goliath fight can still be winnable. In fighting the United States, the Vietnamese paid with tremendous casualties. Between 1965 and 1973, US losses in the Vietnam War were some 58,000, while Communist Vietnamese deaths during the same period were estimated between 0.9 million and 1.1 million! The Vietnamese were prepared to sustain these losses over a long period. The question is, can the United States also be so determined?

China is increasingly being portrayed in the Western mainstream media as an "aggressor," a "threat" or, if those words are too strong, at least a "competitor" to the United States. Many Americans fear a rising China, and those on the hawkish side of the divide would like to contain it. China wants no confrontation with the United States; as a developing country there are still many, especially in the landlocked provinces, still living in abject poverty and China wants nothing more than to raise the living standard for all. Confronting the world's biggest economy and the country with the most powerful army just does not make sense. The danger of the US "hawks" is that their fear can be a self-fulfilling prophecy. By containing, baiting, or forcing China into a corner, it may only transform what was a relatively "benign China" into an active adversary.

This view of the world that I have just outlined may be not what is parroted in the mainstream Western media; however, it is the prevailing view that the Chinese themselves have on the current geopolitical situation. The rise of China is inevitable, and history tells us that empires come and go, no matter how powerful they once were. As the British Empire waned the United States took over as a new global superpower in a peaceful handover; however, in another scenario, in the early 20th century, a rising Germany challenged the all-powerful British Empire and the result was not so pretty. Is a rising China a threat to the West? How will the scenario of a rising China on the world political/economic scene go—a Germany/Britain outcome or a Britain/USA one? I have no definite answer, but the one thing that is certain is that China will be more assertive and more willing to defend its rights. The days when colonial powers could assert their demands through gunboats are over. China has expressed its core interests and is willing to defend those rights, even if only as the last option will it resort to arms.

THE NEW MODEL PLA?

As we step into 2016, President Xi Jinping's military reform, which has been in progress since 2014, has just unfolded the biggest shake-up in the past months, touching almost every military institution.

The aim of these changes are two-fold, to strengthen President Xi's grip on the 2.3 million troops of the PLA and turn the PLA into a more coherent, effective, and efficient fighting force. Despite new weaponry the PLA was not a modern army capable of warfare in the 21st century. One of the key changes was the breaking down of the inter-service rivalry to make the PLA a truly combined and integrated armed force. It has taken almost four years since Xi came to power to make these modernizing changes, reflecting both the importance and difficulties to break down vested interests against changes.

Xi's first action after he was made chairman of the Central Military Commission (CMC) was to cut out the rot that had taken hold at all levels of the military. His nationwide "tiger and flies" anti-corruption campaign (no matter big or small as long as they are corrupt they will not escape the law) has netted more than forty-four senior officers—"tigers"—including general-grade senior officers such as Gu Junshan (谷俊山), Deputy Head of the Logistics Department, Deputy Political Head (commissar) of the Second Artillery Corps, China's strategic nuclear force, Zhang Dongshui (张东水), Lanzhou MR Logistics Department head Zhang Wansong (张万松), Heilongjiang Military Sub-District Deputy Commander Zhang Daixin (张代新), to name a few.

The PLA itself has long admitted that it is lagging behind the US military. The PLA may now have plenty of new weapons—China has admitted that it is building a second conventionally powered aircraft carrier—but its outdated command control and management system failed to make effective use of new capabilities. Before any substantial changes in this area, President Xi felt that the aura of "money-grabbing" practice had to be stamped out and therefore the anti-corruption drive was first on the agenda before the organizational reform.

The reform began at the apogee of the PLA, the CMC, the four headquarters of the PLA—the GSD, the GAD, the GLD, and the GPD—were all disbanded as of December 31, 2015. From January 1, 2016, the functions of these independent departments which once operated virtually as fiefdoms were split up, slimmed down and absorbed into the CMC as sub-functionaries. These are split into six separate departments, six standalone offices and three independent commissions, all for better supervision and control. These new sub-functionaries of the CMC are:

1. General Office (办公厅)
2. Joint Staff Department (联合参谋部)—Founded on January 11, 2016
3. Political Work Department (政治工作部)
4. Logistics Support Department (后勤保障部)
5. Equipment Development Department (装备发展部)
6. Training and Administration Department (训练管理部)
7. National Defense Mobilization Department (国防动员部)
8. Discipline Inspection Commission (纪律检查委员会)
9. Politics and Legal Affairs Commission (政法委员会)
10. Science and Technology Commission (科学技术委员会)
11. Office for Strategic Planning (战略规划办公室)
12. Office for Reform and Organizational Structure (改革和编制办公室)
13. Office for International Military Cooperation (国际军事合作办公室)
14. Audit Office (审计署)
15. Agency for Offices Administration (机关事务管理总局)

Of the three independent commissions reporting directly to the CMC, i.e. to President Xi himself, first and foremost is the "Discipline Inspection Commission," in charge of rooting out corruption, a task previously delegated to a commission that was subordinate to the GPD.

The second reform has been to put the various services on a more equal footing. The land forces have hitherto reigned supreme for many years because the main pillars of the PLA were largely constructed when the main threat to China was from the Soviet Union. The most obvious way this threat would come as a land invasion across the vast Sino-Soviet land border. But now the "threat" is from the South and Eastern Seas, fear of US-led encroachment on China near seas interests, and the protection of China's ambitious "One Belt, One Road" development strategy—a 21st-century silk land and maritime road economic cooperation plan that stretches to Southeast Asia, Central Asia, Africa, Middle East, and even to Europe. The PLA is no more a land-centric force, to accommodate this new outlook, a separate command has been created for the Army which has for many years run things on behalf of the Navy and Air Force. The Air Force and the Navy are now independently run. On top of that there are two new branches of the PLA, a Cyber Command responsible for cyber, intelligence, psych-ops and space warfare called the PLA Strategic Support Force and the Second Artillery Corps. China's nuclear force, once part of the army is now a separate branch, the PLA Rocket Corps. There is also a new joint command to take care of the new structure, something akin to the US Joint Chiefs of Staff concept.

Big changes are afoot in the regional command structures, gone are the seven military regions which ran as more or less self-contained entities. One of the major effects of this reorganization will be on recruit training, which will now be conducted centrally by the various services before regional deployment; previously each MR would have trained their own recruits separately, and the style and content of military education could not be guaranteed. A second indication of this new change is that the arm badge of the new Theatre Command has been changed into a "combined arms" logo bearing the combined symbols of land, air, sea, and rocket forces and the Army badge has been changed from two crossed rifles to a winged wheel logo that symbolized greater mobility.

The new military administration zones have been cut from seven to five. From February 1, 2016, the five new military regions have been renamed and reorganized as:

1. Eastern Theater (the direct translation from Chinese is "battle zone") Command—Least affected, essentially the old Nanjing MR geographical area.
2. Southern Theater Command—covering Guangzhou MR and part of Chengdu MR.
3. Western Theater Command—covering Lanzhou MR and part of Chengdu MR.
4. Northern Theater Command—A new command, joining the Beijing and Shenyang MR and part of the Jinan MR.
5. Central Theater Command—A new command, joining part of the former Guangzhou MR, Beijing, and Jinan MR.

These changes give the PLA more flexibility to face different threats, for example the Eastern Theater Command faces Taiwan and the new Command HQ has been shifted from Nanjing, the land-locked city in Central China to Fuzhou, a city in the coastal province of Fujian province. With the sea in front this new command the operational structure put emphasis on amphibious warfare with a heavy emphasis on the PLA Marine Corps and naval and air capacity.

The culling of the military regions from seven to five will no doubt involve personnel cuts. In September 2015 during the celebration of the seventieth anniversary of VJ Day, Xi announced that the PLA will have to lose 300,000 of its members, bringing the overall numbers of the PLA from 2.3 million down to just two million. How the cuts will occur remains to be seen, no official press release has yet been made, but it is clear that the Army will be hit hardest by the latest cull, rumor has it that of the eighteen army groups, five will be disbanded (27th from Beijing MR, 40th from Shenyang MR, 20th and 26th from Jinan MR, and 14th from Chengdu MR) and part of the other forces will be absorbed into the remaining thirteen Army Groups structure.

There will then be the challenge of absorbing these 300,000 ex-soldiers back into society. State firms have been ordered to give priority to ex-soldiers for jobs and some commentators close to the army has said that up to 5% of its jobs in state-owned corporations are to be reserved for the latest batch of demobbed soldiers.

The latest batch of military reforms will not be the last—as President Xi has announced, this is only the first of the series of military reforms and more changes will come.

New weaponry

The DF-21D (range 1,700 km) and DF-26 (3,500–4,000 km, nicknamed by the West as "Guam Killer" because of its ability to reach US Guam) anti-ship ballistic missiles are much mentioned but never seen until finally revealed to the world during the seventieth anniversary VJ Day parade. The Y-8FQ ASW variant GX-6 Maritime Patrol Aircraft also at last entered PLANAF service with the 6th Regiment, 2nd Aviation Division, the North Sea Fleet, after years of testing. These aircraft are reported to be based in Dalian. The Chinese Ministry of Defense has confirmed that the construction of the second domestically designed and built aircraft carrier is in progress. This is to be a conventionally powered vessel as China still lacks the ability to make a reliable nuclear power propulsion plant. However, speculation is rife that work on a nuclear power aircraft carrier is in the design stage. Besides the high-profile carrier, more warships have been added to the Chinese Navy. The sixth and last 052C-class (NATO: *Lvyang II*) destroyer (Pennant Number: 153, CNS *Xian*) was finally commissioned in early 2015, two 052D-class (NATO: *Lvyang III*) destroyers (Pennant Number: 173, CNS *Changsha*; 174, CNS *Hefei*), four 054A-class (NATO: *Jiangkai II*) frigates (Pennant Number: 576, CNS *Daqing*; 577, CNS *Huanggang*; 578, CNS *Yangzhou*; 579, CNS *Handan*) and six 056/A-class (NATO: *Jiangdao*) corvettes (Pennant Number: 501, CNS *Xinyang*; CNS 502, CNS *Huangshi*; 503, CNS *Suzhou*; 504, CNS *Suqian*; 505, CNS *Qinhuangdao*; 506, CNS *Jiangmen*) were all commissioned into the PLAN fleet. China's amphibious capacity is further enhanced with a new 701-class LSD (Pennant

Number: 988, CNS *Mount Yimeng*) as well as one *Zuber* Class LCAC from Ukraine (Pennant Number: 3326) added to the South Seas Fleet. On the support side two 903A-class AORs (Pennant Number: 966, CNS *Lake Gaoyou*; 960, CNS *Lake Dongping*), not to mentioned a large number of auxiliaries including an ice-breaker (Pennant Number: 722, CNS *Hai Bing*), one Expeditionary Transfer Dock (ESD) heavy lift ship, two Type -072B medium Landing Ship Dock (LSD), two Type-904B General supply ships, one Type 636 hydro-survey research ship and two Type-815A electronic intelligence-gathering ships were also added to the ORBAT of PLAN. Although too late to make the 2015 list of launched, a new high-speed AOE, tailored to the need of supplying the new Chinese aircraft carrier, the 901-class is already undergoing fitting in Guangzhou. In 2016, in addition to the existing designs, we can expect to see an all-new 12,000-ton fleet air defense destroyer, the 055-class being launched. This new vessel is expected to be the aircraft carrier battle group primary air defense guardian.

On the Air Force side confirmation of China's order of twenty-four Su-35s was finally unveiled by both Chinese and Russian governments, ending an almost decade-long negotiation. Progress on the domestically built "Flanker" is continuing. The J-16 long-range multirole strike aircraft has finally been delivered to the PLAAF, the J-11D, a single-seat fighter with modern avionics such as an AESA radar as well as the J-16D, an electronic warfare variant of the J-16 both made their maiden flights but without much fanfare in the Chinese media. The numbers of J-10B/C fighters are gradually increasing; this much-awaited fighter aircraft will replace the older J-10A. It is also worth noting that at least two J-10Bs regiments have been refitted with the WS-10 turbofan, to eventually replace imported Russian-built AI-31 family turbofans aboard J-10B/C production. However, China is well aware that their aero-engine technology is still behind that of the West and there has been a major announcement that the Chinese state will invest US\$ 50 billion in the development of new jet engines, hiring Western experts to be advisors.

Pictures of the J-20, the Chinese stealth fighter which is still undergoing testing, are now a common sight in the Chinese press. In December 2015, images emerged of a J-20 with serial number 2101, which is highly suspected if not virtually confirmed to be the first Low Rate Initial Production (LRIP) model of the J-20, suggesting the aircraft has reached the next stage of development. It is worth noting that at this stage the J-20 is still only being powered by the interim Al-31 family of engines rather than the intended, more powerful WS-15s. On the non-fighter side development, the Y-20, the Chinese wide-body strategic transporter is in steady progress reaching the LRIP stage, along with the development of the airframe. There are hopes that the WS-20 high bypass turbofan will replace the older imported D-30s currently in use.

In November 2015 the US military reported on the third successful tests of the Chinese hypersonic glide vehicle, with its designation changed from WU-14 to DF-ZF, also news of a new generation long-range road mobile solid-fuelled DF-41 ICBM with multiple independent warheads (MIRV) capable of a reach of 12,000–15,000 km is in progress. Also quoting from news from the United States, as the Chinese almost never release news of its strategic force, the Chinese Navy's 094-class SSBNs began their first deterrent patrols, indicating the 094s and their JL-2 SLBMs had likely reached a level of operational readiness such that the Navy was confident in their ability to make long patrols.

As President Xi has pointed out that the emphasis is on seaward threats from the east and south, the development of new land-based weapon systems has been relegated to a sad third place. The only notable new weapon for the Army is a new lightweight "mountain" tank, named by the Chinese media as ZTQ. The mountain tank has been seen deployed in Xinjiang and Tibet in which potential clashes over disputed land at high altitudes against the India remains a source of unease for the Chinese. The PLA land force's main development will focus on command and control, to be more digital, to improve the information flow which will help to build a more integrated armed force, combining not only the traditional sea, land, air dimensions but also space and cyber.

The PLA is also active on the international front. For the first time a combat unit, a reinforced infantry battalion, has been sent to participate in UN peacekeeping operations, to Sudan as part of the UNMISS. In October 2015, President Xi promised to assign an 8,000-man UN peacekeeper force with attached helicopter unit to Africa. Therefore, the footprint of the PLA in the future will be much more overt and visible. However, as we enter 2016, we will see more PLA activities outside that of the UN framework, including combat role. In the last days of December 2015, the Chinese parliament had just enacted the nation's first counterterrorism law that allows the PLA to fight terrorism on a global basis. The Chinese definition of "terrorism" is defined as any proposition or activity—that, by means of violence, sabotage or threat, generates social panic, undermines public security, infringes on personal and property rights, and menaces government organs and international organizations—with the aim of realizing certain political and ideological purposes.

Although in 2014 she was narrowly pipped by Germany, China could still claim to be the world's fourth biggest arms seller. News of Chinese arms sales has been mixed, success is noted with sales of UAVs to Saudi Arabia and Nigeria (deployed in the fight against ISIS and Boko Haram), wheeled armored cars to Kenya, C-28A Corvettes to Algeria, C-701 anti-ship missiles to Indonesia, amphibious tanks, APC and jet trainers to the Venezuelan Marine Corps. Despite the variety the main outlets for Chinese arms are just three countries, Pakistan (mainly FC-1/JF-17 fighter), Bangladesh, and Myanmar, but Turkey chose to cancel an agreed purchase of Chinese SAM under NATO/US pressure citing system integration as an excuse. Good value for money continued to attract buyers.

Potential hotspots

The South China and Eastern Seas remain the two greatest hotspots for China. The disputed Diaoyu Islands (Senkaku Islands to the Japanese) remains a flash point. In 2015 the emphasis shifted to the South Seas, where the reclamation of reef/islands by the Chinese was highlighted and interpreted in Western media as a series of "greedy land-grabbing" actions by Communist China. These disputes are further complicated by the participation in the arguments by the actions of two out-of-area participants, Japan siding with the Philippines and India supporting

Vietnam in confronting the Chinese on this matter. From the Chinese point of view, this is further evidence of "containment" of China and the double standards in administering disputes. Building on and enlarging of reef/island facilities is not only being undertaken by China, but also by other claimants. Malaysia has built extensively on Swallow Reef (Pulau Layang-Layang, Dawan Reef, Celerio) one of the many reefs of the Spratly Islands Group that it occupies that has an airport, Taiwan has just lengthened the runway on Taiping Island (Itu Aba Island, Ligao, Ba Binh), while Philippines has just repaired the previously unpaved runway on Thitu Island (Zhongye Island) using US aid. Many of these reefs/islands are claimed by a number of states, judging by the different names it is known by. A recent move by the Philippines to bring China to the International Court of Arbitration in The Hague is expected to be ruled sometime of 2016. The resolution of these complicated disputes are unlikely to be eased by this move, as China has not agreed to this method of resolution thus this court case is a rather one-sided, with no defendant in the dock. Under these circumstances it is difficult to see how a resolution can be achieved and can only be a strategy to incense China further. Even if the case is ruled in favor of the Philippines, the court has no means of enforcement so one may question what all this work is for.

Recent actions by the US military—USS *Curtis Wilbur* (DDG-54) and USS *Lassen* (DDG-82) sailing close to the Chinese-occupied reefs/Islands—has inflamed Beijing. The justification of these sailings was supposed to be "exercising freedom of navigation," or saying the United States don't recognize the territorial waters claims. To the Chinese this is direct provocation by the United States and China will not back down, it will only further enhance Beijing's determination to build and hold on to these contested reefs/islands. As a signal to the world of China's resolve, during the recent (2016) Chinese New Year celebration holiday, the Chinese news media highlighted a report of "hard-working construction crews working through the holiday period" on the Paracel Islands. Reports of radar and SAM missiles permanently based in the Chinese part of these disputed islands confirm the Chinese determination on safeguarding sovereignty of the islands. Perhaps as a counter tit-for-tat move, against these sailings by the USN, the Chinese PLAN has recently sailed through international waters and conducted a clockwise circumnavigation of Japan (Qingdao Home port, Tsushima Straits, Tsugaru Straits, Osumi Straits back to home port) causing much concern to the Japanese.

APPENDICES

The following appendices list all major weapons in service with the PLA in 2016. As far as possible names are used as they appear in the Chinese press or Chinese PLA designation; NATO names are listed alongside the Chinese PLA names to aid readers.

1

PLA Infantry Weapons

Name	Caliber (mm)	Type	Weight (kg)	Magazine	Range (m)	Comments
QSZ-92	9x19 parabellum 5.8x21 DAP92	QSZ-92-9, QSZ-92-5.8 semi-automatic pistol	0.93 (QSZ-92-9 loaded)	15 (9 mm) 20 (5.8 mm)	50	PLA, PAP
Type-77	7.62x17 (model 64 rounds) 9x19 parabellum	Type-77-7 (7.62 mm) Type-77B (9 mm) semi-automatic pistol	0.5	9 or 15	–	PLA, PAP, Reserves
QQS-05 (P-119?)	4 barrels	Underwater pistol		5	10–15?	Design based on Soviet PPS-01 but highly modified
Type-97	18.4x69.8 Gauge 12	Type-97-1, Type-97-2, Pump action Shotgun	2.75 (T-79), 3.05(T-97-1), 3.2 (T-97-2)	4+1	40	Clone Remington 870
QBS-09	18.4x69.85 Gauge 12	Collapsed Stock Combat Shotgun	3.45	5+1	50	PLA
QSW-06	5.8x21 DAP92 5.8x21 DCV05	QSW-06	< 1 kg	20	50	Pistol (Silenced)

(Continued)

Name	Caliber (mm)	Type	Weight (kg)	Magazine	Range (m)	Comments
Type 95	5.8x42	QBZ-95, QBZ-95 Gai	3.25 (unloaded)	30	400–600	Bullpup Version Assault Rifle
		QBZ-95B, QBZ-95B Gai	2.9 (unloaded)		300–500	Carbine
Type-88		QBB-95	3.95 (unloaded)	30–75	600–800	LSW
		QBU-88 DMR	4.1	10	800–1,000	Designated Marksman rifle
Type-03		QBZ-03	3.5	30	400	Assault Rifle Airborne Forces
Type-05	5.8x21	QCW-05	2.2	50	50	SMG (Silenced)
Type-81	7.62x39	Type-81-1 (Folding butt)	3.4~3.5 (loaded)	30	500	Assault Rifle for second line troops
		Type-81 LMG	5.15	75	500	LMG
Type-56		Type-56-1 (Folding butt) Type-56C (Carbine)	3-70~4.03	20~30	300–400	Assault Rifle For ceremonial and some militia
Type-56		Type-56 Carbine	3.85	10	400	Chinese version of Soviet SKS Carbine. For Honor Guard use only with chrome metal parts
Type-85	7.62x25	Type-85 Silenced	1.9–2.5	30	150–200	SMG, mainly in service with PAP and police
Type-79		Type-79 SMG	1.75	20	200	SMG, mainly with airborne and special force

(Continued)

Name	Caliber (mm)	Type	Weight (kg)	Magazine	Range (m)	Comments
CF-05 (CS/LF-06)	9x19parabellum	CS/LS-05 SMG	2.1 (unloaded)	50	150~100?	SMG for PAP mainly
Type-79	7.62x54 (model 53 rounds)	Type-85 Sniper Rifle	4.31 (unloaded)	10	800	Chinese Copy of Soviet Dragunov SVD, Type-85 is improved version of T-79. Mainly with PAP and Police
JS 7.62		JS-7.62 Sniper Rifle	5.5 (unloaded)	5		In limited service PLA, PAP and Police
QBU-10	12.7x108 (model 54 rounds)	QBU-10 AMR QBU-09 (Older Version of QBU-10)	13.3	5	1,500	Under Trail? Limited Service with Special Force
QJY-88	5.8x42 (model 87 rounds)	QJY-88 GPMG	7.6 (Light), 11.8 (Heavy),	100-200 Belt	1,000	PLA, PAP
Type-80	7.62x54	Type-80 GPMG	12.6	100-250 Belt	700-800	Copy Soviet PKM
Type-67		Type-67 GPMG	11	100-250 Belt	800-1,000	Replace by QJY-88
QJG-02	14.5x114	QJG-02 HMG	75	50 Belt	2000	Also used on Tanks / AFVs
QJZ-89	12.7x108	QJZ-89 HMG	26.5		1500	ReplacedType-77
Type-85	12.7x108	HMG	40 (with tripod)	60 Belt	800-1600	

(Continued)

Name	Caliber (mm)	Type	Weight (kg)	Magazine	Range (m)	Comments
QLZ-87	35x114	AGL	20 (with tripod)	Drums 6,9,12	600	Phasing Out
QLZ-04	35x32		24 (with tripod)	30 Belt	600 (spot), 800 (optical), 1,000 (area)	Replace QLZ-87
QLZ-06	35	SAGL	9.1	Drums 4,6,15	600–800	AMR configuration
PF-98	120 rocket	PF-98A AT rocket launcher	PF-98 (10) PF-98A (7)	–	300~500	HEAT rds
PF-89	80x900 LAW type RPG	PF-89A, PF-89B	PF-89 (3.7) (loaded) PF-89A (4.2) (loaded)	Single shot	200	Single shot throw-away shaped charged RPG
FHJ-84	62	FHJ-84	?	?	?	Over and Under type incendiary and smoke rocket launcher
PP-89	60	60 mm Mortar	?	–	2,700	
PP-93	60	60 mm Mortars	22.4	–	5,564	Battalion asset
PP-87	82	82 mm Mortar	40	–	4,660 (charge 6) 5,700	
PP-89	100	100 mm Mortar	73 (not inc. sights)	–	6,400	Regimental asset
W-86	120	120 mm Mortar	206	–	7,700	

(Continued)

Name	Caliber (mm)	Type	Weight (kg)	Magazine	Range (m)	Comments
W-99	82	82 mm Towed Mortar	650	4 (rapid fire)	4,270	4 rounds in 1.5 Sec
Type-02	–	Type-02A (Two tanks) Type-02C	Type-02A (14.5)	–	–	Flame thrower
QSB-91	7.62x17 (model 64 rounds)	Dagger with pistol port	0.69	4	10	Special Force Only
Type-82-2	5.6	Dagger with pistol port	0.33	3	5–8	
QBS-06	5.8x42 (underwater)	Underwater assault rifle	3.15	25	?	

2

Tanks and AFVs of the PLA

Name	Caliber (mm)	Type	Weight (t)	Range (km)	Crew	Speed (kph)	Comments
ZTZ-99	125/41, 125/50.	ZTZ-99, ZTZ-99A2 (MBT)	51	2+ (APFSDS)	3	65–80	QJC-88 HMG, Coaxial 7.62
ZTZ-98	125/48	MBT	52			70	
ZTZ-96	125	ZTZ-96A (MBT)	43			65	QJC-88 HMG, Coaxial 12.7, 7.62 GPMG
T-88	125	T-88C (MBT)	39		4	56	12.7 mm HMG, 7.62 coaxial,
ZTZ-59D	105	ZTZ-51D1 (MBT)	37+		4	50+	12.7 HMG, 7.62 Coaxial Firefighting variant also exists
T-GCZ110	7.62 GPMG	Tracked Engineering Vehicle	37.5	–	3	?	Based on T-79 MBT tank
T-653	7.62 GPMG	ARV	38	–	5	50 (road)	Base on Type 69 MBT
T-84		AVLB	38.5	–	3	50	Span—16, carry 40 tons in 3-4 minutes. Based on T-79 MBT tank
T-82	Type-54 12.7 HMG	CET	20.5	–	4	48 (road)	Based on T-62 light tank

(Continued)

Name	Caliber (mm)	Type	Weight (t)	Range (km)	Crew	Speed (kph)	Comments
T-62	85	T-62 Gai, T-70, T-79. Light Tank	21	?	4	60 (road), 35 (cross country)	7.62 Coaxial, Being phased out
T-63	85/105	T-63A, T-63A1, T-63AII, T-63HG, Amphibious Light Tank	18-19	?	4	36 (land), 12 (water)	7.62 coaxial, 12.7 mm HMG
T-63	Type-54 12.7 HMG	T-63-1, T-63-2, Many variants: Command, Rebroadcast, Forest Firefighting, APC	12.6	–	2+10	65-46	Type-81: Command APC Most Type-63 are relegated to reserve
Type-77	12.7 HMG	APC with many Variants: Type-77-1, Type-77-2, Type-76, Type GCZ-111:AEV, Type 89 (SPG) Amphibious	16		2+20	60 (land) 12 (water)	Based on the Type-63 Tank but look alike to the Soviet BTR-50

(Continued)

Name	Caliber (mm)	Type	Weight (t)	Range (km)	Crew	Speed (kph)	Comments
Type-85 (ZSD-85)	Type-59 12.7 HMG	Type-85Many variants: Command, Mortar, Artillery survey, SPG, Recce, Ambulance, ARV, Supply, Rebroadcast,	13.6	–	2+13	65	Improvement on Type-63
Type-89 (ZSD-89)	25 Chain Gun 12.7 HMG, 7.62 GPMG	Many variants AFV, AIFV Command, Mortar, Ambulance, Refueling, Artillery survey, ARV, Supply, Recce, Radar, Mine laying, Obstacle removing, Anti-tank Forest Fire fighting (SXD-09), Special Rescue vehicle etc.	14.3	–	2+13	66	Improvement on Type-85 ZSD-89II: AIFV ZJX-93: Recovery; Type-99: Command, ZHB-94: Supply, ZZC-01: Recce, Type-93/ZZC-02: Radar (LLP3 radar/camera that can be elevated 10 m), ZDF-1: ATGM carrier

(Continued)

Name	Caliber (mm)	Type	Weight (t)	Range (km)	Crew	Speed (kph)	Comments
ZSL-90	105, 122 Howitzer	6x6 Wheeled APC	12.5	–	3+9 or 11	85	Problems lead to ZSL-92
ZSL-92	73, 25 12.7 HMG, Type-86 7.62 GPMG HJ-73D ATGM	4x4, 6x6 and 8x8 Wheeled APC, AIFV Many Variants ZSL-92A, ZSL-92B, ATGM carrier, Mortar, Ambulance, ARV, Command, SAM carrier, Police version					Improved ZSL-90 Police Variant has non-lethal weapons
	120 Mortar	PPL-05 (6x6 wheeled APC)	16.5	–	4	80 (land), 8 (water)	12.7 HMG
ZBD-86	73, HJ-73DMissile	ZBD-86 AIFV	13.3	1.3 (HESH), 2.9 (HE)	3+8	65	Clone of Soviet BMP-1
ZBD-97	30, 100	ZBD-97	20	?	3+7	68 (land) 6 (water)	Type-86 7.62 mm GPMG
ZBD-03	30 HJ-73C	ZBD-03 Airborne AIFV	8	?		75	
ZBD-04	100	ZBD-04 AIFV	20	?			
ZBD-05	30 HJ-73D	Tracked Amphibious	26		3+8	40 (water)	PLAMC, 7.62 coaxial
ZBD-09	Missiles	8x8 AIFV	21	?	3+7	100 (road), 8 (water)	7.62 coaxial

(Continued)

Name	Caliber (mm)	Type	Weight (t)	Range (km)	Crew	Speed (kph)	Comments
ZTD-05	105	Amphibious	26	?	4	28–32 knots (water)	7.62 coaxial
Type-85	130x30 AFV	Type-85 130 mm MBRL	14.5	10–15	6	60	
Type-89 (PHZ-89)	122x40 AFV	Type-89 122 mm MBRL	33	40	5	55	12.7 mm HMG, Each AFV carried a 40 rocket reload that can be reloaded in 3 min
Type-90	122x40 Wheeled	Type-90 122 wheeled MBRL	20	40	?	30	6x6 truck
A-100 (PHL-03)	300x12	8x8 Trucked MBRL	43–44	400	WS-2D—400 km for pinpoint or area targets. Warheads includes		Chinese copy of the Soviet 9A52-4 Tornado (Smerch) 8x8-truck base. Different types of munitions WS-2A—70 km for area targets, traditional HE to Anti-radiation for knocking out electronics. Crew is 3 per vehicle, a company consists of 1 command truck, six launchers, and six ammunition carriers. With up to 48 rounds per vehicles
WM-80	273	WM-80 273 MBRL	?	?	3	70–80	8x8 truck

(Continued)

Name	Caliber (mm)	Type	Weight (t)	Range (km)	Crew	Speed (kph)	Comments
Type-83	152	SPG	30	17 Standard	5	55	12.7 mm HMG
PLZ-05	155/52		35	50~100	4	56	QJC-88 12.7 mm HMG
PLZ-07	122/32		24.5	18 Standard 27 Rocket	5	65	PLAMC
PLZ-07B	122/32						QJC-88 12.7 mm HMG
PLZ-45 (Type-88)	155/45		33	24 (HE)30 (ERFB)		55	
PLZ-89	122/32		20	18 Standard 2 (ERFB HB)		60	PLA, PLAMC Replace by PLZ-07
PTL-02	100	Assault gun Wheeled	18	?	4	75	T-86 7.62 GMPG 12.7 mm HMG
PGZ-07	35x2 4 x Missiles	SPAAG AFV	-	?	4	55	T-90 35 mm AA guns
PGZ-95	25x4 QW-2 SAM		22.5	6 (gun)	3	53	Tracked SPAAGA typical PGZ-95 battery consists of six SPAAG, and a single command vehicle with three ammunition re-supply trucks, a test/repair truck and a power supply truck.

(Continued)

Name	Caliber (mm)	Type	Weight (t)	Range (km)	Crew	Speed (kph)	Comments
902 FCS	35x2	SPAAG 6x6 truck	?	?	?	?	?
?	35	SPAAG 8x8 truck	?	?	?	?	?
ZFB-05	35 mm Grenade launcher, 23x2 Chain Gun or 12.7 mm HMG or 7.62 GPMG	4x4 Light Armoured vehicle ZFB-05A, ZFB-05B, Grenade launder, Chain gun, Broadcasting, Police, Ambulance, Anti-riot	4.5–4.7	?	2+7–9	110	Manufactured by Shaanxi Baoji Special Vehicle Factory—China's first private arms manufacturer

3

Artillery of the PLA

Name	Caliber (mm)	Type	Weight (kg)	Range (m)	Comments
Type-63	107x12	Tow MBRL	602	8	Mainly with specialist troops such as mountain
Type-96	122/38	Tow Howitzer	3,290	16–22	Three versions (Type-83, Type 86) each with slight variations of the same—copy of the Soviet D-30
Type-59	130		Type-59 (8,500) Type-59-1 (6,400)	27 Standard 44 Rocket assisted	Developed based on the Soviet M-46 Howitzer
Type-66	152		5,650~5,720	17 Standard 28 Rocket Assisted	Clone of Soviet D-20
Type-83	152		9,700~10,500	30	Replacement of Type-59-1 130 mm Howitzer
Type-83	122	Tow Howitzer	2,700	15.6	Reserve units mainly
W-88	155		12,000 (with self-propulsion)	30–39	Self-propulsion 18 km/h (WA-021 is trade name for overseas sales)
Type-86	100	Tow ATG	?	–	–
PLL-05	120	Howitzer/ Mortar SPG	16,500	9.5–8.5	Type-85 12.7 mm HMG 6x6 wheeled base

(Continued)

Name	Caliber (mm)	Type	Weight (kg)	Range (m)	Comments
Type-85	23x2	Tow AAA	950	2.5	Integrated air defense system Shengong consisted of eight towed T-85 twin 23 mm AAA, and a command vehicle. Similar to Soviet ZU-23-2
Type-59	57		4,660	4–6	Chinese version of Soviet S-60
Type-90	35x2	PG-99 Tow AAA	6,300	3–4	Based on Swiss Oerlikon GDF-002 35 mm AA gun
Type-74	37x2	Tow AAA, Many variants Type-74SD, Type 79III, P-793, JP-113	3,100 9,000 (JP-113)	6.7–8.5 7.8–9.4 (JP-113)	Developed from the T-55 Model which single barrel.

4

Ships of the PLAN

Class (NATO name)	Pennant Nos	Type	Numbers	Displacement (tons)	Fleet	Comments
			Submarines			
T-094 "晉" *Jin*	–	SSBN	2 or more	9000	North South	–
T-092 "夏" *Xia*	406		1	8,000	North	CNS *Changzheng 6*
T-093 "商" *Shang*	407–408	SSN	4	6,500	North	2–4 More under construction
						CNS *Changzheng 7, 8*
T-091 "汉" *Han*	403–405		5 built (2 decomm.)	4500–5500	North	CNS *Changzheng 3, 4, 5*
T-032 "清" *Qing*		Experimental ballistic missile submarine	1	6,628		
Project 629 "Golf"			1	3,553		
T-039A/B "元" *Yuan*	330–332, 334, 336, 340 ??	Attack	12	3,600	North East	

(Continued)

Class (NATO name)	Pennant Nos	Type	Numbers	Displacement (tons)	Fleet	Comments
T-039 "宋" Song	320–326		13	2,250		
T-877 & T-636 Kilo	364–375		12	3,076	East South	Import from Russia.
T-035 "明" Ming			12? 17?	1,500		
Surface Vessel						
T-001 Admiral Kuznetsov-class aircraft carrier	16	Aircraft Carrier	1	67,500	Not part of fleet	Training Vessel, CNS Liaoning
Sovremenny-class типа Современный	136–139	Guided missile destroyer	4	7,940	East	CNS Hangzhou, Taizhou, Fuzhou, Ningbo
T-051 "旅大" Lvda	109–110, 133–134, 163–166.		8	3,670	North East South	CNS Kaifeng, Dalian, Chongqing, Zunyi, Nanchang, Guilin, Zhanjiang, Zhuhai
T-051C "旅洲" Lvzhou	115–116		2	7,100	North	CNS Shenyang, Shijiazhuang
T-051B "旅海" Lvhai	167		1	6,100	South	CNS Shenzhen
T-052 "旅沪" Lvhu	112–113		2	4,800	North	CNS Harbin, Qingdao
T-052B "旅洋" I Lvyang I	168–169		2	6,500	South	CNS Guangzhou, Wuhan
T-052C "旅洋" II Lvyang II	150–153, 170–171		6	7,000	East South	CNS Changchun, Zhengzhou, Jinan, Xian, Lanzhou, Haikou

(Continued)

Class (NATO name)	Pennant Nos	Type	Numbers	Displacement (tons)	Fleet	Comments
T-052D "旅洋" III Lvyang III	118–120, 172–175		8	7,500?	North South	CNS Kunming, Changsha, Guiyang, Nanning, Yinchun, Xining, Taiyuan, Dalian (Not yet in service, however Kunming will be the lead boat for commission in 2014 follow by Changsha and Guiyang)
T-053H "江卫" Jiangsu I	516 517	Fire Support Training	1+1	1,662	East (CNS Nanping 517 is a training ship at Dalian Naval Academy)	CNS Jiujiang
T-053H1 "江卫" II Jianghu II	533–534, 543, 545, 544, 553, 555.	Frigate	6+1	1,700	South (Except for 544 CNS Siping Training ship in Dalian Naval Academy)	CNS Taizhou, Jinhua, Dandong, Linfen, Shaoguan, Shaotong,

(Continued)

Class (NATO name)	Pennant Nos	Type	Numbers	Displacement (tons)	Fleet	Comments
T-053H2 "江卫" III *Jianghu III*	537		1	1,960	North	CNS *Cangzhou,*
T-053H1G "江卫" V *Jianghu V*	558–563		6	1,661	South	CNS *Beihai, Foshan, Dongguan, Shantou, Jiangmen, Zhaoqing*
T-053H2G "江卫" I *Jianwei I*	539–542		4	2,300	East	CNS *Anqing, Huainan, Huaibei, Tongling*
T-053H3 "江卫" II *Jianwei II*	521–524, 527–528, 564–567.		10	2,500	North East	CNS *Jiaxing, Lianyungang, Putian, Sanming, Luoyang, Mianyang, Yichang, Huludao, Huaihua, Xiangyang*
T-054 "江凯" I *Jiangkai I*	525–526		2	3,900	East	CNS *Ma'anshan, Wenzhou*
T-054A "江凯" II *Jiangkai II*	529–530, 538, 546–550, 568–575		16 (additional four—CNS *Hangshi, Sanmenxia* to be commissioned in 2014)	4,400–5,000	North East South	CNS *Zhoushan, Xuzhou, Yantai, Yancheng, Linyi, Yiyang, Changzhou, Weifang, Hengyang, Yulin, Huangshan, Yuncheng, Hengshui, Liuzhou, Sanya, Yueyang*

(Continued)

Class (NATO name)	Pennant Nos	Type	Numbers	Displacement (tons)	Fleet	Comments
T-056 "江岛" *Jiangdao*	580–587, 596–597.	Corvettes	More than 50 is ordered, so far 10	1,440	North East South Hong Kong	CNS *Datong, Yingkou, Bengbu, Shangrao, Meizhou, Baise, Jian,Jieyang,Huizhou, Qinzhou*
T-037-II "沪建" *Hujian*	770–775	Missile Boats	6	520	South	CNS *Yangjiang, Shunde, Nanhai, Panyu, Lianjiang, Xinhui*
T-037-ID "沪新" *Huxin*	?, 694, 697		4	?	East South	CNS *Nanhui, Yongjia, Ruian, Anji*
T-037-IG "沪新" *Huxin*	651–656, 751–760, 764–767.		30	478	?	?
T-022 "沪北" *Hubei*	2208–??		83	220	North East South	Catamaran design
T-024 "河谷" *Valley*	615, 1103, 1108, 2128, 8107, 9106		50	79	East?	?
T-082II "武藏" *Wuzang*	804, 818	Mine hunter	2	575	East	CNS *Huoqiu, Kunshan*

(Continued)

Class (NATO name)	Pennant Nos	Type	Numbers	Displacement (tons)	Fleet	Comments
T-081 "武池" *Wuchi*	805, 810, 839–845		10	996 (batch 1) 1,200 (batch II)	North East South	CNS *Zhangjiagang, Jingjiang, Liuyang, Luxi, Xiaoyi, Taishan, Changshu, Heshan, Qingzhou*
T-082 "武扫" *Wusao*	801–803, 854	Minesweeper	4	320	East	CNS *Xiangshan, Songming, Fenghua, Doumen,*
T-082 I "武扫" *Wusao*	806–807, 816–817, 820–827		12	320	?	Often misquoted as *Wosao*. *Wu Sao* is Chinese for "Armed Sweep." *Wo* is whirlpool which makes no sense
T-6610T-43 ("抚顺" *Fushun Class*)	?		30? (some transfer to reserve)	570	North East South	CNS *Changxindian, Shajiadian, Zhoukoudian* etc.
T-918 "武雷" *Wulei*	814	Minelayer	1	2418	North	?
T-071 "玉州" *Yuzhao* (PLAN Name: "昆仑山" *Kunlun Shan*)	989, 998, 999.	Landing Ship Dock	3 +2 building	20,000	South	CNS *Kunlunshan, Jinggangshan, Changbaishan*
Pomornik	?	Hovercraft	1 fitting, +3 more	555	? First boat to be commissioned in 2014	?

(Continued)

Class (NATO name)	Pennant Nos	Type	Numbers	Displacement (tons)	Fleet	Comments
T-726 "王义" Yuyi	?		2	160	South	Brand new, still some teething trouble
T-724	?		50+	6.5	South	?
T-072A "玉亭" II Yuting II	911–913, 992–997	Landing Ship Tank LST	9	4,800	North East South	CNS Tianchushan, Daqingshan, Baxianshan, Huadingshan, Luoxiaoshan, Daiyunshan, Wanyangshan, Laotieshan, Yunwushan
T-072III "玉亭" I Yuting I	908–910, 934–937, 939–940, 991		10	4,800	East South	CNS Yandangshan, Jiuhuashan, Huanggangshan, Danxiashan, Xuefengshan, Haiyangshan, Qingchengshan, Putuoshan, Tiantaishan, Emeishan.
T-072II "玉亭" Yuting	930–933		4	4,170	East	CNS Lingyanshan, Dongtingshan, Jialanshan, Liupanshan

(Continued)

Class (NATO name)	Pennant Nos	Type	Numbers	Displacement (tons)	Fleet	Comments
T-072 "玉康" *Yukan*	927–929		3	4,170	East	CNS *Yuntaishan, Wufengshan, Zijinshan*
T-073III "玉登" *Yudeng*	950	Landing Ship Medium LSM	1	2,000	East	CNS *Jinchengshan*
T-073A "玉登" *Yudeng*	941–950		10	2,000	East South山	CNS *Shengshan, Lüshan, Mengshan, Yushan, Huashan, Lanshan, Lishan, Xueshan, Henshan, Taishan.*
T-079II "玉连" *Yulian*	957–986		29 (most may have been paid off or move to reserved)	1,100	South	?
T-074A "玉北" *Yubei*	3,128–29, 3,232–35, 3,315–18	Landing Ship Light LSL	10	800	North East South	?
T-074 "玉海" *Yuhai*	7,593?		12	?	North East South Hong Kong	?
T-271-III "玉盆" *Yupen*	?	Landing Ship Tank LST	500+?	500	North East South	No names just pennant numbers
T-066 "玉寨" *Yuzhai*	Y-XXX		30+?	70	North East South	In auxiliary service as general transport
T-069 "玉清" *Yuqing*			300+	128	North East South	No names just pennant numbers

(Continued)

Class (NATO name)	Pennant Nos	Type	Numbers	Displacement (tons)	Fleet	Comments
T-062IG " 上海" Shanghai (T-0111 or 125 tonne Defence boat)	1,201–08, 1,231–42, 1,271–82		32	135	North East South	No names just pennant numbers
T-037 "海南" Hainan	259, 278–283, 267–270, 295–298, 610, 615–630, 641–648, 664–669, 670–672, 676–677, 680–683, 685–687, 692, 695–696, 699–709, 721–732, 740–742, J505, J-303, J125 medical boat Hujiu 1 (Shanghai Rescue 1), Binhai 409		Approx.96 +3 converted to medical boats +2 rescue boat	392	North East South	?

(Continued)

Class (NATO name)	Pennant Nos	Type	Numbers	Displacement (tons)	Fleet	Comments
T037I "海鸠" Haijiu	688, 693–694, 697.	?	4	450	?	?
T-037 IS "海青" Haiqing	611–614, 631–635, 710–713, 743–744, 761–763, 786–789		22	478	North East South	CNS Haiyang, Zhangqiu, Renqiu, Changli, Yongji, Changhai, Suizhong, Baofeng, Yichun, Jimo, Luoning, Jijiang, Longhai, Yunhe, Fuyang, Xiaoshan, Shangyu, Wangning, Ledong, Dingan, Ligao
T-903 "福池" Fuchi	886–887, 889–890.	Auxiliary Cargo and Explosives AKE	4	23,000	North East South	CNS Qiandaohu, Weishanhu, Taihu, Chaohu
T-904 "大运" Dayun	884	Auxiliary Oiler Explosives AOE	2	10,975	?	CNS Jingpohu
T-908 "南仓" Nancang Komandram Fedko (ex-Soviet)	885	Auxiliary Oiler Replenisher AOR	1	37,000	South	CNS Qinghaihu
"福清" Fuqing (PLAN Name: "大仓") Taichang Class)	881–882		2	21,750	?	CNS Hongzehu, Poyanghu

(Continued)

Class (NATO name)	Pennant Nos	Type	Numbers	Displacement (tons)	Fleet	Comments
T-920	866	Hospital Ship	1	14,000	?	CNS Daishan Dao or The Peace Ark
(PLAN Name: "琼沙" Qiongsha Class)	832–833		2	30,000	South?	CNS Nankang
?	865		1	5,548	?	CNS Zhuanghe
T-917 Trimaran	143	Rescue	1	550	North	Beijiu 143
T-946 (PLAN Name: "大舟" Dazou Class)	137, 502	Submarine Rescue	2	1,100	South	Beijiu 137, Nanjiu 502
T-946A	304		1	1,500	East	Dongjiu 304
T-926	861, 864–865, 867		4	9,500	North, South?	CNS Haiyangdao, Changda, Liugongdao, Changxingdao
T-925 (PLAN Name: "大江" Dajiang Class)	862		1	13,500	East	CNS Chongmingdao
T-922111A (PLAN Name: "大浪" Dalang II Class)	122, 138, 510, 332	Salvage	4		North East South	Beijiu 122, Beijiu 138, Nanjiu 510, Dongjiu 332
T-648	911	Submarine Repair	1	1,962	East	Dongxiu 911
T-0891A	82	National Defense Mobilization	1	9,150	Naval Academy	CNS Deng Shichang

(Continued)

Class (NATO name)	Pennant Nos	Type	Numbers	Displacement (tons)	Fleet	Comments
T-795	81	Training Vessel	1	6,000	Naval Academy	CNS Cheng He
T-813	852	Intelligence Gathering Vessel	1	4,590	South	CNS Haihuangxing (Neptune)
T-814A	900		1	2,198	North	Beitiao 900
T-851 Modified	853		1		?	CNS Tianhuangxing (Jupiter)
T-851	851		1	6,000	East	
?	88	Aircraft Carrier support Passenger/ Crew Ship	1	23,000+	?	CNS Xuxiake
?	22	Survey	1	?	Space and missile tracking	Yuanwang 22
	21		1	9,080		Yuanwang 21
	6		1	24,966		Yuanwang 6
	5		1	?		Yuanwang 5
	3		1	18,000		Yuanwang 3
	2		1	21,000		Yuanwang 2
?	22		1	?	Ocean Survey	Qiansanqiang
T-636A	872	Ocean Survey	1	5,883	?	Zhu Ke Zhen
?	228–229		2	?	East	Dongce 228, Dongce 229

(Continued)

Class (NATO name)	Pennant Nos	Type	Numbers	Displacement (tons)	Fleet	Comments
T-639 Catamaran	991, 992	Sonar Survey	2	1,500	North	Beitiao 991, Beitiao 992
T-646	426	Survey	1	676	South	Nance 426
T-690 (Converted from T-069 Landing Craft)	230, 231		2	?	East	Dongce 230, Dongce 231
T-625C	411, 412		2	3,000	South	Nantiao 411, Nantiao 412
T-068 (Converted from T-068 Landing craft)	907		1	?	North	Beitiao 907
?	721	Ice Breaker	1	?	?	

5

PLAN Torpedoes and Depth Charges

Torpedoes	Origin	Role	Version	Guidance	Range (km) (max)	Comments
Yu-1 (mod) Yu-2 (mod) Yu-3 (mod)	China	ASuW, ASW, CAPTOR Mine	Yu-1, 3 (553 mm) Yu-2 (450 mm)	AAH, PAH	50~39	Oldest torpedoes in PLAN, but modified with new Electronics
Yu-5		AsuW, ASW	ET34, ET-36 (553 mm)	AAH, PAH, Wire	Up to 25	
Yu-6			553 mm	PAH, AAH, Wake homing	45	Similar to US Mk 48
Type 53	Russia				19?	Russian Designation 53-65KE
Yu-7	China		324 mm	PAH, AAH	7.3?	Similar to US Mk 46
S3V Zagon	Russia	AsuW	211 mm	Sonar Guided	600 m Depth	Especially for Ka-28 helicopter

6

Principal Aircraft of the PLA, PLAAF and PLANAF

Aircraft	NATO Name	Origin	Role	Version	Estimated Nos	Comments
			Fixed-Wing Aircraft			
Ilyushin Il-76	Mainring	Russia/ China	AWACS	KJ-2000	4–5?	Conversion to AWACS by Shaanxi Aircraft Company
	Candid (IL-76)		Transport	IL-76MD	9–10?	PLAAF
Shaanxi Y-8	Cub (An-12)	China	AWACS	Y-8W (KJ-200 Balance Beam)	4	PLAAF
				Y-8J	4	PLANAF
			Battlefield Surveillance/ Airborne Command	Y-8G, Y-8T	5+2	PLAAF
			Drone Launcher	Y-8E	1+?	
			Psy-Ops aircraft	Y-8XZ		
			Maritime Patrol	Y-8FQ/ Y-8X.	6	PLANAF
			Reconnaissance	Y-8CA, Y-8CB, Y8DZ	3+	PLAAF
				Y-8JB / Y-8DZ / Y-8EW (ELINT)	5	PLANAF

(Continued)

Aircraft	NATO Name	Origin	Role	Version	Estimated Nos	Comments
			Transport	Y-8, Y-8A/C	7?	PLA
					39	PLAAF
					12	PLANAF
Tupolev Tu-154	Careless	USSR	Reconnaissance	Tu-154MD (ELINT)	4	PLAAF
Xian H-6	Badger (Tu-16)	China	Bomber	H-6A H-6F.	65	
				H-6H, H-6M, H-6K (missile strike)	11++	
				H-6 Drone Launcher	1	
				H-6D, H-6M (missile strike)	23	PLANAF
			EW	H-6D ECM	?	
			Tanker	HY-6U or HU-6 (Air force)	11	PLAAF
				HY-6DU (Navy)	7	Similar capacity to the British Victor K.2. Total fuel uplifts about one half of a KC-135. Each HY-6U can support two fighters

(Continued)

Aircraft	NATO Name	Origin	Role	Version	Estimated Nos	Comments
Sukhoi Su–27	Flanker (Su–27)	Russia	Fighter	Su-27 SK	46	PLAAF
			Fighter /Combat Trainer	Su-27 UBK	39? / 47?	
Sukhoi Su-30MKK	Flanker (Su–30)		Fighter	Su-30MKK	58	
				Su30MK2	23	PLANAF
J-20	?	China		J-20	?	Prototype Stealth Fighter
Shenyang J-15	?		Naval Fighter	J-15	16+ (Mass production approve Dec 2013)	PLANAF Carrier Capable
Shenyang J-11	Flanker (Su-27)		Fighter	J-11	59+	Local Production Version of Su-27
				J-11B	7+	
				J-11BH	24	PLANAF
Chengdu J-10	?		Fighter	J-10	50	PLAAF
			Fighter/Combat Trainer	J-10A, J-10AS	14	
			Fighter	J-10B	2+	
			Aerobatic Display	J-10SY	12?	
			Fighter	J-10	20?	PLANAF
Xian JH-7	Flounder	China	Fighter Bomber	JH-7A	37+	PLAAF
				JH-7	43+	PLANAF
				JH-7 (ECM)	2-3+??	
				JH-7A	31+	

(Continued)

Aircraft	NATO Name	Origin	Role	Version	Estimated Nos	Comments
Shenyang J-8	Finback		All Weather Interceptor	J-8IE, J-8B (J-8 II), J-8D, J-8H	84-	PLAAF (Obsolete)
				J-8F	8-	
			Reconnaissance (Tactical)	JZ-8F	4	
			All Weather Interceptor	J-8IE, J-8B, J-8D, J-8F:	37-	PLANAF
Chengdu J-7	Fishbed (MiG –21)		Interceptor	J-7E, J-7G.	71-	PLAAF (Obsolete)
Guizhou JJ-7	Mongol (MiG-21U)		Interceptor/Combat Trainer	JJ-7, JJ-7II	40-	
Chengdu J-7	Fishbed (MiG –21)		Interceptor	J-7EH	19-	PLANAF (Obsolete)
Guizhou JJ-7	Mongol (MiG-21U)		Interceptor/Combat Trainer	JJ-7, JJ-7II	6-	
Nanchang Q-5	Fantan		Strike	Q-5, Q-5I, Q-5II,	106-	PLAAF (Obsolete)
Hongdu Q-5D				Q-5D, Q-5E	27-	
Nanchang Q-5D			Conversion Trainer	Q-5J	?	
Nanchang Q-5			Strike	Q-5I	13-	PLANAF(Obsolete)
Harbin SH-5	–		Maritime patrol	SH-5	4	PLANAF

(Continued)

Aircraft	NATO Name	Origin	Role	Version	Estimated Nos	Comments
Ilyushin IL-78	Midas	Russia	Tanker	IL-78MK	8 on order	PLAAF
Shaanxi Y-9	–	China	Transport	Y-9	7	
Xian Y-7	Coke (An-24) –			Y-7H, Y-7G	3+?	PLA
				Y-7H, Y-7G, An-24B, An-24RV	59	PLAAF
			Bomber Transport Trainer	HYJ-7	2+	
			Transport	Y-7G	9	PLAAF/United Airlines
			Experimental Carrier AWACS	JZY-01	1	PLAAF Experimental
			Bomber Transport Trainer	HYJ-7	1+?	PLANAF
			Transport	Y-7G	16	
Antonov An-26	Clank	USSR	Reconnaissance (Tactical)	An-30A	18+	PLAAF/CAAC
			Transport	An-30	70	
Nanchang CJ-6	Max (Yak-18)	China	Primary Trainer (Propeller)	CJ-6A	100?	PLAAF
					14	PLANAF
Yakovlov/ Hongdu CJ-7	–	China/ Russia Join venture		CJ-7 or L-7	?	PLAAF/PLANAF

(Continued)

Aircraft	NATO Name	Origin	Role	Version	Estimated Nos	Comments
Hongdu JL-8	–	China	Jet Trainer	JL-8	200? + (Total 400 ordered)	PLAAF
					12? +	PLANAF
Hongdu L-15	–		Supersonic Trainer / Light Attack	L-15	4++?	PLAAF
Guizhou JL-9	–		Supersonic Trainer/ Light Attack	JL-9	5 (testing)	
				JL-9G	12	PLANAF
Harbin Y-12	–		Utility	Y-12II	94	Also used by China Marine Surveillance, Redevelopment of the not too successful Y-11
Harbin Y-11	Chan				41 was produced in total limited service in PLAAF	?
Shijiazhuang Y-5	Colt (An-2)	China	Utility / Paratroop Trainer	Y-5B, Y-5B(T)	293	PLAAF
			Utility	Y-5	2?	PLA
			Bomber Crew Trainer	Y-5D	?	PLAAF
			Utility	Y-5B/ Y-5C (with floats)	3	PLANAF
			Trainer	Y-5	4	
Gates Learjet	–	USA	Reconnaissance (ELINT)	Learjet 36A	5	PLAAF (China United Airlines)

(Continued)

Aircraft	NATO Name	Origin	Role	Version	Estimated Nos	Comments
Bombardier CRJ200	–	Canada	Utility VIP transport	Challenger 600	2	PLANAF
				Challenger 800	5	PLAAF (China United Airlines)
Bombardier CRJ700				Challenger 870	5	
Boeing B737-300	–	USA	Airborne Command Post	B-737-300	2	
Boeing B-737	–		Utility VIP transport	B-737-300/700	10	
Rotary Wing Aircraft						
Changhe Z-10W	–	China	Attack	Z-10W	60+?	PLA
Harbin Z-9	Haitun		Multirole Utility (inc Artillery Spotting, ECM)	Z-9W, Z-9WA; Z-9A, Z-9B, Z-9EW	66+?; 23	
			ASW/SAR	Z-9C	16+ ~ 25?	PLANAF
			Ship borne Attack	Z-9D	?	
Aerospatiale SA-365 Dauphin	–	France	ASW/SAR	SA-365	8	
Kamov Ka-28	Helix	Russia	ASW	Ka-28	17?	
Kamov Ka-31			AEW	Ka-31	9	

(Continued)

Aircraft	NATO Name	Origin	Role	Version	Estimated Nos	Comments
Harbin Z-19	-	China	Attack & Reconnaissance		80+?	PLA
Changhe Z-11	-		Attack Battlefield Surveillance	Z-11W	40+	
			Trainer	Z-11J	10	
			Utility Multirole		60+	
Mil Mi-171	Hip	Russia/China.	Transport/Assault, Attack	Mi-17-1 (Mi-17C), Mi-17 V5, Mi-171 Sh, Mi-171 P, Mi-17 V7	132+	
Mil Mi-8		USSR/Russia	Transport, Assault	Mi-8T	9+	
			Transport		5	PLANAF
Sikorsky S-70 Blackhawk	-	USA	Transport	S-70C-2	24	PLA
Changhe Z-8	-	China	Transport/	Z-8A	6+ ??	
			SAR	Z-8K, Z-8KA	12	
Aerospatiale SA-321	-	France	Utility	SA-321 Ja	10 (one converted for Polar expedition)	PLANAF

(Continued)

Aircraft	NATO Name	Origin	Role	Version	Estimated Nos	Comments
Changhe Z-8	–	China	Utility	Z-8E, Z-8F	9	
			ASW	Z-8 ASW	?	
			Gunship (local conversation for Somalia Anti-Piracy Patrol)	Z-8W?	?	PLANAF (Total production over 130+)
			AEW	Z-8 AEW	1?	
			Medevac/ SAR	Z-8 JH, Z-8S	6+?	
Eurocopter AS-532 Cougar	–	France	Transport	AS-532	6	PLA
Eurocopter HC-120 Colibri	–	China/ Singapore/ France	Utility	HC-120	9+	
Aerospatiale SA-342 Gazelle	–	France	Attack	SA-342 l1	6-8?	
Aerospatiale SA-316 Alouette III	–	France	Utility	SA-316	14-?	

(Continued)

7

Aircraft of the PAP

Aircraft	NATO Name	Origin	Role	Version	Estimated Nos	Comments
Chenghe Z-8	–	China	Firefighting	Z-8FA (Z-9WJS)	18+	
Aerospatiale AS-365N	–	France	Public Order	AS-365N	1+	PAP
Harbin Z-9	Haitun	China	Public Order	Z-9B	3+	

8

Missiles used by the PLAAF, PLAN, and PLA

Missiles	Origin	Role	Version	Guidance	Range (km) (max/min)	Comments
PL-12/SD-10	China	AAM Med	SD-10, SA-10A	Inertial / Data-link (mid-course) ARH (Terminal phase)	21/0	PLAAF
			LD-10		60/?	ASM PLAAF
		SAM	DK-10, DK-10A		50/?	PLA
PL-10		AAM	K/AKK-10	SARH, ARH		
		SAM	HQ-6, HQ-64, HQ-64D		18/?	PLAAF; PLAN.
PL-9		AAM Short	PL-9C	Multi-element	22/?	PLAAF
		SAM Low	DK-9	IR gas cooled	>8	Divisional AD
PL-8	Israel/China	AAM	PL-8	Passive IR	20/0.5	Licensed production of Python 3
	China		PL-8B			
		SAM Low	PL-8H			
PL-7		AAM Short	PL-7	IR	14/0.5	Clone version of Magic R550 of France
PL-5			PL-5B, PL-5E	SARH, IR	16++/1.3	Development of PL-2

(Continued)

Missiles	Origin	Role	Version	Guidance	Range (km) (max/min)	Comments
PL-2			PL-2, PL-2A, PL-2B, PL-2 J72, PL-2 512	IR	21.2/ 2.7	Development of Soviet Vvmpel K-13 (NATO: Atoll)
HJ-10		AAM (Helicopter)	HJ-10	TV, ImIR, SARHMillimeter wave (MMW)	10+/?	For Z-10W, Z-11W attacked helicopter
		ASM	AKD-10	radar	?	For unarmored ground targets
			AR-1	Depends on what version	10/?	For use by UAVs
			CM-502KG		25/?	For manned aircraft and UAV use
		SSM	LJ-7, BA-7	Semi-active laser guided	7/2	Penetration 1400 mm armor
TY-90	China	AAM (helicopter)	TY-90	ImIR, IR	6/0.5	PLA
		SAM	SG-II (ADS)		?	
			LS, YT (ADS)		6/0.3	
		SAM (Naval)	FL-3000M	RF &ImIR or ImIR only	9~6/0.5	For PLAN

(Continued)

Missiles	Origin	Role	Version	Guidance	Range (km) (max/min)	Comments
QW Series		MANPAD SAM	QW1, QW-1M, QW-1A,	IR	5/0.5	Supposedly based on 9K310 (SA-16 Gimlet) Igla-1 missile
			QW-11, QW11G, QW-18			Terrain hugging cruise missiles
			QW-2	ImIR	6/0.5	Fire and Forget
			QW-3	Semi-active laser guidance	8/0.8	Similar to French Mistral missile
		MANPAD SAM + SS	TB-1	?	?	With anti-armor capability—Testing?
		MANPAD SAM	FLS-1	?	?	PLAN
FN-6			FN-6, FN6A, HN-6	IR	6/?	PLA, PLAAF
HQ-18/ S-300	Russia/China	SAM Long	S-300PMU2/ HQ-18	TVM	200-27/ 5-0.01	PLA
HQ-10/ S-300			S-300PMU1/ HQ10		150-27/ 5-0.01	
HQ-9	China		HQ-9, HQ-9A, HQ-9B.	INS with ARH	200/?	
			HHQ-9, HHQ-9A, HHQ-9B.			PLAN

(Continued)

Missiles	Origin	Role	Version	Guidance	Range (km) (max/min)	Comments
HQ-16	Russia/China	SAM Med	HQ-16, HQ-16A, HQ-16B	SARH	50/3 land 32-12/2.4 naval	Improved Soviet SA-17 Buk Missile
HQ-2	China		HQ-2 Upgrade	RC	80/?	Uprated SA-2 Guideline (S75 Dvina)
HQ-7		SAM Short	HQ-7 Land & Naval version	Command + electro-optical tracking	15-12/?	Clone Thomson-CSF Crotale missile
HJ-9		ATGM	HJ-9, HJ-9A, HJ-9B	Laser Beam Riding & MMW radar	5.5/0.1	PLA
HJ-8			HJ-8B, HJ-8C, HJ-8E, HJ-8H	SACLOS wire guided	6-3/?	
HJ-73	China		HJ-73, HJ-73B, HJ-73C	MCLOS, SACLOS	5/0.3	Similar to AT-3 Saggar (9M14 Malyutka)
CY Series		Anti-Submarine	CY-1, CY-2, CY-3	INS in flight, PAS in water	10/?	PLAN
CJ-1			CJ-1	ARH, TV, ImIR	80-50/?	
YJ-82 (C-802)		AShM, ASM.	YJ-83 (C-802A), YJ-83K (C-802AK), KD-88 (C-802KD) YJ-85 (C805)	INS and Terminal ARH	500-120/?	PLAN, PLAAF, PLANAF K is air-launch version
C-704			C-704K, C-705KD	ARH, ImIR, IR, TV	35/?	PLAN, PLAAF, PLANAF

(Continued)

Missiles	Origin	Role	Version	Guidance	Range (km) (max/min)	Comments
YJ-62 (C-602)		AShM, ASM, LACM.	CM-602G		400/?	PLAN, PLA
YJ-91		AShM, ARM, ASM.	YJ-91	ARH,PRH	120/5	PLAN, PLAAF, PLANAF
YJ-12			YJ-12	ARH, PRH, TV,ImIR	400/?	
CJ-10		LACM	CJ-10A, CJ-10K, YJ-100	INS, GPS, possibly COMPASS	2200-2000/?	PLA (2nd Artillery)
DH-10			DH-10	INS, GPS, TERCOM, DSMAC, COMPASS	4000+/?	
CF-1			CF-1, CF-2	TERCOM, ARH, TV, ImIR	800~400/?	
DF-31		ICBM.	DF-31, DF-31A,	INS, Stellar Updates	12000~7200/?	
DF-21	China	MRBM, ASBM.	DF-21, DF21A, DF-21C	INS, Terminal radar guidance	1450~1770/?	
DF-15		SRBM	DF-15, DF-16	INS, Beidou (GPS), Ring-laser gyroscope	600/?	PLA(2nd Artillery)
DF-11			DF-11		300/?	
DF-5		ICBM	DF-5	INS, On-board computers	1500/?	

(Continued)

BIBLIOGRAPHY

English

ANDREW, Martin K. *Tuo Mao: The Operational History of the People's Liberation Army*. Australia: Bound University, Doctor of Phil. thesis, 2008.

BLASK, Dennis O. *The Chinese Army Today*. London: Routledge, 2006.

BURKITT, L.; SCOBELL, A.; WORTZEL, L. M. (ed.). *The Lessons of History: The Chinese People's Liberation Army at 75*. USA, PA: Strategic Studies Institute, US Army War College, 2003.

COLE, Bernard D. *The Great Wall At Sea Second Editions, China's Navy in the Twenty-first Century*. Annapolis MD: Naval Institute Press, 2010.

CORDSMEN, Anthony H.; YAROSH, Nicholas S. *Chinese Military Modernization and Force Development—A Western Perspective*. Washington DC: Center for Strategic & International Studies, 2012.

GAO, Xiao Xing. *Series of Chinese Army—The PLA Navy*. Beijing: China Intercontinental Press, 2102.

GORDON, Yefim; KOMISSAROV, Dmitriy. *Chinese Air Power—The Current Organization and Aircraft of the Chinese Air Forces*. London: Midland Publishing, 2010.

HALLON, Richard P.; CLIFF, Roger and SAUNDERS, Philip C. *The Chinese Air Force—Evolving Concepts, Roles and Capabilities*. Washington DC: National Defense University Press, 2012.

KIM, Jae Chang; LI, Or Shih. *The Chinese military strategic Culture and Chinese use of Force during the Cold War. USA: Fetcher School of law and Diplomacy, Doctor of Phil. thesis, 2002.*

LILLEY, James; SHAMBURGH, David (ed.). *China's Military Faces the Future.* East Gate Book, American Enterprise Institute for Public Policy Research, 1999.

LU, Xiao Ping. *Series of Chinese Army—The PLA Air Force.* Beijing: China Intercontinental Press, 2012.

O'DOWD, Edward. *The last Maoist War—Chinese cadres and conscripts in the third Indochina war 1978–1991.* Dissertation presented to the faculty of Princeton University in the candidacy for the degree of Doctor of Philosophy, 2004.

O'ROURKE, Ronald. *China Naval Modernization: Implications for US Navy Capabilities—Background and Issues for Congress.* Washington DC: CRS, 2011.

QIANG, Zhang. *China & The Vietnam Wars, 1950–1975,* London: The University of North Carolina Press and Chapel Hill Press, 2000.

RYAN, Mark A.; FINKELSTEIN, David M.; McDEVITT, Michael A. and CNA Corporation (ed.). *Chinese War Fighting—the PLA Experience since 1949;* New York: East Gate Book, 2003.

SAUNDERS, Philip C.; YUNG, Christopher; SWAINE, Michael and YANG, Andrew N-D. *The Chinese Navy—Expanding Capabilities, Evolving Roles;* Washington DC: National Defense University Press, 2011.

Chinese

LIU Bin Jie et al. *30 years of Reform of the PLA.* Beijing: Military Science Publishing

LIU Ming, TONG Xu. *Main Battle Weapons of China.* Hohhot: Inner Mongolia People's Press, 2009.

LIU Wen Xiao. *The Lost Voodoo Pilots.* Taipei: Wings of China Press, 1992.

LIU Wen Xiao. *The History of the PLA Air Force*. Taipei: Wings of China Press, 1993.

LIU Wen Xiao, LU Xiliang. *Piercing the Bamboo Curtain from the Sky*. Taipei: Wings of China Press, 1996.

LIU Wen Xiao. *Defected From Formosa*. Taipei: Wings of China Press, 1998.

NI Chuang Hui. *Ten Years of Sino Vietnam War*. Hong Kong: M+N Publishing Co., 2010.

PLA General Logistics Department. *Sword of the Blue Sky*. Beijing: Blue Sky Press, 2011.

QIAN Jiang. *The Secret War—Chinese Military Advisory Group Goes to War in Vietnam*, Zhengzhou: Henan People's Press, 1992.

SHEN Wei Ping, LIU Wen Xiao. *The Battle of Jinmen—Crisis of the Taiwan Straits*. Taipei: Wings of China Press, 2007.

TIAN Yue Ying. *Pictorial Guide—Contemporary National Defense of China*. Hong Kong: Chong Hwa Books, 2013.

WANG, Hui. *ZTZ-98 MBT Special*. Inner Mongolia: Inner Mongolia Cultural Publisher, 2002.

WANG Zhen Hua et al. *The History of the Chinese Military Advisory Group in the Vietnamese anti-French War*. Beijing: China PLA Press, 1990.

WANG Zhi Jun. *My Personal Combat Experience in the Sino Vietnam War 1979*. Hong Kong; Thinker Publishing (HK) Limited. 2008.

XU Ping, XU Hai Yen. *Expanded Edition 100 Years of Chinese Military Uniform*. Beijing: Gold Wall Press, 2009.

XU Miao. *Fleet Ahoy Gulf of Aden—A record of the PLA Escort Fleet*. Beijing: CAPH, 2011.

YANG Si Ying. *High Altitude Anti-Espionage Battle—PLA Air force SAM interception of High Altitude Reconnaissance planes*; Beijing: Blue Sky Press, 2012.

ZHAO Fu Yun. *Sea Power between the Chinese Communist and Nationalist*. Taipei: Dongcha Press

Western military magazines:
Air Forces Monthly
Jane's Defence Weekly

Chinese military magazines:
Defense International, Modern Ships (现代舰船)
Naval & Merchant Ships (舰船知识)
Tank & Armored Vehicle (坦克装甲车辆)
Weapon (兵器)
Light Weapons (轻兵器)
Aviation Archives (航空档案)
Battlefield (战场文集)
Military Power (军事力量)
Ordnance Knowledge (兵器知识)

Taiwan military magazines:
Asia-Pacific Defense Magazine (亚太防务)
Defense International (军事家)
National Defense Digest (国防译粹)

INDEX